BROOKLANDS BOOKS

PORSCHE 928
PERFORMANCE PORTFOLIO
—1977-1994—

Compiled by
R.M.CLARKE

ISBN 1 85520 2697

BROOKLANDS BOOKS LTD.
P.O. BOX 146, COBHAM,
SURREY, KT11 1LG. UK

PRINTED IN HONG KONG

A-POC77PP

BROOKLANDS BOOKS

MOTORING

BROOKLANDS ROAD TEST SERIES

Abarth Gold Portfolio 1950-1971
AC Ace & Aceca 1953-1983
Alfa Romeo Giulietta Gold Portfolio 1954-1965
Alfa Romeo Giulia Berlinas 1962-1976
Alfa Romeo Giulia Coupés 1963-1976
Alfa Romeo Giulia Coupés Gold P. 1963-1976
Alfa Romeo Spider 1966-1990
Alfa Romeo Spider Gold Portfolio 1966-1991
Alfa Romeo Alfasud 1972-1984
Alfa Romeo Alfetta Gold Portfolio 1972-1987
Alfa Romeo Alfetta GTV6 1980-1986
Allard Gold Portfolio 1937-1959
Alvis Gold Portfolio 1919-1967
AMX & Javelin Muscle Portfolio 1968-1974
Armstrong Siddeley Gold Portfolio 1945-1960
Aston Martin Gold Portfolio 1972-1985
Aston Martin Gold Portfolio 1985-1995
Audi Quattro Gold Portfolio 1980-1991
Austin A30 & A35 1951-1962
Austin Healey 100 & 100/6 Gold P. 1952-1959
Austin Healey 3000 Gold Portfolio 1959-1967
Austin Healey Sprite 1958-1971
Barracuda Muscle Portfolio 1964-1974
BMW Six Cylinder Coupés 1969-1975
BMW 1600 Collection No.1 1966-1981
BMW 2002 Gold Portfolio 1968-1976
BMW 316, 318, 320 (4 cyl.) Gold P. 1975-1990
BMW 320, 323, 325 (6 cyl.) Gold P. 1977-1990
BMW M Series Performance Portfolio 1976-1993
BMW 5 Series Gold Portfolio 1981-1987
Bricklin Gold Portfolio 1974-1975
Bristol Cars Gold Portfolio 1946-1992
Buick Automobiles 1947-1960
Buick Muscle Cars 1965-1970
Cadillac Allanté 1986-1993
Cadillac Automobiles 1949-1959
Cadillac Automobiles 1960-1969
Charger Muscle Portfolio 1966-1974
Checker ☆ Limited Edition
Chevrolet 1955-1957
Chevrolet Impala & SS 1958-1971
Chevrolet Corvair 1959-1969
Chevy II & Nova SS Muscle Portfolio 1962-1974
Chevy El Camino & SS 1959-1987
Chevelle & SS Muscle Portfolio 1964-1972
Chevrolet Muscle Cars 1966-1971
Chevy Blazer 1969-1981
Chevrolet Corvette Gold Portfolio 1953-1962
Chevrolet Corvette Sting Ray Gold P. 1963-1967
Chevrolet Corvette Gold Portfolio 1968-1977
High Performance Corvettes 1983-1989
Camaro Muscle Portfolio 1967-1973
Chevrolet Camaro Z28 & SS 1966-1973
Chevrolet Camaro & Z28 1973-1981
High Performance Camaros 1982-1988
Chrysler 300 Gold Portfolio 1955-1970
Chrysler Valiant 1960-1962
Citroen Traction Avant Gold Portfolio 1934-1957
Citroen 2CV Gold Portfolio 1948-1989
Citroen DS & ID 1955-1975
Citroen DS & ID Gold Portfolio 1955-1975
Citroen SM 1970-1975
Cobras & Replicas 1962-1983
Shelby Cobra Gold Portfolio 1962-1969
Cobras & Cobra Replicas Gold P. 1962-1989
Cunningham Automobiles 1951-1955
Daimler SP250 Sports & V-8 250 Saloon Gold P. 1959-1969
Datsun Roadsters 1962-1971
Datsun 240Z 1970-1973
Datsun 280Z & ZX 1975-1983
DeLorean Gold Portfolio 1977-1995
Dodge Muscle Cars 1967-1970
Dodge Viper on the Road
ERA Gold Portfolio 1934-1994
Excalibur Collection No.1 1952-1981
Facel Vega 1954-1964
Ferrari Dino 1965-1974
Ferrari Dino 308 1974-1979
Ferrari 328 • 348 • Mondial Gold Portfolio 1986-1994
Fiat 500 Gold Portfolio 1936-1972
Fiat 600 & 850 Gold Portfolio 1955-1972
Fiat Pininfarina 124 & 2000 Spider 1968-1985
Fiat-Bertone X1/9 1973-1988
Fiat Abarth Performance Portfolio 1972-1987
Ford Consul, Zephyr, Zodiac Mk.I & II 1950-1962
Ford Zephyr, Zodiac, Executive, Mk.III & Mk.IV 1962-1971
Ford Cortina 1600E & GT 1967-1970
High Performance Capris Gold Portfolio 1969-1987
Capri Muscle Portfolio 1974-1987
High Performance Fiestas 1979-1991
High Performance Escorts Mk.I 1968-1974
High Performance Escorts Mk.II 1975-1980
High Performance Escorts 1980-1985
High Performance Escorts 1985-1990
High Performance Sierras & Merkurs Gold Portfolio 1983-1990
Ford Automobiles 1949-1959
Ford Fairlane 1955-1970
Ford Ranchero 1957-1959
Ford Thunderbird 1955-1957
Ford Thunderbird 1958-1963
Ford Thunderbird 1964-1976
Ford GT40 Gold Portfolio 1964-1987
Ford Bronco 1966-1977
Ford Bronco 1978-1988
Goggomobil ☆ Limited Edition
Holden 1948-1962
Honda CRX 1983-1987
International Scout Gold Portfolio 1961-1980
Isetta 1953-1964
Iso & Bizzarrini Gold Portfolio 1962-1974
Jaguar and SS Gold Portfolio 1931-1951
Jaguar XK120, 140, 150 Gold P. 1948-1960
Jaguar Mk.VII, VIII, IX, X, 420 Gold P. 1950-1970
Jaguar Mk.1 & Mk.2 Gold Portfolio 1959-1969
Jaguar C-Type & D-Type ☆ Limited Edition
Jaguar E-Type Gold Portfolio 1961-1971
Jaguar E-Type V-12 1971-1975
Jaguar S-Type & 420 ☆ Limited Edition
Jaguar XJ12, XJ5.3, V12 Gold P. 1972-1990
Jaguar XJ6 Series I & II Gold P. 1968-1979
Jaguar XJ6 Series III 1979-1986
Jaguar XJ6 Gold Portfolio 1986-1994
Jaguar XJS Gold Portfolio 1975-1988
Jaguar XJS Gold Portfolio 1988-1995
Jeep CJ5 & CJ6 1960-1976
Jeep CJ5 & CJ7 1976-1986
Jensen Cars 1946-1967
Jensen Cars 1967-1979
Jensen Interceptor Gold Portfolio 1966-1986
Jensen Healey 1972-1976
Lagonda Gold Portfolio 1919-1964
Lamborghini Countach & Urraco 1974-1980
Lamborghini Countach & Jalpa 1980-1985
Lancia Aurelia & Flaminia Gold Portfolio 1950-1970
Lancia Fulvia Gold Portfolio 1963-1976
Lancia Beta Gold Portfolio 1972-1984
Lancia Delta Gold Portfolio 1979-1994
Lancia Stratos 1972-1985
Land Rover Series I 1948-1958
Land Rover Series II & IIa 1958-1971
Land Rover Series III 1971-1985
Land Rover 90 110 Defender Gold Portfolio 1983-1994
Land Rover Discovery 1989-1994
Land Rover Story Part One 1948-1971
Lincoln Gold Portfolio 1949-1960
Lincoln Continental 1961-1969
Lincoln Continental 1969-1976
Lotus Sports Racers Gold Portfolio 1953-1965
Lotus Seven Gold Portfolio 1957-1974
Lotus Caterham Seven Gold Portfolio 1974-1995
Lotus Elite 1957-1964
Lotus Elite & Eclat 1974-1982
Lotus Elan Gold Portfolio 1962-1974
Lotus Elan Collection No. 2 1963-1972
Lotus Elan & SE 1989-1992
Lotus Cortina Gold Portfolio 1963-1970
Lotus Europa Gold Portfolio 1966-1975
Lotus Elite & Eclat 1974-1982
Lotus Turbo Esprit 1980-1986
Marcos Cars 1960-1988
Maserati 1970-1975
Mazda RX-7 Gold Portfolio 1978-1991
Mercedes 190 & 300 SL 1954-1963
Mercedes 230/250/280SL 1963-1971
Mercedes G Wagen 1981-1994
Mercedes Benz SLs & SLCs Gold P. 1971-1989
Mercedes S & 600 1965-1972
Mercedes S Class 1972-1979
Mercedes SLs Performance Portfolio 1989-1994
Mercury Muscle Cars 1966-1971
Messerschmitt Gold Portfolio 1954-1964
MG Gold Portfolio 1929-1939
MG TA & TC Gold Portfolio 1936-1949
MG TD & TF Gold Portfolio 1949-1955
MGA & Twin Cam Gold Portfolio 1955-1962
MG Midget Gold Portfolio 1961-1979
MGB Roadsters 1962-1980
MGB MGC & V8 Gold Portfolio 1962-1980
MGB GT 1965-1980
MG Y Type & Magnette ZA/ZB ☆ Limited Edition
Mini Gold Portfolio 1959-1969
Mini Gold Portfolio 1969-1980
High Performance Minis Gold Portfolio 1960-1973
Mini Cooper Gold Portfolio 1961-1971
Mini Moke Gold Portfolio 1964-1994
Mopar Muscle Cars 1964-1967
Morgan Three-Wheeler Gold Portfolio 1910-1952
Morgan Plus 4 & Four 4 Gold P. 1936-1967
Morgan Cars 1960-1970
Morgan Cars Gold Portfolio 1968-1989
Morris Minor Collection No. 1 1948-1980
Shelby Mustang Muscle Portfolio 1965-1970
High Performance Mustang IIs 1974-1978
High Performance Mustangs 1982-1988
Nash-Austin Metropolitan Gold P. 1954-1962
Oldsmobile Automobiles 1955-1963
Oldsmobile Muscle Cars 1964-1971
Oldsmobile Toronado 1966-1978
Opel GT Gold Portfolio 1968-1973
Packard Gold Portfolio 1946-1958
Pantera Gold Portfolio 1970-1989
Panther Gold Portfolio 1972-1990
Plymouth Muscle Cars 1966-1971
Pontiac Tempest & GTO 1961-1965
Pontiac Muscle Cars 1966-1972
Pontiac Firebird & Trans-Am 1973-1981
High Performance Firebirds 1982-1988
Pontiac Fiero 1984-1988
Porsche 356 Gold Portfolio 1953-1965
Porsche 911 1965-1969
Porsche 911 1970-1972
Porsche 911 1973-1977
Porsche 911 Carrera 1973-1977
Porsche 911 Turbo 1975-1984
Porsche 911 SC & Turbo Gold Portfolio 1978-1983
Porsche 911 Carrera & Turbo Gold P. 1984-1989
Porsche 914 Gold Portfolio 1969-1976
Porsche 924 Gold Portfolio 1975-1988
Porsche 928 Performance Portfolio 1977-1994
Porsche 944 Gold Portfolio 1981-1991
Range Rover Gold Portfolio 1970-1985
Range Rover Gold Portfolio 1986-1995
Reliant Scimitar 1964-1986
Riley Gold Portfolio 1924-1939
Riley 1.5 & 2.5 Litre Gold Portfolio 1945-1955
Rolls Royce Silver Cloud & Bentley 'S' Series Gold Portfolio 1955-1965
Rolls Royce Silver Shadow Gold P. 1965-1980
Rolls Royce & Bentley Gold P. 1980-1989
Rover P4 1949-1959
Rover P4 1955-1964
Rover 3 & 3.5 Litre Gold Portfolio 1958-1973
Rover 2000 & 2200 1963-1977
Rover 3500 1968-1977
Rover 3500 & Vitesse 1976-1986
Saab Sonett Collection No.1 1966-1974
Saab Turbo 1976-1983
Studebaker Gold Portfolio 1947-1966
Studebaker Hawks & Larks 1956-1963
Avanti 1962-1990
Sunbeam Tiger & Alpine Gold P. 1959-1967
Toyota MR2 1984-1988
Toyota Land Cruiser 1956-1984
Triumph Dolomite Sprint ☆ Limited Edition
Triumph TR2 & TR3 Gold Portfolio 1952-1961
Triumph TR4, TR5, TR250 1961-1968
Triumph TR6 Gold Portfolio 1969-1976
Triumph TR7 & TR8 Gold Portfolio 1975-1982
Triumph Herald 1959-1971
Triumph Vitesse 1962-1971
Triumph Spitfire Gold Portfolio 1962-1980
Triumph 2000, 2.5, 2500 1963-1977
Triumph GT6 Gold Portfolio 1966-1974
Triumph Stag Gold Portfolio 1970-1977
TVR Gold Portfolio 1959-1986
TVR Performance Portfolio 1986-1994
VW Beetle Gold Portfolio 1935-1967
VW Beetle Gold Portfolio 1968-1991
VW Beetle Collection No.1 1970-1982
VW Karmann Ghia 1955-1982
VW Bus, Camper, Van 1954-1967
VW Bus, Camper, Van 1968-1979
VW Bus, Camper, Van 1979-1989
VW Scirocco 1974-1981
VW Golf GTI 1976-1986
Volvo PV444 & PV544 1945-1965
Volvo Amazon-120 Gold Portfolio 1956-1970
Volvo 1800 Gold Portfolio 1960-1973
Volvo 140 & 160 Series Gold Portfolio 1966-1975

Forty Years of Selling Volvo

BROOKLANDS ROAD & TRACK SERIES

Road & Track on Alfa Romeo 1949-1963
Road & Track on Alfa Romeo 1964-1970
Road & Track on Alfa Romeo 1971-1976
Road & Track on Alfa Romeo 1977-1989
Road & Track on Aston Martin 1962-1990
R & T on Auburn Cord and Duesenburg 1952-84
Road & Track on Audi & Auto Union 1952-1980
Road & Track on Audi & Auto Union 1980-1986
Road & Track on Austin Healey 1953-1970
Road & Track on BMW Cars 1966-1974
Road & Track on BMW Cars 1975-1978
Road & Track on BMW Cars 1979-1983
R & T on Cobra, Shelby & Ford GT40 1962-1992
Road & Track on Corvette 1953-1967
Road & Track on Corvette 1968-1982
Road & Track on Corvette 1982-1986
Road & Track on Corvette 1986-1990
Road & Track on Datsun Z 1970-1983
Road & Track on Ferrari 1975-1981
Road & Track on Ferrari 1981-1984
Road & Track on Ferrari 1984-1988
Road & Track on Fiat Sports Cars 1968-1987
Road & Track on Jaguar 1950-1960
Road & Track on Jaguar 1961-1968
Road & Track on Jaguar 1968-1974
Road & Track on Jaguar 1974-1982
Road & Track on Jaguar 1983-1989
Road & Track on Lamborghini 1964-1985
Road & Track on Lotus 1972-1981
Road & Track on Maserati 1952-1974
Road & Track on Maserati 1975-1983
R & T on Mazda RX7 & MX5 Miata 1986-1991
Road & Track on Mercedes 1952-1962
Road & Track on Mercedes 1963-1970
Road & Track on Mercedes 1971-1979
Road & Track on Mercedes 1980-1987
Road & Track on MG Sports Cars 1949-1961
Road & Track on MG Sports Cars 1962-1980
Road & Track on Mustang 1964-1977
R & T on Nissan 300-ZX & Turbo 1984-1989
Road & Track on Pontiac 1960-1983
Road & Track on Porsche 1951-1967
Road & Track on Porsche 1968-1971
Road & Track on Porsche 1972-1975
Road & Track on Porsche 1975-1978
Road & Track on Porsche 1985-1988
R & T on Rolls Royce & Bentley 1950-1965
R & T on Rolls Royce & Bentley 1966-1984
Road & Track on Saab 1972-1992
R & T on Toyota Sports & GT Cars 1966-1984
R & T on Triumph Sports Cars 1953-1967
R & T on Triumph Sports Cars 1967-1974
R & T on Triumph Sports Cars 1974-1982
Road & Track on Volkswagen 1951-1968
Road & Track on Volkswagen 1968-1978
Road & Track on Volkswagen 1978-1985
Road & Track on Volvo 1957-1974
Road & Track on Volvo 1977-1994
R&T - Henry Manney at Large & Abroad
R&T - Peter Egan's "Side Glances"

BROOKLANDS CAR AND DRIVER SERIES

Car and Driver on BMW 1955-1977
Car and Driver on BMW 1977-1985
C and D on Cobra, Shelby & Ford GT40 1963-84
Car and Driver on Corvette 1956-1967
Car and Driver on Corvette 1968-1977
Car and Driver on Corvette 1978-1982
Car and Driver on Corvette 1983-1988
C and D on Datsun Z 1600 & 2000 1966-1984
Car and Driver on Ferrari 1955-1962
Car and Driver on Ferrari 1963-1975
Car and Driver on Ferrari 1976-1983
Car and Driver on Mopar 1956-1967
Car and Driver on Mopar 1968-1975
Car and Driver on Mustang 1964-1972
Car and Driver on Pontiac 1961-1975
Car and Driver on Porsche 1955-1962
Car and Driver on Porsche 1963-1970
Car and Driver on Porsche 1970-1976
Car and Driver on Porsche 1977-1981
Car and Driver on Porsche 1982-1986
Car and Driver on Saab 1956-1985
Car and Driver on Volvo 1955-1986

BROOKLANDS PRACTICAL CLASSICS SERIES

PC on Austin A40 Restoration
PC on Land Rover Restoration
PC on Metalworking in Restoration
PC on Midget/Sprite Restoration
PC on Mini Cooper Restoration
PC on MGB Restoration
PC on Morris Minor Restoration
PC on Sunbeam Rapier Restoration
PC on Triumph Herald/Vitesse
PC on Spitfire Restoration
PC on Beetle Restoration
PC on 1930s Car Restoration

BROOKLANDS HOT ROD 'MUSCLECAR & HI-PO ENGINES' SERIES

Chevy 265 & 283
Chevy 302 & 327
Chevy 348 & 409
Chevy 350 & 400
Chevy 396 & 427
Chevy 454 thru 512
Chrysler Hemi
Chrysler 273, 318, 340 & 360
Chrysler 361, 383, 400, 413, 426, 440
Ford 289, 302, Boss 302 & 351W
Ford 351C & Boss 351
Ford Big Block

BROOKLANDS RESTORATION SERIES

Auto Restoration Tips & Techniques
Basic Bodywork Tips & Techniques
Camaro Restoration Tips & Techniques
Chevrolet High Performance Tips & Techniques
Chevy Engine Swapping Tips & Techniques
Chevy-GMC Pickup Repair
Chrysler Engine Swapping Tips & Techniques
Engine Swapping Tips & Techniques
Ford Pickup Repair
How to Build a Street Rod
Land Rover Restoration Tips & Techniques
MG 'T' Series Restoration Guide
MGA Restoration Guide
Mustang Restoration Tips & Techniques
Performance Tuning - Chevrolets of the '60's
Performance Tuning - Pontiacs of the '60's

MOTORCYCLING

BROOKLANDS ROAD TEST SERIES

BSA Twins A7 & A10 Gold Portfolio 1946-1962
BSA Twins A50 & A65 Gold Portfolio 1962-1973
Norton Commando Gold Portfolio 1968-1977
Triumph Bonneville Gold Portfolio 1959-1983

BROOKLANDS CYCLE WORLD SERIES

Cycle World on BMW 1974-1980
Cycle World on BMW 1981-1986
Cycle World on Ducati 1982-1991
Cycle World on Harley-Davidson 1962-1968
Cycle World on Harley-Davidson 19781-1983
Cycle World on Harley-Davidson 1983-1987
Cycle World on Harley-Davidson 1987-1990
Cycle World on Harley-Davidson 1990-1992
Cycle World on Honda 1962-1967
Cycle World on Honda 1968-1971
Cycle World on Honda 1971-1974
Cycle World on Husqvarna 1966-1976
Cycle World on Husqvarna 1977-1984
Cycle World on Kawasaki 1966-1971
Cycle World on Kawasaki Off-Road Bikes 1972-1979
Cycle World on Kawasaki Street Bikes 1972-1976
Cycle World on Norton 1962-1971
Cycle World on Suzuki 1962-1970
Cycle World on Suzuki Off-Road Bikes 1971-1976
Cycle World on Suzuki Street Bikes 1971-1976
Cycle World on Triumph 1967-1972
Cycle World on Yamaha 1962-1969
Cycle World on Yamaha Off-Road Bikes 1970-1974
Cycle World on Yamaha Street Bikes 1970-1974

MILITARY

BROOKLANDS MILITARY VEHICLES SERIES

Allied Military Vehicles No.1 1942-1945
Allied Military Vehicles No.2 1941-1946
Complete WW2 Military Jeep Manual
Dodge Military Vehicles No.1 1940-1945
Hail To The Jeep
Land Rovers in Military Service
Military & Civilian Amphibians 1940-1990
Off Road Jeeps: Civ. & Mil. 1944-1971
US Military Vehicles 1941-1945
US Army Military Vehicles WW2-TM9-2800
VW Kubelwagen Military Portfolio 1940-1990
WW2 Jeep Military Portfolio 1941-1945

CONTENTS

ACKNOWLEDGEMENTS

When our regular Road Test book on the Porsche 928 went out of print, we searched through our archives to see if there was more material on these cars which might prove of interest to enthusiasts. There was, and so we have put it together with material from our first book to produce this new and enlarged 928 Performance Portfolio.

As always, we are indebted to the copyright holders of the articles we reproduce. Without their help and understanding, we would simply not be able to publish books like this one, so we are pleased to record our sincere thanks to them. They are the publishers of *Autocar, Autocar and Motor, Automobile Magazine, Car South Africa, Car and Driver, Drive, Motor, Motor Manual, Motor Sport, Motor Trend, Performance Car, Road & Track, Road & Track Specials, Sports Car World, Thoroughbred and Classic Cars* and *What Car?*
Our thanks also go to motoring writer James Taylor for agreeing once again to write a brief introduction.

R. M. Clarke

I can well remember seeing a 928 for the first time, back in 1977, and wondering how anybody could even conceive of that check upholstery, let alone live with it. I also had my doubts about what Porsche were up to: was this a front-engined V8 supercar aimed specifically at the American market, and were Porsche about to ditch their allegiance to flat-sixes and rear-mounted engines?

I need not have worried. The 911 with its flat-six mounted at the rear is still with us, and has never been more highly regarded. And, paradoxically, the current versions of the 928 are also held in higher esteem than any versions before them.

The 928 certainly did come as a shock at the end of the 1970's and it took a few years before it gained acceptance among enthusiasts. However, progressive development in the Porsche tradition produced a progressively better car. There was the 928S in 1979, the 32-valve 5-litre engine in 1986, the 928GT in 1989 and 928GTS in 1992. The Weissach engineers used the 928 as their technological flagship: it was the first car to have onboard tyre-pressure checking, the first with a full diagnostic system, and the first with an electronically controlled differential.

This Brooklands Performance Portfolio provides both inspiration and nostalgia for 928 enthusiasts - inspiration to get out on the road and enjoy their cars, and nostalgia for the early days when 928s were controversial cars, and few and far between.

James Taylor

PORSCHE 928 ... On the road

SOMEHOW it sounded like a Porsche the moment it started but perhaps only at that moment; the 928's 4·5-litre light-alloy V-8 is an all-new engine designed to be as tractable, quiet and economical as possible – which is why its single overhead camshafts are belt driven and use hydraulic cam followers and why it is water-cooled. Bosch K-Jetronic allows 2-star fuel and oil change intervals are 20,000km.

At the time the 928 concept was in planning during 1971, the law-makers were beginning to get more than usually obstructive and Porsche felt that they were going to have a better chance of long term survival if they conformed to the universal standard car; thus the 928 and the 924, which actually came out first although its development started later, have front-mounted engines. It had to be a sports car, but more comfortable, more economical to run and safer, but still a Porsche.

For optimum weight distribution and the high polar moment of inertia required for stability the gearbox is in a transaxle at the rear, in front of the final drive in the case of the 928 to give better rear seat capacity, but behind for the more compact 924. After generations of rear-engined motor-cars Porsche engineers are perhaps more sensitive to lift-off tuck-in (foot-off tail-out) than most; considerable research into this and the rate of such response involved an engineer counter-steering on Opel Admiral equipped with rear wheel steering. The result is the patented Weissach axle which gives toe-in on a trailing throttle – but not as a function of suspension movement; basically it is equivalent to a double wishbone set-up, although the upper one is just a single transverse link, but the lower forward arm has a rubber jointed knuckle with limited articulation near its chassis pick-up end. The movement is precisely controlled by rubber rate *versus* decelerative forces and certainly appears to work in practice – lift-off half way round and it maintains its line, but you have to be going ridiculously fast to be at a level to check this. The body is as neat and clean as a bumperless car can look, only there are controlled crushing bumpers behind a polyurethane skin; a 5mph wall nudge causes no damage while an Opel Ascona making frontal and rear assaults at around 22kph could only manage to bend a shock absorbing tube on the 928 despite considerable detriment to itself. That is part of reduced running costs with lower insurance claims, and the 928 has a lower insurance rating than the 911 in Germany.

In creating the 928 shape Porsche have continued a line which is recognisable in all Porsches so far; the claim for a 0·4 drag coefficient seems pretty conservative against other claims of nearer 0·3 but some scepticism over such figures was expressed. Against the 924 it certainly looks a little cleaner in minor details although there are headlamp scoops for swivelling lights, which are cockpit adjustable for load compensation – a 1979 EEC regulation.

In the car it is easy to tailor the driving position to suit any needs; the idea is that instruments should always be visible through the steering wheel, so the whole

Right, Dr Fuhrmann, Porsche engineer, surveys the chef's attempt at styling a puff pastry flan at the Hotel Mas d'Artigny near Nice.

Top, 928 (nearest) and 924 compare front end treatments; 928's concealed bumpers are more evident from behind where the rounded tail makes a 911 look almost pointed.

binnacle moves with the rake adjustable wheel. Seats have the usual range plus height variation. And there really is room for adult rear passengers as I sat in the back seat for a reasonable distance; at average height I could sit square behind my own driving position, although a pair of six-footers may not get on so well.

The performance is completely effortless with very little noise until you wind the engine beyond 4500rpm; road noise is partially subdued and wind noise almost totally absent so that country road driving is simply a question of steering, because you hardly ever need to brake, there is plenty of torque available and there is no noise distraction. I had forgotten that the car had ZF power assisted steering and didn't remember it until I had driven some 30 miles, so well weighted is it. It is nicely geared, too, and the nose is instantly responsive to wheel movement on those very low very fat Pirellis – 50% aspect ratio, nominal 9in tyre width.

On public roads one never reached the handling stage other than a mild correction on a gritty corner; the roadholding is just very good indeed. In keeping with usual Porsche characteristics the instrumentation is beautifully clear and controls and switchgear nicely laid out for easy familiarisation in a short time.

What is so different about this Porsche is that you can drive it entirely according to your mood in the knowledge that it will never bite should your concentration relax for a bit. Even at high speed it is utterly stable and you never feel the need to grip the wheel more firmly as you go faster. I found it very satisfying to stay in as high gear as possible and just waft the car smoothly through the corners in complete safety, if quickly; others found it just as satisfying to play rally drivers in the mountains using lower gears, higher revs and heavier brakes. It is because it is such a complete car, totally designed in every aspect, that the 928 will be a great success.

Production will start this autumn – our test cars were pre-production prototypes – and will build up gradually to around 5000 units a year. At present Zuffenhausen's production is 13,500 911s a year with 20,000 924s coming from Neckarsulm; capacity is 15,000 a year at Zuffenhausen, so some of the 911 production will switch to 928s, but the plan is still to produce two 911s for one 928; so the 911 will be around for some time yet with the 928 having a life expectancy of a similar period of 10–15 years. Thus one might reasonably call the 928 a car for the 'nineties! ●

It looks like a big, up-market copy of the cheaper 924 but the 928 was actually conceived first and shelved for a while. Its new front-mounted 4.5-litre light-alloy V8 drives the rear wheels through a five-speed transaxle. Anti tuck-in rear suspension and a luxurious 2 + 2 interior are also features of this exciting new 140 mph Supercar described by Anthony Curtis overleaf

THE NEW PORSCHE

Tail lamp cluster is deeply inset into rear bumper

Instruments and stalks are linked to the wheel

Rear wiper has pantograph action for bigger sweep

New-style alloy wheels are an attractive feature

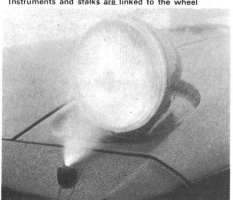

The new all-alloy V8 is a tight fit

With a low nose, pop-up lamps are almost inevitable

CUTAWAY KEY

1 Alloy, liner-less water-cooled 4474 cc V8 engine.
2 Bosch K–Jetronic fuel injection system.
3 Front suspension by cast double wishbones.
4 Power-assisted rack and pinion steering.
5 Instrument binnacle which adjusts in unison with steering column.
6 Aluminium alloy doors.
7 Five-speed transaxle mounted at the rear.
8 Rear suspension by double wishbones with anti-tuck-in geometry.
9 Battery and exhaust system slung from transaxle.
10 Space-saving spare wheel.
11 Folding rear seats.
12 Aluminium alloy tailgate.

BECAUSE PORSCHE have been producing a model of such individuality and excellence as the 911 for so many years, they may well have found it difficult to decide what sort of car should augment or replace it. One possibility might be a car with the mid-engine layout—still acknowledged to give the ultimate combination of high cornering power and responsive handling—in view of the company's long-standing reputation for high standards of roadholding. For although the 911 exemplifies these in nearly every respect, the location of its engine at the back, overhanging the rear wheels, probably puts a limit on further possible improvements in stability, especially at the limit of adhesion or in a violent manoeuvre.

But the mid-engine configuration is a space-wasting arrangement in which it is difficult to fit more than two seats—though Bertone showed how it could be done with their Trapeze styling exercise—and like many other manufacturers of high performance cars, Porsche regard the provision of a pair of occasional rear seats, no matter how vestigial, as being essential. Another possibility, therefore, might be to complement the 911 with a larger and more luxurious car offering ample space for four adults.

Both these ideas were rejected by the management of Porsche who felt strongly that their best market would always be for sporting 2 + 2 coupes: It was what the public expected of them and what they knew very well how to create. But they had noticed a certain drift, especially amongst their older customers, from their own cars to more luxurious models with similar interior space, like the Mercedes SLC. At the same time Porsche wanted to widen their appeal, so the logical solution, in their view, was to introduce a slightly larger and much more refined, luxurious and expensive—yet sporting

—car above the 911, which with the new 924 below it should increase their sales significantly.

The location of the engine was partly decided by external events. At the time the decisions were being made, some five years ago, the ballyhoo surrounding the American ESV programme and its associated proposed handling tests made the total exclusion of rear- or even mid-engined cars from the States seem a serious possibility. But it was felt that prospective customers would not take kindly to a nose-heavy Porsche, so it was decided to mount the gearbox of the new car at the rear, as it is in the 924. In fact the basic design of the car was laid down before that of the 924, the project being dropped for a while to concentrate on the cheaper, mass market model.

The result of all these considerations is the Porsche 928, a three-door hatchback very similar in appearance to the 924, with a Porsche-styled rounded shape. It is, however, significantly larger, with rear seats which, although very definitely occasional in nature, do provide more space and comfort than those in the 911. It is also much more powerful than the 924 and much more refined and luxurious with an interior featuring instruments and stalks which move with the adjustable steering wheel.

The 928's front-mounted engine is an all-new watercooled 4.5–litre light alloy V8 developing 240 (DIN) bhp at 5250 rpm and 267.5 lb ft of torque at 3600 rpm. By comparison a Carrera engine develops 200 bhp and 188 lb ft of torque, but since the new car is considerably heavier despite the use of aluminium for the bonnet, bootlid and doors,weighing over 30 cwt, it is not quite as fast, the claimed maximum speed being just over 140 mph, while the 0-60 mph acceleration time is likely to be slightly more than 6 seconds.

Following current design trends the engine is composed of a stack of diecastings including a massive one-piece "ladder" into which the caps of the five main bearings are formed. More unusually, though the block is cast in a special high-silicon aluminium alloy so that, as in the Chevrolet Vega engine, the coated aluminium pistons can run directly in the bores without liners. There is a single, belt driven overhead camshaft for each bank of cylinders and the fuel is metered by a Bosch K-Jetronic continuous injection system.

To cut down rotational inertia, this engine drives through a small-diameter two-plate clutch instead of the normal single-plate unit. This in turn drives a propeller shaft enclosed within a torque tube and coupled to the completely new five-speed gearbox/rear transaxle unit. Double wishbone independent suspension is used at both ends of the car, but the system at the rear incorporates an ingenious modification minimising the tuck-in effect which can occur if a car is forced to slow or brake in mid-corner.

Styling and structure

In appearance the 928 is very similar to the 924, having the same rounded shape and hatchback layout, differing mainly in having a pair of rear side-windows in place of a single wrap-around tailgate window. It is, however, a good deal bigger than the 924, being 4 in longer in the wheelbase and around 9½ in longer overall. But its rear seats, although more comfortable and spacious than those of the 924 or 911, are still very definitely of the occasional sort.

The torsionally rigid structure is made of galvanised steel, and like all current Porsches carries a six-year guarantee. The bodyshell meets all the various safety regulations and incorporates bumpers integrated into the shape. Made of aluminium for lightness, these are covered with a deformable polyurethane foam and finished in a special flexible paint. Aluminium is also used for the doors, bolt-on front wings and bonnet (not the tailgate as stated in the colour section — and the claimed weight of the car is 28.5 cwt, not over 30 cwt).

Engine

If the 928 engine is not the first with watercooling to be designed by Porsche — they laid out a unit of this sort for Studebaker in the Fifties — it is very nearly so, and the minds of its creators can hardly have been much cluttered by precedent. Since those minds are also renowned for their high quality, the combination of design features they finally selected is of considerable interest. The first of these — watercooling itself — need hardly raise any eyebrows: endless complaints about the sensitivity to engine speed and other defects of the 911's heating system must have had their influence, in addition, perhaps, to the less well-founded belief that watercooling cuts noise.

In other respects, though, the engine is an ingenious mixture. Like any large and woolly American V-8 it has hydraulic tappets, which also reduce noise, but have the more important virtue of eliminating the need for adjustment. Like any respectable advanced European engine, however, the new unit also has overhead camshafts — one for each bank of cylinders operating in-line valves. In the same tradition, too, it is also made of aluminium for lightness, but with the simplicity of construction conferred by the Reynolds 390 high-silicon alloy. Developed for the General Motors' Vega engine — and used for the 928's cylinder block — it eliminates the need for cast-iron liners by allowing the steel-coated aluminium pistons to run directly in the aluminium cylinder bores.

With a bore of 95.0 mm and a stroke of 78.9 mm the new 4,474 cc engine is comfortably oversquare. It also has the usual 90 deg vee angle, and a forged steel two-plane crankshaft which runs in five main bearings. Following an increasingly popular modern design practice, the caps of these are not separate components but are formed into a massive one piece ladder frame. The

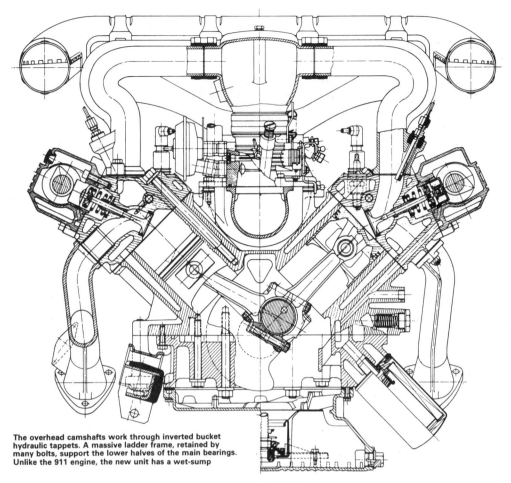

The overhead camshafts work through inverted bucket hydraulic tappets. A massive ladder frame, retained by many bolts, support the lower halves of the main bearings. Unlike the 911 engine, the new unit has a wet-sump

A pair of hoses (removed here) connect the airbox at the rear of the engine with the front of the car. Ahead of the camshaft drive system, a complex array of belts drives the auxiliaries, the alternator and steering pump being on the right-hand side of the engine and the air injection and air conditioning pumps (when fitted) on the other side

Despite rounded lines — and Porsche's reputation with the 911 — the new body is not very slippery, its drag coefficient being about 0.4

A twin-plate clutch cuts rotational inertia and eases the load on the synchromesh units of the rear-mounted gearbox

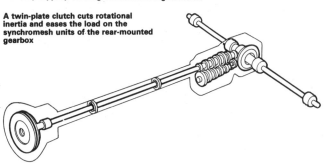

In essentials the rear suspension is of the double-wishbone type. The sub-frame is rigidly mounted to the body and supports the rubber-mounted gearbox which is restrained by a pair of dampers: only one is visible here

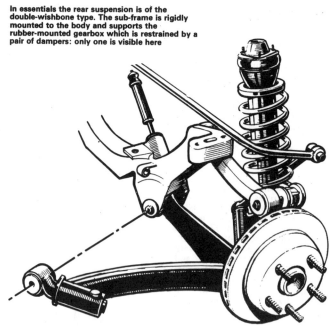

block, cast in the special high-silicon alloy, is of the open-deck type and has generous water spaces all round each cylinder.

The fuel is metered by a Bosch K-Jetronic fuel injection system which forms part of a complex inlet duct arrangement. Air enters through a pair of intakes at the front of the engine compartment on either side, passes to a collector box at the rear of the engine compartment and is then led downwards through the orifice and swinging plate of the K-Jetronic air flow meter. It then passes forward again through a duct which lies between the two banks of cylinders and upwards to the throttle. Above this in turn a plenum chamber is located and it is connected to the eight curved induction pipes which lead to the cylinders.

Wedge-shaped combustion chambers are used, the tops of the pistons being substantially flat except for small valve cut-outs, and the compression ratio is 8.5:1. The exhaust gases leave through ports on the outer sides of the cylinder banks and pass along four-branch manifolds to join a common expansion chamber behind the engine.

By Porsche standards the power output — 240 bhp at 5250 rpm — is pretty modest for a 4.7-litre power unit yet the 3600 rpm at which the 267.5 lb ft of maximum torque is developed is rather high for a lazy V-8. Combustion is clean, though, according to the Porsche engineers, the engine meeting the very stringent 1978 Californian standards with exhaust gas recirculation, an air pump and a catalytic converter.

The valves are operated through tappets which hydraulically take up free play and are of the inverted bucket type. A single toothed rubber belt drives the two camshafts, and it is tensioned by a jockey pulley bearing on its reverse side. The camshaft belt also drives the water pump mounted between the cylinder banks and the oil pump which is mounted low down on the right-hand side (viewed from the front) of

the engine, while the distributor of the breakerless electronic ignition system is driven off the right-hand camshaft.

In front of the casing which encloses the camshaft belt, a complete system of V-belts drives further auxiliaries. From a pulley on the nose of the crankshaft, one belt drives the air pump which lies on the left-hand side of the engine and, through a viscous coupling, the centrally-mounted cooling fan. Another belt drives the steering pump on the right-hand side of the engine, the alternator just beneath it and yet another the air conditioning pump (when fitted) on the left-hand side of the engine.

Transmission

One of the disadvantages of the form of transmission adopted for the 928 is that the propeller shaft as well as the clutch driven plate, gearbox input pinion and layshaft becomes one of the parts that have to be speeded up or slowed down by the synchromesh units when a gearchange is made. Although the propeller shaft is slender, being supported by two bearings within the torque tube linking engine to gearbox, its length of several feet must mean a significant addition to the rotary inertia involved. Accordingly, Porsche have decided to use a twin-plate clutch of small diameter in place of a larger single-plate clutch, thereby achieving a significant reduction in rotary inertia.

The five-speed gearbox is an all-new two-shaft unit, fifth being straight through and direct. It lies ahead of the rear wheel axis — not behind it as in the 924 — driving to a differential immediately behind it which is not of the limited-slip type. From this differential the drive passes to the rear wheels through a pair of equal-length drive-shafts with plunge-accepting constant velocity joints.

A three-speed plus torque converter automatic transmission will be an option.

Suspension and running gear

In many respects the 928's suspension system is quite straightforward — it is unusual only in its subtle detail. Conventional double-wishbone suspension is used at the front, for example, with an ordinary one-piece upper wishbone and a T-shaped lower link similar to that of the Austin Maxi. To reduce unsprung weight, though, both these wishbones are aluminium alloy castings. Coil springs are fitted; these encircle telescopic dampers and there is an anti-roll bar operated by short pushrods. According to the Porsche engineers, the most important elements in achieving the noise insulation essential to a luxury car of this calibre are the rubber mountings between the springs and the bodyshell; the rearward wishbone pivot points, the power-assisted rack and pinion steering and the engine are all carried on a sub-frame but this is rigidly fixed to the body. To this sub-frame are also connected the pair of small hydraulic dampers which Porsche deem necessary to attenuate engine vibrations, though a 90° V-8 is in complete primary and secondary balance.

An anti-roll bar — also operated by short pushrods — coil springs and telescopic dampers are again used at the rear, as are double wishbones. But the upper wishbone is a single transverse link and the lower wishbone is composed of a transverse blade and a tubular radius arm giving fore-and-aft location, both made of steel. For mechanical convenience the lower wishbone axis is inclined to the longitudinal axis of the car which certainly gives some understeer-inducing toe-in to the heavily loaded outside wheel in a corner — but this is not the important feature of the system.

This is the short link through which the forward end of the lower tubular radius arm is connected to the body. Under normal conditions, this arm swings about the inboard of

the two pivot points but when the outside rear wheel is subjected to a braking force in a corner, the radius arm and short link are pulled backwards to ensure toe-in rather than toe-out. The steel blade giving transverse location is strong in tension and compression but flexible enough in the fore-and-aft direction to accommodate this movement which is carefully restrained by large rubber bushes so that the normal suspension geometry is not adversely affected.

This patented arrangement springs from Porsche's strong belief that the sudden change to oversteer (or at least marked reduction in understeer) exhibited by many cars when a driver is forced by modern traffic conditions to slow in the middle of a corner is highly dangerous. We wholeheartedly concur: many years ago our present Editor coined the phrase "lift-off tuck-in" to describe this phenomenon which is useful if mild, but alarming or dangerous if severe.

Porsche's further contention is that it is nearly always due to rear-end "compliance steer" — though when this happens in their own 911 model, its marked rearward weight bias must surely have a lot to do with it. When a conventional semi-trailing rear suspension system is suddenly subjected to a braking force, they point out, the effect is usually to cause the outside loaded wheel to toe out — hence creating unwanted rear-end oversteer. To prove the point to their own satisfaction, they experimentally converted a car to rear wheel steering, appointed a second, back-seat driver and watched him struggle to keep the car on course when the front-seat driver lifted-off! The results of these tests told the engineers how large the toe-in change must be for stability.

As at the front a sub-frame is used, and to this is attached the upper transverse link and the rear pivot of the lower wishbone. Also mounted on this rear sub-frame is

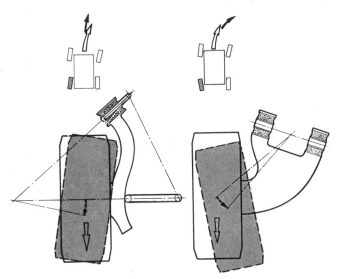

How the anti-tuck-in system works. In most conventional rear suspensions — such as the semi-trailing link type shown here — the effect of the compliance or flexibility introduced to cut road noise is to cause the heavily loaded outer wheel to toe-out (right) or at least to reduce its toe-in, if the driver slows or brakes. Toe-in of the outside wheel in turn creates oversteer. The short swinging link of the rear suspension (left) ensures that the loaded rear wheel toes in under the same conditions

GENERAL SPECIFICATION

ENGINE

Cylinders	8 in V
Capacity	4474 cc (273 cu in)
Bore/stroke	95.0/78.9 mm (3.74/3.11 in)
Cooling	Water
Block	High-silicon
Head	Light alloy
Valves	Sohc
Compression	8.5:1
Fuel metering	Bosch K-Jetronic injection
Bearings	5 main
Fuel pump	Twin electric
Max power	240 bhp (DIN) at 5250 rpm
Max torque	267.5 lb ft (DIN) at 3600 rpm

TRANSMISSION

Type	5-speed manual (3-speed automatic optional)
Clutch	Twin-plate
Internal ratios and mph/1000 rpm	
Top	1.000:1
4th	1.343:1
3rd	1.819:1
2nd	2.466:1
1st	3.601:1
Rev	3.162:1
Final drive	2.75:1

BODY/CHASSIS

Construction	Unitary steel with aluminium front wings, doors and bonnet
Protection	galvanized, extensively protected and guaranteed for 6 years

SUSPENSION

Front	Ind. by wishbones with coil springs, telescopic dampers and an anti-roll bar
Rear	Ind. by wishbones with coil springs, telescopic dampers, an anti-roll bar and an anti-tuck-in system

STEERING

Type	Rack and pinion
Assistance	Yes

BRAKES

Type	Ventilated discs
Servo	Yes
Circuits	Split diagonally

WHEELS

Type	Alloy 7 in rims
Tyres	225/50 VR 16

ELECTRICAL

Battery	12V, 66Ah
Polarity	Negative earth
Generator	1360W altenator

DIMENSIONS

Wheelbase	8 ft	2.4 in
Length	14 ft	7.1 in
Track-front	5 ft	0.8 in
rear	4 ft	11.6 in
Width	6 ft	0.3 in
Height	4 ft	3.7 in
Weight	28.5 cwt.	

AVAILABILITY AND PRICE

The 928 will not be available in Britain until next year, and in price, Porsche say, it will lie somewhere between the Carrera and the Turbo.

---

the gearbox/differential unit, forming with the torque and engine a complete rigid unit which is isolated from the bodyshell and has a large mass which helps to damp out the vibrations generated within it. To increase its mass still further — and also to shift the position of a troublesome vibrational node, the battery and the rear end of the exhaust system are also supported by the sub-frame. As a further defence against vibration, a second pair of small hydraulic dampers is connected between the sub-frame and the gearbox.

In its braking system the 928 is rather more conventional. Four floating-caliper ventilated discs are fitted, mounted outboard and operated with servo-assistance through circuits which are split diagonally in conjunction with negative offset steering. Alloy wheels with 7 in rims are standard, and 255/50-16 tyres are fitted.

Fittings and furniture

To 911 owners, one of the most welcome features of the new car may well be its comprehensive heating and ventilation system, largely made possible by the water cooling of the engine, for which air conditioning is an option. But the 928 has several unusual luxury features in addition to the more ordinary items such as a vacuum-operated central door locking device and a seat which is adjustable for height as well as backrest angle and fore-and-aft position (with electrical operation as another option).

Take the instruments, for example. These are handsome, well-located, and in the best modern fashion grouped behind a single glass which is tilted to minimise unwanted reflections. They are also ample in number, consisting of a speedometer, a rev-counter, a voltmeter and fuel, water temperature and oil pressure gauges. But the unusual feature of the display is its warning light system. Any malfunction in the system monitored is signalled by a light which flashes in front of the driver; the nature of the malfunction is displayed on a separate panel in the central console. If the fault is minor — such as an empty washer bottle — the driver can cancel the flashing warning and

attend to the problem at his leisure, but if the problem is serious — a low brake fluid level, say — the warning light continues to flash.

Nor is that all. The complete instrument binnacle, carrying the stalks and several other switches and controls as well as the instruments themselves, moves up and down with the steering wheel which is adjustable for rake. This, Porsche say, maintains the instruments in the correct viewing position for the individual driver, but we attach as much if not more importance to the advantage of maintaining the stalks in a constant position relative to the wheel. The steering wheel is not adjustable for reach as well as rake, but with the help of spacers, the pedals are. Other luxury features of the 928 are a speed control device, a special additional bottle of screen-wash fluid for exceptionally dirty conditions and a specially developed four-speaker radio/cassette player.

Driving impressions

A short session on a factory test track — even one as magnificent as Porsche's Weissach mountain circuit — is a poor way of assessing a car as sophisticated and significant as the 928. In the space of a few minutes, though, the car managed to convey several important impressions — all of them favourable. Perhaps the most surprising of these was the way in which the car contrived to feel almost *more* responsive than a Carrera that I also drove. It was perhaps helped by a power-steering system which was difficult to distinguish from a good manual steering mechanism. As might be expected from a Porsche — and from those huge fat tyres — the cornering power was tremendous, while the lift-off tuck-in system worked admirably, the car feeling completely stable during various antics on the steering pad.

The engine has the characteristic V-8 throb, albeit a subdued and remote throb — and I don't think many owners will complain about the performance! It would pull strongly from low rpm, but fifth gear is very high.

Personally, I don't like the gearshift pattern Porsche have chosen for the car — the old-fashioned arrangement with first out on a dogleg — but I found the change precise and unobstructive, if a little slow.

The 928 has a light and airy interior and a comfortable driving position with ample legroom for the tallest of drivers. The seat matched Porsche's established high standard of comfort combined with outstanding lateral and lumbar support.

Wind noise was very low, and on the perhaps untypical test-track surface there wasn't much road noise.

I OF ALL people should have approached the Porsche 928 with confidence. After all, my present long-term test car is a 924, and is the 928 not simply a bigger and better version of it?

No, it is not. When you see the two cars side by side, they don't even look the same. The 924 is a lightweight, its waistline delicately scooped, its airy back window all space and nothingness. Contrast the 928 with its starkly level waistline, its flying buttresses flanking the smaller rear hatch, above all its extra width — and the headlamps idly reclining, pointing skyward instead of being tucked away under flaps.

Nor is it reassuring to sit inside. Now the extra width is even more apparent. Tall as I am, I cannot be sure enough of judging it to (I hope) my customary inch. It rolls away out of sight. Sharp-eyed styling has its uses. At least the controls and instruments are not unfamiliar. There are more of them, that is all. The one that mostly matters is the speed control, something which will surely become more common as its virtues, fuel- as well and licence-saving, become apparent. Five speeds in the gearbox instead of four. A heavier clutch. The steering powered, yet feeling almost as heavy as in my unpowered 924.

My passenger for the morning — an unnerving one, were he not so relaxed and pleasant — is John Wyer, dropping in on his old friends at Porsche to have a look at their latest car. Our task is a simple one: out along the twisting upper road through and beyond Grasse to Draguignan, south to the *autoroute* and home. It is Saturday morning, as pleasant a spring morning as the South of France can provide. Much of the province is one the move, to market, to friends, to *le picnic* perhaps. We move out to join them.

The 928 feels big but smooth. There can be no doubting the beauty of the 4½-litre V8, developed as Porsche say for torque rather than power. It pulls superbly from 1,000 rpm in fifth gear, a steady push in the back. One could never talk of this engine "coming on the cam". The torque is there smoothly, continuously, helped by the friction-free accelerator linkage which

is one of the marks of careful development and concern for the driver. Of course, the potential for more power is there as well. No doubt we shall one day see how great it is. For the moment, there is enough to whisk the 928 rapidly to high speed — though for the moment the high speeds must wait for the clear roads to the west of Grasse.

The steering is a marvel. One must consciously recall that it *is* powered. Nothing about the feel gives the game away, only the suspicion, something short of awareness, that one is not working hard enough. It is precise. There is even some fight-back over a potholed surface. The lock is surprisingly tight. At low speeds, the ride is lumpy and the Pirelli P7s create some bump-thump and rumble. Baulked, we follow the main traffic stream patiently into Grasse.

Grasse lives · on perfume. Why else would it be there? It sits in a tight fold of herb-flowered hills, and its side roads twist and dart about to meet the main street at acute angles. People attempt impossible turns, try to squeeze into impossible parking places. We stop, start,

stop again. The 928 takes the whole thing in its stride, muttering through the traffic, quiet, self-effacing except for its looks which instantly attract the young enthusiasts of the town.

Out of Grasse, not up the famous *Route Napoleon*, his road back from Elba, but along the less popular N562. It skirts the foothills of the Alpes Maritimes, crossing the river valleys one by one, always in the same pattern: turn right up the valley, some kind of hairpin left over a bridge, along the other side and swing right again round the shoulder of the hill. How many times does it do that between Grasse and Draguignan? Fifty? A hundred? Often enough, at least, to find out all about the handling of the 928.

Suddenly, the car no longer seems a lump. The sense of width, of the hidden nearside, vanishes. The 928 will proceed with grace, yet does not altogether appreciate it. Down in the valley, stuck in the traffic, it was too far within its limits to come to life. Up here where I am determined to get to grips with it, the response is immediate, almost defiant. Limit? What limit?

We have been told, of course, about the Weissach rear axle. We are all somewhat sceptical. Slowly that scepticism vanishes. The Weissbach arrangement works. dive deep into a corner, wind on the steering, lift off the accelerator. The 928 doesn't care. I try it again, this time dipping the clutch as well to take out the engine torque reaction. It still doesn't care. It sits on the road, hugging the line, the grip of the low, wide Pirellis so much more than one dreams of in normal cars.

To lift off in mid-corner, I hasten to add, is not my usual practice. I hope John Wyer appreciates that. I try to make amends by settling down to drive the 928 as I might a 911: for each corner, judge the line, slow just a bit more than enough, then feed in the power all the way round. When you get it right, it is the most satisfying feeling. In a way, the 928 feeds me more of that satisfaction than most cars. Most of the way along this astonishing road, I stay in third gear: fourth whenever a kilometre of straight comes up, second for the tight bridge-hairpins.

The handling, no less than the sheer grip, is astonishing. Faster

Practical

Road impressions of the new V8-engined Porsche 928 in the mountains and on the autoroutes of the South of France

By Jeffrey Daniels

ound each succeeding corner, urely with a sideways force pproaching 1g. Even a mid-corner ump seems not to worry this stonishing car. The 911 would flick ut its tail and call for instant orrection, but not the 928: if it goes t all, it skitters sideways with all our wheels, a few inches of give to egain its composure? Certainly not ack of power, nor of steering lock. here is no understeer to speak of, nerely a sense that the front wheels are going exactly where hey are intended. Nor control, ither. That superb steering, the alance, the wonderfully esponsive throttle, deny that. So it nust, in the end, be grip; yet Pirelli nave built a tyre to match the car.

And the brakes, what of them? I nave driven 50 miles, me, a rofessional test driver, and not given the brakes a thought . . . vhich is, of course, the ultimate ompliment. We do not notice hings which behave perfectly, which do exactly as we ask without omplaint. That is the measure of he 928 brakes, whether you are alking about response or ultimate topping power or fade resistance.

So is there anything to complain bout? Perhaps there is. The

gearchange is wide-gated. In the Porsche tradition, it has immaculate syncromesh, and the lever movements are light, the gate precise. Yet it seems wrong, somehow, that when the rest of the car is so little effort to drive, one should be slamming this lever around from position to position. The first time I selected fifth, my right elbow thumped John Wyer smartly in the ribs. Purists may scoff, but I feel the 928 may be even better to drive when it gets its promised Mercedes automatic transmission.

Down the final hill into Draguignan, provincial capital of the Var until it was usurped by upstart Toulon. A flatter town, this, though still set in a valley. The traffic gets worse again. We turn left, feeling much more in charge now, and set off towards sea and *autoroute*.

The *autoroute* which bypasses Frejus and Cannes is a major engineering achievement, picking its way through the parched hills behind the coast. Here the 928 is able to demonstrate an extension of its character — not simply its ability to rush up to 100 mph or so,

but its stability at 120 mph or better. Even then, there is plenty more to come: but no room in which to use it. The sun is hotter, falling through the deep windscreen, and the interior of the car is too warm for comfort. I am partly to blame. Along the road, the sheer effort of staying in place — not of actually driving the car — was enough to make me sweat. At least the motorway allows one to relax; until, that is, we round a bend to find the ultimate lunacy, a Frenchman stopped in the overtaking lane to assist a colleague on the hard

Happiness is a 4½ litre Porsche — the Editor (left) like his Technical colleague, found it a supercar with impeccable manners.

shoulder. The 928 brakes do their work well, almost too well for the gentleman behind us, and for a moment I think we are going to see the energy-absorbing, self-repairing rear bumper put to the test.

It is our last moment of excitement. We have learned a lot about the car. By no means everything; it didn't rain, it wasn't dark. But enough to know that the Porsche 928, like its predecessors, is a *practical* supercar. It will do as much, in total, as any other car I know. Accelerating, handling, stopping, smoothly riding at high speed, here is matches its rivals. But in detail design, the feeling that here is something solid, dependable, something one can live with and drive every day whatever the conditions: here the 928 scores most highly.

It will be a year yet before it arrives on the British market, though hopefully we will get our first look at it before then (no Motor Show this year, remember). When it comes, who can yet say what the price will be? However much it costs for a lucky few, it will be worth it. ☐

supercar

PORSCHE
Eight for the ROAD

cooled, front-engined, 8-cylinder 928. It may be the best Porsche yet   by KARL LUDVIGSEN

And we thought the sports car business was in trouble. This is the time to think of fuel economy and safety, we were told. In this polluted, fuel-poor world there was to be no place for such anachronisms as sports cars. Driving would no longer be allowed to be fun. Against all such logic, Porsche has just introduced a completely new sports car, the 928, built from scratch in every detail to be an instrument of personal pleasure. In this it is incredibly successful.

In creating the 928, which will go on sale in the fall of this year, Porsche did not shut its eyes to these realities. On the contrary, it opened them wide. But it did so with the conviction that a world that absorbs 25 million new cars a year must have room for 25 thousand or so purebred sports cars a year from a small company in Stuttgart that has always specialized in that kind of car.

Though it's in no sense a "safety car," the Porsche 928 was designed to allow it to survive in this age of governmental regulation of car design. One of the main reasons it has a front engine and rear-wheel-drive is that this layout is so widely accepted that most future auto laws will have to take it into account. It gives more room for catalysts and mufflers between the engine and the exhaust pipe tip, and it spreads out the sources of noise that register on a microphone when a car drives past a measurement point. It also offers energy-management advantages in a crash. Even the body shape of the

928, with its massive, sloping roof pillars, is planned to offer high roof strength and crush resistance.

In the 928, Porsche carries even further its passion for longevity and serviceability. Corrosion-resistant aluminum is used liberally. It's the material of the cast wheels, the doors, hood and detachable front fenders, the transaxle housing, the front suspension wishbones, the rear suspension uprights, upper links and main crossmember, and the heads, block and crankcase of the V-8 engine.

Those parts of the body that aren't of aluminum are made of galvanized steel or, at the nose and tail, plastic. Painted in body color, the plastic bumpers are carried on aluminum frames backed by hydraulic energy absorbers. They far exceed the requirements of the bumper rules.

The 928 should need service less often than other Porsches and, indeed, most other cars. Its valves don't need adjusting, because hydraulic lash adjusters are built into its cup-type tappets. Its contactless ignition needs no adjustment. Its battery is a large, long-life type hidden deep under the rear floor. Its fuel and oil filters are extra-large, and in Europe its oil-change interval is set at 12,500 miles (20,000 kilometers).

These features are part of the largest and heaviest production Porsche yet made. Its wheelbase of 98.4 in. (2500 mm) is 9 in. longer than that of the 911, 4 in. longer than the 924, and even half an inch longer than the Corvette's wheelbase. Its 59.6-in. rear track is about the same as the

Corvette's, and the 60.8-in. front track is 2 in. wider than that car's. Compared to the Corvette, the 928 is 10 in. shorter, 3 in. wider and almost 4 in. higher. At a curb weight of 3197 lb (1450 kg), the 928 is a hefty 639 lb more than a 911S and 337 less than a base Corvette.

With its V-8 engine up front, the Porsche 928 resembles the Corvette in another way. But its interior layout is vastly better than that of Chevrolet's sports car. Lengthened 4½ in. from that of the 911, the 928 interior has room for two narrow yet useful rear seats flanking a big hump above the transaxle. The rear seatbacks can be folded forward to clear more space in the trunk compartment, which is a deep tray under a lift-up rear hatch. Below the trunk floor are the space-saver spare, the plastic 22.7-gal. fuel tank, and the battery. A lavish tool kit is fitted into a container across the rear of the trunk.

For most people the 928 will be a roomy 2-seater with extra space for kids or for a couple with whom you want to have dinner downtown. The two front-seat occupants are in typical Porsche seats, facing a dash that's smooth, clean and handsome. The driver has a normal 3-spoke Porsche wheel, which gives him a welcome sense of continuity with the older Porsche models. Minor controls for the heater, radio and electric windows are all on the center console.

Four instrument dials are deeply recessed into a cove in a control pod behind the steering wheel that has a unique feature: You can adjust the

14

wheel up and down by about an inch and a half, and the whole instrument unit goes up and down with it! Various switches, including the ignition, also are carried on the control pod. That assures that drivers of different heights have a good wheel position and also are able to see the dials through the wheel. Optional is an electrically adjustable driver's seat with a height adjustment.

Surrounding the cockpit is the strongest steel monocoque body/ frame structure yet used in any Porsche. Through the deep tunnel down the center of its floor runs a drivetrain of the type we're already familiar with from the 924 (and from recent Ferraris, up to and including the Daytona): a steel tube rigidly connecting the engine and clutch up front to a combined transmission and axle at the rear. In the 928, however, there are important differences from the 924.

The clutch is a twin-disc design, to get a high torque capacity in a small diameter. Thanks to the V-8's smoothness, there are only two support bearings inside the tube for the 25mm driveshaft. And the transmission is placed ahead of the final drive gears instead of behind them. This is a lighter form of construction, and it offers several other advantages.

With the transmission ahead of the axle, Porsche could and did arrange for a direct drive in the top gear of the 5-speed transmission. In all other Porsches, the power has to go through a pair of gears, plus the final drive gears, in every ratio. This should give quieter and more efficient top-gear cruising.

This position also makes it easier to install the automatic transmission that'll be optional in the 928. Made by Mercedes-Benz and recalibrated to suit the Porsche, it has a torque converter plus 3 forward speeds. Models with the automatic will have a different floor pan with a larger bulge in the center hump between the rear-seat passengers.

Emphatically *not* made by Mercedes-Benz—in spite of many rumors to that effect—is the 928's engine. It is pure Porsche, and it is certainly the most advanced V-8 engine, and one of the most advanced power units of any kind, now being made. What else would we have expected from the Weissach engineers?

An 8-cylinder engine of 4474cc (273cid), the 928 power unit has the largest cylinders, in displacement, ever used in any Porsche. This has 559cc per cylinder, and no Porsche before has had more than 499cc per cylinder. It has the same 95mm bore used in the 3-liter Turbo, plus a longer stroke, 78.9mm. It's more oversquare (bigger bore than stroke) than the other eights in its size class, those of the Mercedes-Benz 450SL and Maserati Bora.

There are no iron liners in the 928's aluminum block. It uses steel-plated pistons running in aluminum bores in a block die-cast of Reynolds 390 alloy, the same kind used in the Vega and in the cylinders of 2.7-liter Porsche sixes since 1974. Under the block is an aluminum "girdle" that combines all the five main-bearing caps in a single massive casting. The bottom end is closed off by a shallow oil pan for the wet-sump lubrication system. It has a crescent-type pressure pump and an oil/water heat exchanger built into the left-hand header tank of the crossflow radiator.

Cylinder head design is dead conventional in the 928, with wedge-type combustion chambers and in-line valves, slanted at 20 degrees outward from the cylinder centerline. A cogged rubber belt drives the single camshaft running above each row of valves, and the back of the belt turns the water pump, which is nestled into the front of the block. Spark plugs and fuel injection nozzles are easy to get at, above the heads, and passages for emissions-reducing air injection are drilled into the heads.

This V-8 may be the first engine designed expressly for use with the Bosch K-Jetronic fuel injection system. The center vee of the block is completely clear over the back six cylinders to make room for the duct that carries air down from the injection metering unit, at the rear, and

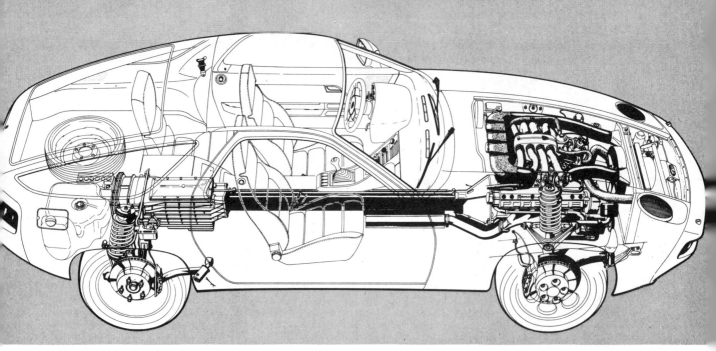

up again through the throttle to the plenum chamber above the engine. From there, individual ram pipes take the air down to each cylinder.

The ignition distributor is driven by the left-hand camshaft. At the nose of the forged steel crankshaft there's a cluster of four pulleys driving belts to the power steering pump and alternator on the left, the air pump and air conditioning compressor on the right, and the 6-bladed cooling fan at the center. The crankshaft also has a vibration damper at its nose. Complete with all these accessories, and with the air cleaner and radiator too, the engine weighs 584 lb (265 kg).

With an 8.5:1 compression ratio, the European 928 engine runs on 91-octane fuel and produces a maximum of 240 bhp at 5250 rpm. It keeps on revving up to 6200 rpm, at which point the power has dropped off to 210 bhp. Maximum torque is 268 lb-ft at 3600 rpm. In the United States and other low-emissions markets the car will be catalyst-equipped, and the power rating will drop to 225 net hp.

This powerful and hefty Porsche will be stopped by ventilated discs at all four wheels, gripped by floating calipers. The brake system is power-assisted, and its twin circuits are divided up diagonally, so braking power will always be maintained on one front and one rear wheel. A massive lever on the left side of the driver's seat applies the handbrakes, formed as small drum brakes inside the rear discs.

Production Turbo techniques were carried over to the wheels and tires of the 928, which are 16 in. in diameter. The rims are 7 in. wide, and the tires are Pirelli's Cinturato P7 pattern with a 225/50 section. Porsche has

found no tire that measures up better to its need for good all-weather grip combined with a good ride on this chassis.

In the 928, Porsche uses, for the first time, a suspension of racing car derivation on a road car. At both front and rear it's basically of coil-and-wishbone layout, topped by coil springs concentric with tubular shock absorbers. Gone are the torsion bars, struts and modified swing axles that have been used on all previous volume-production Porsches.

At the front, the kingpin geometry adopts the negative scrub radius first used by Audi and then by Volkswagen to give more stable braking

on surfaces of unequal grip. The power-assisted steering is of rack and pinion type, with a power effect that tapers off as the car goes faster. There are 3.2 turns of the steering wheel from lock to lock.

The Porsche engineers added a new trick of their own to the rear suspension. Its upper arm is a simple lateral link, and its lower arm a wide-based steel wishbone. Porsche found that the rubber suspension bushings tended to let the rear wheels toe out when the car was decelerating or being braked, and this in turn made the car swerve inward on a turn. It put a special rubber-bushed link in the front joint of each lower wishbone, designed to compensate for that toe-out tendency. This patented "Weissach axle," named after the Porsche engineering center, keeps the rear wheels from steering the car that way.

This is not the 928's only trick. It is packed with intriguing and useful technical goodies. Automatic speed control *(Tempomat)* is standard. The pop-up headlights have their lenses exposed so they're cleaned when the car is washed, and a knob on the left of the driver's seat adjusts the angle of the beams to suit the way the car is loaded.

The first true production of this complex new Porsche was scheduled for May. By August this is to be stepped up to 20 cars a day in a new assembly plant across the street from the main Porsche factory. The aim for the first full year of production is to build 5000 cars, half of which may make it to Porsche's main market, America. In the fall the 928 will be put on sale in all of Porsche's important markets.

What will it cost? Porsche has already announced that the base price in West Germany will be DM 55,000, about $22,900. In the United States, where air conditioning will be standard, it will be "definitely under $25,000." This places it in a slot between the Turbo and the rest of the 911 Porsche line.

With the arrival of the 928, the Porsche range takes on a completely new look. Said Dr. Ernst Fuhrmann, the head of Porsche, "For the first time our firm can offer a range of models in which the proven 911 is supplemented by the 928, above, and the smaller 924 below." It is the new concept, that of the front engine and rear transaxle, that will eventually rule. The 911 has been a magnificent car, one of the greatest in all auto history. But in the 928 it has met its match. [MT]

Porsche 928

Specifications

GENERAL

No. of U.S. dealers	305
Warranty	NA
Base price	NA
Price as tested	NA

POWERTRAIN

Engine type	SOHC V-8
Bore & stroke	95.0mm x 78.9mm
Displacement	4474cc/273cid
Horsepower at rpm	240 at 5250
Torque (lb-ft) at rpm	268 at 3600
Compression ratio	8.5:1
Carburetion	Bosch K-Jetronic F.I.
Transmission	5-spd manual
Final drive ratio	2.75:1

CHASSIS

Body/frame	Unitized
Suspension, front	Independent, double trailing arms, coil springs, hydraulic shocks
rear	Independent, diagonal trailing arms, upper transverse trailing arms (Weissach axle), coil springs, hydraulic shocks
Steering type	Rack and pinion, pwr-assisted
Turns lock-to-lock	3.2
Turning circle diameter	NA
Brakes, front	Ventilated discs
rear	Ventilated discs
Wheel size	cast alloy, 7Jx16
Tires, make & size	Pirelli 225/50 VR 16

DIMENSIONS

Wheelbase	98.4 in.
Track, front	60.8 in.
rear	56.9 in.
Length	175.2 in.
Width	72.3 in.
Height	51.7 in.
Curb Weight	3197 lb
Fuel Capacity	22.7 U.S. gals.

Test Data

ACCELERATION

0-60 mph	6.7 sec
0-80 mph	11.0 sec
0-90 mph	13.0 sec
0-100 mph	17.0 sec
Standing quarter mile	15.2 sec

PORSCHE 928

Ring out the old, ring in the new

WHAT IS A Porsche 928? It's driving farther and farther down your favorite twisty road for the sheer exhilaration of driving. It's braking for a corner you always brake for and then asking yourself afterward: Why did I slow down?

It's a V-8 engine with the sort of tach-twisting throttle response rarely experienced in these days of low emissions, low compression and low performance. It's using wide-open throttle for no other reason than to surround yourself with the mellow guttural roar of a fuel-injected, 4.5-liter, single-overhead cam V-8. It's the smooth surge of power that can result in blaring sirens and flashing red lights unless you watch the speedometer (and rearview mirror) closely.

It's a feeling of total command: an excellent driving position, comfortable individual seats with just the right body-gripping contours, an expansive view of the road up front and the world all around. It's the feeling that even if you were blindfolded you'd know exactly where each important control is located.

It's the precision of rack-and-pinion steering with speed-sensitive assist that's so unobtrusive you're never consciously aware that the steering is assisted. It's the awe and confidence-inspiring grip of 225/50VR-16 Pirelli P7 radials. It's a feeling of balance and security that urges you to drive faster and faster—and discovering each time when you're sure you've reached the limit that the car can be pushed even harder.

It's finding yourself in the middle of a fast decreasing-radius turn on an unfamiliar road with metal-bending rock walls on either side and hearing the tires take on that characteristic juddering squeal as they fight for grip at the limit of adhesion. And that heart pounding, adrenaline pumping, throat tightening, derriere puckering sensation you experience as the turn gets tighter and tighter and the tail starts to slide. And that feeling of complete euphoria as you snick the front wheels into mild opposite lock and exit in complete control, saying to yourself, I made it, and knowing deep inside that the car was probably 70 percent responsible for the save. And it's reflecting on the incident later and realizing that if you'd been in the same situation in virtually any other car, right now somebody would probably be peeling you and that car off those very unforgiving rock walls.

It's a Toyota Celica driver who goes seven miles out of his way to follow you into your driveway and who admits he'd have driven 70 miles to get a better look at your car. It's being followed by vans, gawked at by Volvo drivers, eyed by 18-wheelers and pursued by Porsche 924s and 911s that make U-turns and run red lights to get another glimpse of this newest Porsche.

What else is a Porsche 928? It's hard cold facts and a scrutiny of details and a battery of acceleration, braking, noise and handling tests. Does the 928 disappoint in these areas? Judge for yourself.

18

The styling is . . . well . . . the words that first come to mind are different, rounded, controversial, love it/hate it (choose one). Porsche's Chief Stylist, Tony Lapine, is an American, so we'd be the last to cry "foul" if you likened the shape to such American image cars as the Chevrolet Corvette and the Pontiac Firebird Trans-Am. Nor would you be wrong if you placed your money on the Datsun 280Z and the Ferrari Daytona.

Two of the most controversial design elements are the flat exposed headlights and the super-stubby rear end. Despite what you may think, the headlight treatment is no fluke. Porsche says they're uncovered because most owners of cars with concealed headlights forget to keep them clean. That's a logical answer when you consider that most German designs are logical and practical to the nth degree. But how do you explain the 924's headlights and the headlight washers Porsche has fitted to the 928 to cover that contingency? Unless, of course, Porsche believes the typical owner will forget he has this convenience at his fingertips. Porsche also says the uncovered lamps accent that expansive hood. Probably true and also probably to keep the 928 from being mistaken for a 924.

One staffer described the rear end this way: "If it were the year 2001 I could almost believe the rear was the front with some new type headlight treatment and a single wiper for the windshield." Another said he had the sensation of being stared at when viewing the car from about 10 ft away at a rear three-quarter angle. The shape of the rear is, to be sure, aggressive and thus quite in keeping with the behavior of the typical Porsche driver.

Taken as a whole, the 928 is, as Tony Lapine says, "A car that should grow on the public and become more appealing with age."

The 928 is the most comfortable Porsche ever built. The driving position and seating comfort rate with the world's finest and the controls, with only a few minor exceptions, are properly placed and close at hand. For instance, the shorter drivers on our staff thought the gearshift lever was positioned a little too far rearward. But there was unanimous praise for the ingenious steering-column height adjustment. The instrument pod containing the central round speedometer and tachometer plus smaller round dials for auxiliary gauges and critical warning lights moves with the column. So there's no way for these gauges to be blocked from view when the wheel is moved up or down. Neat.

Other minor controls are grouped on either side of the steering wheel as either round push buttons or rotary switches. And, surprise, the driver-actuated hydraulic control for aiming the

headlights to compensate for changes in car loading and ride height made it past the feds.

The primary gauges are supplemented by a central warning system that monitors the most important operating functions of the car. A warning light located in the center of the instrument cluster comes on automatically to report a defect in the car. At the same time, another indicator light tells the driver whether a critical component (oil pressure, oil level, brake fluid level, brake failure, coolant temperature, coolant level) or an important component (brake pad wear, fuel level, windshield washer fluid level, stop lights, taillights, parking lights) has failed. For non-critical failures, a reset button on the indicator board allows the driver to turn off the central warning light after a defect has been reported.

Column controls are used for major functions, the left stalk for directionals and high/low beams and the two on the right side for windshield wipers/washers and the standard cruise control. Surprised that the 928 has cruise control? Don't be. The 911SC

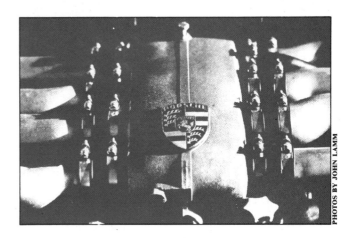

offers it as an option and we have to agree when Porsche explains, "Nowadays comfort is just as important as sportiness." That statement also explains standard features such as air conditioning, an electrically adjustable and heated outside mirror (the one on the right side of our test car is a $90 option), a central door locking system, electric window lifts and an impressive Blaupunkt AM/FM/cassette sound system with electric retract-

ing antenna and separate controls for left/right and front/rear speaker balance.

The comprehensive heater/vent/air conditioning system is the best of any Porsche but in the vent mode it has one flaw. The two central adjustable dash-level vents duct air only on the air conditioning setting and most drivers complained that the adjustable vents integrated into the door panel armrests couldn't be angled far enough to blow sufficient air low on the body. The heater, like the 911's, will practically fry eggs and burn toast. And how Porsche manages to make the heater smell the same as it does in its air-cooled cars is a perplexing question.

If you remember that the 928 is a 2+2, you won't be disappointed with the rear seating. It's occasional at best with barely adequate head room for a person 5 ft 8 in. tall. And that same 5 ft 8 incher has to sit in those deeply contoured seats with his knees splayed on either side of the front seat when the driver's seat is comfortably adjusted for a person of the same height. But to help compensate for lack of space, Porsche provides rear seaters with appreciated amenities including grab handles, an ashtray and lighter, a shallow, locking central console, a map light and sun visors that rotate 180 degrees to shade the leading edge of the *rear* window. The visors can also be positioned as blinds in front of the eyes of squeamish passengers. When these seats aren't occupied, the backs can be folded flat to increase the luggage capacity from 6.3 to 20.5 cu ft.

Full credit must go to Porsche for designing as much room as they did into the rear compartment. Like the 911, the 928 is an impressively roomy car for its compact size. High marks also for the lightweight aluminum doors which are easy to open and close despite their length.

Rumors circulated during the 928's gestation period that this newest Porsche's sohc 4.5-liter V-8 was a Mercedes-Benz power-plant proved totally false. (For technical details see June 1977 R&T.) In U.S. smog trim, this compact, watercooled, aluminum 8-cylinder produces 219 bhp at 5250 rpm and generates 254 lb-ft of torque at 3600. It's equipped with Bosch K-Jetronic injection that's fed with fuel from two surprisingly noisy pumps. Distribution of the fuel/air mixture is via a cast-aluminum spider-like manifold mounted between the cylinder banks. Call it heresy if you wish, but the engine sounds and feels like a smoother and quieter small-block Chevrolet; and with throttle response that belies its 8.5:1 compression ratio. Around 3500 rpm the engine takes on a mild rough growling note that continues to about 5000. Then the sound smooths out again and the V-8 revs without strain to its 6000-rpm redline. Cold starting and warmup in our rather mild coastal California climate were exemplary.

Porsches are expected to go fast. And the 3410-lb (curb weight) 928 is quick, reaching 60 mph in 7.0 sec, covering the quarter mile in 15.6 sec at 93.0 mph and topping out at six score and 18 mph. But what's even more impressive, particularly to someone used to the somewhat peaky response of earlier Porsches, is the big V-8's flexibility. Let the revs fall to 1000 rpm in 5th gear, step on the throttle and the 928 picks up speed, admittedly slowly, without the slightest protest. There's just no substitute for cubic inches and the low-speed torque of a V-8 engine . . . unless it's an engine with even more cylinders.

Of course, the typical 928 driver won't be caught dead lugging his engine in this fashion. He'll be taking full advantage of the five speeds at his disposal. The shift pattern, with reverse ahead of 1st gear, is not our favorite. We prefer having reverse out of the way, over to the right below 5th. The 928's gearbox represents a reversal of current Porsche practice (the first 911 5-speeds also had reverse in line with 1st) and most of our staffers said they'd prefer a positive reverse lockout, not just spring tension to prevent catching reverse by mistake. Despite the long distance between the shifter mechanism and the rear gearbox, the shift linkage is precise and accurate but not as crisp feeling as the best front engine/front gearbox designs. As usual, the Porsche synchronizer action is excellent, except for a little balkiness when the gearbox is cold. Those drivers who desire the convenience of clutchless shifting can order a 3-speed automatic transmission in place of the 5-speed manual with no increase in price.

For most driving conditions the combination of vented discs and fat Pirelli P7s yielded impressive braking. The one sour note was the moderate rear locking and slewing encountered during our 80–0 mph panic stops. Considerable pedal modulation was required, but even so, these stops averaged a short 248 ft.

No previous Porsche has had the finely balanced handling characteristics exhibited by the 928, the near 50/50 weight distribution resulting in race car-like neutral response. Yes, it will oversteer if the driver so commands, but anyone who gets into trouble driving this car should be stripped of his driver's license, issued a pair of Adidas and banished to a class for remedial joggers.

We wouldn't be surprised if you took one look at those low-section P7s pumped up to 36 psi and said the 928 must ride like a truck. And you'd be wrong. True, those tires are harsh over sharp inputs such as lane-divider dots and tar strips and they're also noisy on all but the smoothest asphalt surfaces, but otherwise the ride is wonderfully supple and well controlled. The softness of the suspension on our California freeways had some drivers expecting a floaty, wallowy ride on fast, twisty undulating roads. Nothing could be farther from reality. The 928's suspension soaks up dips, bumps and every other pavement irregularity in stride with never an unwanted change in direction. Most impressive. And it bears repeating: The steering is superb, with road feel, feedback and precise control few other systems, assisted or not, can match.

If you've gotten the impression we love the 928, you're right. Its combination of comfort, sportiness and civility (it's the quietest Porsche we've ever tested) rank it with the world's great GTs. In describing the 911, R&T has said, "There's no other sports car like it. And if you want one, you pay the price or do without." The same can be said of the 928. At $26,000 it can hardly be considered a bargain, but clever engineering doesn't come cheaply and few automotive design teams are more clever than the one residing in Zuffenhausen, West Germany.

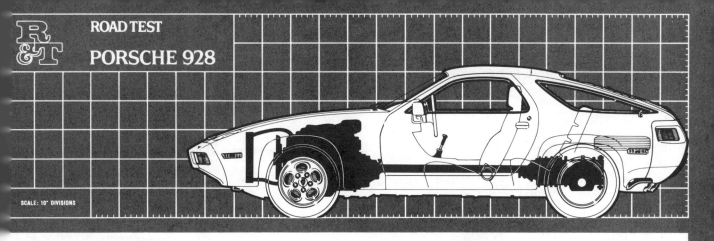

PORSCHE 928

SCALE: 10" DIVISIONS

PRICE

List price, all POE $28,500
Price as tested, west coast....$28,900
  Price as tested includes: standard equipment (air cond, AM/FM stereo/cassette, forged alloy wheels & Pirelli P7s), elect. adj right side mirror ($90), dealer prep (est $200), Calif. emissions ($110)

IMPORTER

Porsche-Audi Div, VW of America
818 Sylvan Ave
Englewood Cliffs, N.J. 07632

GENERAL

Curb weight, lb 3410
Test weight 3510
Weight distribution (with
  driver), front/rear, % 51/49
Wheelbase, in. 98.3
Track; front/rear 60.8/59.6
Length 175.7
Width 72.3
Height 51.6
Ground clearance..................... 4.7
Overhang, front/rear 39.7/37.7
Usable trunk space, cu ft....6.3+14.2
Fuel capacity, U.S. gal. 22.4

ENGINE

Type .... sohc V-8
Bore x stroke, mm........ 95.0 x 78.9
  Equivalent in. .... 3.74 x 3.11
Displacement, cc/cu in.....4474/273
Compression ratio 8.5:1
Bhp @ rpm, net .... 219 @ 5250
  Equivalent mph 145
Torque @ rpm, lb-ft .. 254 @ 3600
  Equivalent mph 99
Fuel injection ....Bosch K-Jetronic
Fuel requirement ..unleaded, 91-oct
Exhaust-emission control equipment: catalytic converter, exhaust-gas recirculation, air injection

DRIVETRAIN

Transmission .... 5-sp manual
Gear ratios: 5th (1.00) 2.75:1
  4th (1.34) 3.69:1
  3rd (1.75) 4.81:1
  2nd (2.47) 6.79:1
  1st (3.60) 9.90:1
Final drive ratio.................. 2.75:1

ACCOMMODATION

Seating capacity, persons .. 2 + 2
Seat width, f/r, in....2 x 20.0/2 x 15.0
Head room, f/r 36.5/32.0
Seat back adjustment, deg 70

CHASSIS & BODY

Layout .... front engine/rear drive
Body/frame: unit steel with aluminum doors, hood, front fenders
Brake system: vented discs; 11.1-in. front, 11.4 in. rear, vacuum assisted
  Swept area, sq in. 440
Wheels ....forged alloy, 16 x 7J
Tires .... Pirelli P7, 225/50VR-16
Steering type: rack & pinion, power assisted
  Overall ratio 17.8:1
  Turns, lock-to-lock 3.1
  Turning circle, ft 31.5
Front suspension: upper A-arms, lower trailing arms, coil springs, tube shocks, anti-roll bar
Rear suspension: upper transverse links, lower trailing arms, coil springs, tube shocks, anti-roll bar

CALCULATED DATA

Lb/bhp (test weight) 16.2
Mph/1000 rpm (5th gear) 27.3
Engine revs/mi (60 mph) 2200
Piston travel, ft/mi 1140
R&T steering index 0.98
Brake swept area, sq in./ton .. 251

INSTRUMENTATION

Instruments: 170-mph speedo, 7000-rpm tach, 999,999 odometer, 999.9 trip odo, oil press., coolant temp, voltmeter, fuel level, clock
Warning lights: central warning system (see text), hand brake, ignition, hazard, seatbelts, high beam, directionals

MAINTENANCE

Service intervals, mi:
  Oil change......................... 7500
  Filter change 15,000
  Tuneup 15,000
  Warranty, mo/mi........ 12/20,000

RELIABILITY

From R&T Owner Surveys the average number of problem areas for all models surveyed is 12. An average of 7 of these problem areas is considered serious enough to constitute reliability areas that could keep the car off the road. As owners of earlier-model Porsches reported 11 problem areas and 4 reliability areas we expect the overall reliability of the 928 to be better than average.

ROAD TEST RESULTS

ACCELERATION

Time to distance, sec:
  0-100 ft. 3.3
  0-500 ft 8.7
  0-1320 ft (¼ mi) 15.6
Speed at end of ¼ mi, mph ...93.0
Time to speed, sec:
  0-30 mph 2.5
  0-40 mph 3.7
  0-60 mph 7.0
  0-80 mph 11.5
  0-100 mph 18.5
  0-110 mph 25.8

SPEEDS IN GEARS

5th gear (5000 rpm)............. 138
4th (6000)............................ 121
3rd (6000)............................. 91
2nd (6000)............................ 67
1st (6000) 47

FUEL ECONOMY

Normal driving, mpg 16.0
Cruising range, mi (1-gal. res)....342

HANDLING

Speed on 100-ft radius, mph 34.8
Lateral acceleration, g............ 0.811
Speed thru 700-ft slalom, mph...59.7

BRAKES

Minimum stopping distances, ft:
  From 60 mph 138
  From 80 mph 248
Control in panic stop................good
Pedal effort for 0.5g stop, lb 18
Fade: percent increase in pedal effort to maintain 0.5g deceleration in 6 stops from 60 mph ....nil
Parking: hold 30% grade? ....yes
Overall brake rating.........very good

INTERIOR NOISE

All noise readings in dBA:
Idle in neutral........................66
Maximum, 1st gear 83
Constant 30 mph 68
  50 mph...............................71
  70 mph...............................73
  90 mph...............................78

SPEEDOMETER ERROR

30 mph indicated is actually 29.5
50 mph 50.5
60 mph 60.0
70 mph 70.0
80 mph 82.0
Odometer, 10.0 mi.....................9.9

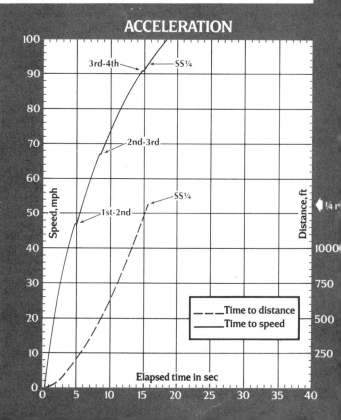

ACCELERATION

3rd-4th — SS¼
2nd-3rd
SS¼
1st-2nd

Speed, mph

Distance, ft

¼

- - - Time to distance
——— Time to speed

Elapsed time in sec

Star Road Test
PORSCHE 928

1978 Car of the Year and now, at last, available in England — is Porsche's all-new supercar really all that it's cracked up to be?

HOW DO you follow up on a legend? That was the dilemma faced by Porsche when it took the decision to add a larger, more luxurious and dearer car to its range, up-market of that charismatic pleasure-machine, the 911.

As a manufacturer that only produces sports cars, Porsche knew its new car would have to live up to an almost unrivalled sporting reputation. But then again, as a manufacturer *dependent* on the sports car, Porsche knew it would have to safeguard its future by designing a car that is compatible with a political and ecological climate ever more hostile to the idea of the sports car as a temperamental, anti-social plaything for the selfish hedonist.

Porsche's solution was the 928, a 2+2 coupé with striking curvaceous contours, introduced to an awe-struck world last year, and subsequently winner of the 1978 Car of the Year award. Technically, it is no surprise that the 911's fundamentally unsound rear engine layout was discarded, but more surprising is the rejection of the theoretically supreme — in sporting terms — mid-engine layout. Instead, for the sake of space and practicality the 928 has an essentially conventional front engine/rear wheel drive layout, though it's rather less conventional in detail, with the five-speed gearbox mounted at the rear in unit with the final drive. It has all-

independent coil spring suspension employing double wishbones at the front and lower wishbones with upper transverse links at the rear, while all four wheels are braked by ventilated discs.

The all-new water-cooled engine is a 90-deg V8 of all-alloy construction with pistons running directly in the alloy bores of its cylinders that add up to a capacity of 4474 cc. Fuel is supplied by Bosch K-jetronic injection through in-line valves that are actuated by a single overhead cam on each bank. On a compression ratio of 8.5:1 it produces 240 bhp (DIN) at 5500 rpm. A respectable output, but hydraulic tappets and 2-star fuel requirement also reflect the overall emphasis on durability, and low maintenance costs.

Because it was a new, bigger and supposedly better car from the people who gave us the 911, the 928 created expectations that no new car should, in fairness, be burdened with. And only now, a year and a half since its introduction, do UK car buyers get their chance to find out whether the expectations are realised. At a price of £19,499, Porsche GB has already taken orders for almost all the 300 cars destined for the UK in 1979.

The 928's price may well be less than many had expected: it's £4,000 more than the 911SC Sport, certainly, but £4,500 cheaper than the

911 Turbo, and cheaper than some rivals such as the Aston Martin V8 (£23,999 in manual form) or Maserati Kyalami (£21,996). On the other hand it is undercut by such as Jaguar's XJS (£15,149), the BMW 633 CSi (£15,379) or Ferrari 308 GT4 (£15,250).

On balance, though, the 928 is competitively priced within its market and perhaps the fact that it is not even the dearest Porsche is also a clue to why the 928 does not entirely live up to all the expectations we had of it. Impressive though the performance and handling are, they do not set new standards, while overall refinement is let down by excessive road noise.

In the final analysis, while the 928 undoubtedly *is* a most desirable car even by the exacting standards of its class, it isn't, after all, The Ultimate.

PERFORMANCE

★★
★★ It is perhaps a sad comment on the motoring times that when a company like Porsche has the opportunity to design a new engine starting with a clean piece of paper, such parameters as performance and sheer driver appeal must cede, to a certain extent, to requirements relating to emissions, economy, noise and easy maintenance.

Thus, in contrast to the 911's glorious rev-for-ever flat six with its high specific output and unmistakable sound of power, we have an essentially 'soft' V8 with hydraulic tappets producing fewer than 54 bhp per litre — a total of 240 bhp

(DIN) from its 4474 cc — and peaking at a modest 5500 rpm. With its all-alloy construction, overhead cams, oversquare (95 × 78.9 mm) cylinder dimensions and K-Jetronic fuel injection the potential is obviously there, but has yet to be fully realised.

But if the 928 does not raise Porsche performance standards on to an even higher plane (outright, the current 911 is a quicker car) it does introduce a new docility and effortlessness as exemplified by 257 lb ft of torque peaking at 3600 rpm and the ability to accelerate sweetly and sturdily from below 500 rpm in fourth gear. Adequate performance, with (almost) unmatched civility, seems to be the message.

For the truth is that by Supercar standards the 928's outright performance is unexceptional. To accelerate from 0-60 mph in 7.0 sec and to 100 mph in 17.8 sec makes the 928 no sluggard, but the Jaguar, the Aston and the Ferrari do it faster. In top gear, too, the 928 sets no new standards.

We were unable to record a true maximum speed in the 928, but the speeds we *were* able to reach suggest that 140 mph is about it, all out, even though Porsche claims 143 mph plus. It's more than enough, of course, but again the Aston, the Ferrari and the Jaguar do better.

But, to coin a cliché, it's not what the car does, but the way it does it. So quiet is the Porsche's V8, and so smooth (apart from a slight throbby vibration over 4000 rpm) that what performance it has can be more fully exploited than in many of its rivals, though the XJS, for one, is even better. It feels able to maintain maximum speed all day in its loping fifth gear, or for vivid overtaking acceleration (30-50 mph in 5.4, 50-70 mph in 5.2 and 70-90 mph in 5.6 sec) you can stay in fourth all day on give and take roads without a hint of strain from the engine. Or you can simply trickle along in traffic with fewer than 1000 rpm on the clock and know that when your chance comes to open up again, the engine will respond without a hint of hesitation or temperament. There *is* a power band — concentrated between 3000 and 5500 rpm — but it is a broad and barely perceptible one, the engine pulling as sweetly from 1000 rpm as it revs freely to 6000.

ECONOMY

By Supercar standards the 928's overall fuel consumption of 14.9 mpg is reason-

ably thrifty, though by Porsche's own standards — in comparison to what past 911 test cars have achieved — it is nothing special. It should be borne in mind, though, that unlike most of its rivals, the 928 only requires the cheaper 2-star fuel.

As the 928 is fitted with electronic fuel injection we were unable to measure steady-speed fuel consumption and so compute our usual Touring mpg figure. However, on a couple of occasions we approached 18 mpg on motorway-type runs even with much cruising in the 90 to 100 mph range. By observing the speed limit in the UK it should be possible easily to exceed 20 mpg — an estimate that is in keeping with Porsche's claim of 21.7 mpg at a steady 75 mph. Even at 18 mpg the 928 would have a range of well over 300 miles on its 18.9 gallon tank.

TRANSMISSION

★★
★★

In virtually every aspect of its design the 928's transmission is unconventional, from the gate pattern of its gearchange, through the twin-plate clutch and torque-tube-enclosed propshaft, to the mounting of its five-speed gearbox in unit with the final drive at the rear axle.

The gate pattern places the top four forward gears in a conventional H pattern, with first over to the left and back (with reverse opposite) and so requiring a dog-leg movement for the first-to-second change. The resulting gearchange does take some getting used to: there is a strong spring loading from the 1st/Reverse plane to the 2nd/3rd plane, and you must learn to leave it to the spring loading to find the 2nd gear slot when changing up — if you consciously try to guide the lever across the gate you may well end up in 4th instead. On the other hand, the lack of spring loading between 2nd/3rd and 4th/5th does require some conscious guidance from the driver when changing up and (especially) when changing down.

Once the change is learned, however, it proves fast and light, though the powerful synchromesh means that downchanges are considerably eased by double declutching. The clutch has an unusually long travel — which must be used to its full extent for clean gearchanges — and is light to operate, though prone to judder if you try to pull away with two few revs.

Spacing of the gearbox ratios is generally very good, with a very long-legged fifth giving 26.5 mph per 1,000 rpm, though fourth could usefully be made a little taller and so closer to fifth.

HANDLING

★★
★★

It is in this area more than perhaps any other that you would expect any new Porsche to excel — the 928 certainly has the right ingredients, with its engine located behind the front axle line and the rear-mounted gearbox further aiding good weight distribution. Wide 7J × 16 alloy wheels are shod with ultra-low-profile 225/50 VR 16 Pirelli P7 tyres, and it has independent suspension with coil springs damper struts all round. At

the front are double wishbones of cast alloy, and an anti-roll bar, while the rear suspension features upper transverse links, and lower wishbones, with a difference: the Porsche-Weissach axle's special geometry is designed to cause rear wheel toe-in, rather than usual toe-out, upon sudden deceleration in mid-corner and so prevent sudden oversteer. A rear anti-roll bar is also used.

The specification is completed by power-assisted rack and pinion steering that must be among the best available on any car — you are rarely aware that there is any assistance. Direct, very precise and nicely weighted, the only possible criticism of the steering is a degree of lifelessness about the straight ahead position compared with that of, say, an Aston — it improves on lock and does provide real 'feel' of what the front wheels are doing.

Although the steering is not especially high geared, the sheer 'bite' of the low profile tyres ensures sharp response to the helm. So far as most drivers will ever experience it, the 928's handling is of the Proverbial 'on rails' variety as the dry road adhesion of the P7s is very high. The car can be flicked through tight corners at very high speeds with little of the expected scrubby understeer, tyre squeal or body roll.

As speeds rise still further there is a steady increase in safe stable understeer, and although the 928 can be persuaded to oversteer it needs to be deliberately provoked. You can do it by throwing the car into a corner, or by really pouring on the power in a low gear. The Porsche-Weissach rear axle ensures that there is no instant oversteer should you lift off the throttle in mid-bend, but there is a pronounced tuck-in effect which can be used to counter excessive understeer near the limit.

But if and when you do get the tail to step out of line, the breakaway is not always as tidy and progressive as we would like, especially if the road is less than smooth. The 928 does not always inspire total confidence at speed on an uneven road, when the wheels tend to follow cambers and you may even experience a tendency to float on humps.

We were generally highly impressed by the 928's stability at speed on a motorway and the way it sits four-square on the road through long bends at desperately illegal speeds, but there are times when it causes disquiet. If you need to brake hard for a bend at three-figure speeds the 928 feels unstable as it enters the bend — a tendency to float and weave disconcertingly, though once committed to the bend its usual imperturbability is restored. Thus it does not always inspire the total confidence that its lower speed stability might suggest. In the wet the P7s retain a respectable measure of their dry road grip, but obviously, with so much power on tap, you should not take liberties with it.

BRAKES

★★
★★

Large ventilated discs on all four wheels, with floating calipers and servo assist-

ance, add up to a braking specification that is well matched to the 928's weight and speed. Porsche's engineers have not deemed a rear pressure limiting valve to be necessary, while the handbrake operates on the rear wheels, by means of small drums inside the rear discs.

At low speeds the brakes feel rather dead, and need a hefty push for maximum deceleration, but they are nicely progressive, giving a maximum deceleration of 1.0 g plus, for 95 lb pedal pressure. An extra safety bonus is the extreme reluctance of the wheels to lock up and skid even in a panic stop.

Predictably, the Porsche sailed through our fade test (involving 20 successive 0.5 g stops at 1 minute intervals from 90 mph) with ease, the required pressures actually dropping a little towards the end of the test as the brakes warmed to their task.

A good 0.38 g deceleration was achieved using the handbrake only from 30 mph, though a very hefty yank on the handbrake lever was required to hold the car facing down the 1 in 3 hill.

ACCOMMODATION

★
★★

Considered purely as a 2-seater the 928 is extremely spacious, with an enormous amount of legroom in the front and good headroom (though this is achieved partially by a very low seating position); with the rear seats folded forward we were able to accommodate 14.2 cu ft of our Revelation test luggage without harming rearward visibility.

As a four-seater, however, the 928 must be considered strictly as a 2+2. To travel four up, even with passengers of only average height, entails a degree of compromise on legroom that could only be tolerated for short journeys, while headroom in the rear is very limited.

With the rear seat in use, only 5.3 cu ft of luggage can be accommodated if you want to have the luggage cover in place, though another 2 cu ft can be squeezed if you don't clip the cover right down. This would leave the contents of the boot exposed to prying eyes, but for smaller valuables there is a locking glove box on the facia (with a parcel tray below it), small compartments hidden under the door armrests, and a shallow tray under the rear seat central armrest.

RIDE

★
★★

It is usual (though by no means compulsory) among cars of this class to sacrifice some ride comfort — especially at low speeds — in pursuance of taut and sporting handling. The Porsche is no exception to this norm, and in its overall ride/handling compromise the 928 is not as successful as some rivals. It is distinctly firm and restless at low speeds on small bumps, accompanied by a lot of bump thump, and large sharp disturbances can cause quite a sharp jolt.

At speed the ride does improve, but not to the same degree as in some rivals, and we were a little surprised and disappointed to observe a very slight tendency to float at times on humps and bumps, especially when the car was laden with passengers and luggage.

AT THE WHEEL

★★
★★ A notable feature of the 928's cockpit is that when you adjust the rake of the steering wheel, the whole steering column and instrument binnacle moves with it, thus maintaining the correct relationship between wheel, switches and instruments.

This feature, in combination with sensible location of major and minor controls, enables most drivers to find a comfortable attitude at the wheel, though the very low seating position was commented on even by our tallest testers and the shorter ones found it awkward to see out: we would like to see the optional electrically-adjustable seats with height adjustment made available on the UK market, as this should also meet our other criticisms concerning too coarse fore/aft adjustment and, in the case of some taller testers, insufficient thigh support. However, these are minor complaints: the majority of our testers did find the Porsche a comfortable car.

Most of the minor switches are well located, with two column stalks for wash/wipe and indicators/dip/flash respectively. To the left of the instruments are three large rotary knobs for driving lights, and front and rear fog lamps respectively, with two similar knobs on the right for the rear wipe and heated rear window. All the aforementioned fall very easily to hand, but less satisfactory are the two knurled wheels hidden on the underside of the instrument binnacle, for the instrument lighting rheostat and wiper delay adjustment respectively.

VISIBILITY

★★
★   Even quite tall drivers found the 928 awkward to see out of, especially for parking, when the drooping nose of the car is invisible and the bulbous sides make it very difficult to judge the car's width. For short drivers the low seating position only aggravates the situation.

It's not all bad, however: the twin door mirrors (optional on the passenger side) with electric adjustment provide excellent rearward vision in conjunction with a rear screen wiper (no rear wash, though), and two-stage rear window heater for de-

icing or demisting respectively.

Forward visibility on the move is also good, with effective windscreen wipers, and excellent headlamps with beam height adjustment from the driver's seat.

INSTRUMENTS

★★
★★ In terms of both their quantity and quality it is hard to fault the 928's instruments. There are six beautifully calibrated gauges, well located in a single housing under an angled pane of glass that effectively banishes all reflections.

In the centre are the large speedometer and tachometer, the former having a trip odometer that can be zeroed at the touch of a button.

To the left are water-temperature and fuel gauges, to the right the oil pressure gauge and voltmeter. There is also a clock that is clearly calibrated, but is located rather a long glance away on the console.

The instruments are beautifully illuminated at night, though the rheostat is awkward to find in its location under the instrument binnacle.

Additionally, the Porsche has a comprehensive warning lamp system that operates in two stages. If something requires attention, two 'master' warning lights flash continuously: in the case of 'priority 1' functions — ie brake circuit pressure, brake fluid level, engine oil level and engine oil pressure — the warning light cannot be cancelled. In the case of 'Priority 2' functions

If you are prepared to leave the luggage compartment partially unclipped, right, you can squeeze 7.3 cu ft (above right) into the boot — otherwise subtract 2 cu ft. But luggage capacity can be enormously increased by folding down the rear seats

Top to Bottom: most found the seats comfortable but disliked the check pattern. Rear seats are very cramped. Low-slung driving position, but well laid out controls. Instrumentation is crisp and clear. Left: centre console houses fresh air vents, heating and ventilation/air conditioning controls and stereo radio/cassette (warning of brake pad wear, hand brake, water level, water temperature, fuel tank reserve, screen washer water level, brake lights and tail lamps) it can be cancelled.

HEATING

★★
★★

The 928's heating and ventilation controls are fairly straightforward, with a rotary knob for the 5-speed fan, and upper and lower slides governing temperature and distribution respectively. In addition to the usual footwell and windscreen vents, there are also heater vents in the door armrests which can be individually opened or closed, and directed either towards your face or at the side windows for demisting.

Over most of its range the temperature slide control gives fine graduation of temperature, except for one point in its travel where the transition from merely warm to hot occurs very abruptly. As the slide approaches the 'Def' position the face level central vents are automatically closed to increase flow to the windows, and the ultimate heat output is considerable. We disliked the temperature slide's lack of a detent at the 'Def' position, and its generally rather stiff action.

The fan is only acceptably quiet at the lowest three of its five speeds, but is capable of an impressive throughput of air.

VENTILATION

★★
★★

In addition to its very effective air conditioning unit fitted as standard, the Porsche also has a fairly versatile fresh air ventilation system, with two face-level vents in the centre of the facia which supply air at ambient temperature but with a flow that can be fan boosted, and their own individual volume control.

These provide an adequate flow of air provided the fan is used, though maximum throughput is reduced progressively as the heater temperature is increased: at least it is possible, unlike with many air conditioned cars, to have cool air to the face along with warm to the footwells, even if it is not always easy to achieve the right combination of both, so sometimes resulting in a stuffy effect.

NOISE

★★
★★

When a manufacturer with Porsche's pedigree introduces an all-new luxury sports car with a low-stressed V8 engine, you might expect the level of refinement to be something special. But if considered in these terms, the 928 proves somewhat of a disappointment.

This is certainly not to say that it's a noisy car; the engine is virtually silent at modest speeds and remains refined even at peak revs; in the right conditions it is entirely feasible to cruise at 120 mph or more in complete relaxation.

But in adverse conditions of road surface and wind strength, the 928 shows up rather poorly compared to, say, a Jaguar XJS. Even at very modest speeds there is excessive bump thump and, above all, tyre roar on all but the finest surfaces —

PERFORMANCE

CONDITIONS

Weather	Wind 0-15 mph
Temperature	50-54°F
Barometer	29.9 in Hg
Surface	Dry tarmacadam

MAXIMUM SPEEDS

	mph	kph
Max speed	140*	225*

*See text

Terminal Speeds:

	mph	kph
at ¼ mile	92	148
at kilometre	117	188

Speed in gears (at 6000 rpm):

	mph	kph
1st	44	71
2nd	65	105
3rd	91	146
4th	119	191

ACCELERATION FROM REST

mph	sec	kph	sec
0-30	2.7	0-40	2.3
0-40	3.7	0-60	3.5
0-50	5.4	0-80	5.4
0-60	7.0	0-100	7.5
0-70	9.0	0-120	10.1
0-80	11.2	0-140	13.2
0-90	14.5	0-160	17.7
0-100	17.8	0-180	23.9
0-110	22.6		
0-120	31.3		
Stand'g ¼	15.2	Stand'g km	27.7

ACCELERATION IN TOP

mph	sec	kph	sec
20-40	8.0	40-60	4.7
30-50	7.8	60-80	4.9
40-60	7.9	80-100	5.0
50-70	7.9	100-120	5.0
60-80	8.4	120-140	5.4
70-90	8.7	140-160	6.1
80-100	9.4		
90-110	10.9		

ACCELERATION IN 4th

mph	sec	kph	sec
10-30	6.0	20-40	3.8
20-40	5.6	40-60	3.5
30-50	5.4	60-80	3.4
40-60	5.4	80-100	3.3
50-70	5.2	100-120	3.0
60-80	5.2	120-140	3.6
70-90	5.6	140-160	4.2
80-100	6.4	160-180	6.1
90-110	8.3		
100-120	14.0		

FUEL CONSUMPTION

Overall	14.9 mpg
	19.0 litres/100 km
Govt. tests	10.6 mpg (urban)
	25.2 mpg (56 mph)
	21.7 mpg (75 mph)
Fuel grade	91 octane
	2 star rating
Tank capacity	18.9 galls
	80 litres
Max range	340* miles
	547 km
Test distance	1476 miles
	2375 km

*Based on estimated 18 mpg touring consumption.

BRAKES

Pedal pressure deceleration and stopping distance from 30 mph (48 kph).

lb	kg	g	ft	m
25	11	0.30	100	30.5
50	23	0.55	55	16.8
75	34	0.96	31	9.5
95	43	1.00+	30	9.1
Handbrake		0.38	79	24.1

FADE

20 ½g stops at 1 min intervals from speed midway between 40 mph (64 kph) and maximum (90 mph, 145 kph).

	lb	kg
Pedal force at start	32	14.5
Pedal force at 10th stop	32	14.5
Pedal force at 20th stop	28	12.7

STEERING

Turning circle between kerbs

	ft	m
left	33.9	10.3
right	34.2	10.4
lock to lock	3.05 turns	
50ft diam. circle	1.05 turns	

CLUTCH

	in	cm
Free pedal movement	5.0	12.7
Additional to disengage	1.0	2.5
Maximum pedal load	28lb	12.7 kg

SPEEDOMETER (mph)

Speedo

30	40	50	60	70	80	90	100

True mph

29.5	38.5	49.0	58.5	68.5	78.5	88.5	98

Distance recorder: 0.75 per cent fast

WEIGHT

	cwt	kg
Unladen weight*	28.9	1468
Weight as tested	32.6	1656

*with fuel for approx 50 miles

Performance tests carried out at 3500 miles by Motor's staff at the Motor Industry Research Association proving ground, Lindley.

Test Data: World Copyright reserved; no unauthorised reproduction in whole or part.

GENERAL SPECIFICATION

ENGINE

Cylinders	V8
Capacity	4474 cc (273 cu in)
Bore/stroke	95.0/78.9 mm (3.74/3.11 in)
Cooling	Water
Block	Alloy
Head	Alloy
Valves	Sohc per bank
Cam drive	Belts

Valve timing

inlet opens	8° atdc
inlet closes	55° abdc
ex opens	38° bbdc
ex closes	2° btdc
Compression	8.5:1
Fuel	Bosch K-Jetronic injection
Bearings	5 main
Max power	240 bhp (DIN) at 5500 rpm
Max torque	257 lb ft (DIN) at 3600 rpm

TRANSMISSION

Type	5 speed manual rear mounted transaxle
Clutch	8.7 in
Actuation	Hydraulic

Internal ratios and mph/1000 rpm

Top	1:1/26.5	
4th	1.34:1/19.8	
3rd	1.75:1/15.2	
2nd	2.46:1/10.8	
1st	3.60:1/7.4	
Rev	3.16:1	
Final drive	2.75:1	

BODY/CHASSIS

Construction	Steel monocoque, alloy doors, bonnet, front wings
Protection	Galvanised steel body, underbody protection: 6-year long-life guarantee

SUSPENSION

Front	Double wishbones, strut type dampers with co-axial coil springs, anti-roll bar
Rear	Independent, lower wishbone, upper transverse link (Porsche-Weissach patent geometry) coil springs, telescopic dampers, anti-roll bar.

STEERING

Type	Rack and pinion
Assistance	Yes

BRAKES

Front	11.1 in ventilated discs
Rear	11.4 in ventilated discs
Park	On rear, drum in disc
Servo	Yes
Circuit	Split diagonally
Rear valve	No
Adjustment	Automatic

WHEELS/TYRES

Type	7Jx16 Alloy
Tyres	Pirelli P7 225/50 VR 16
Pressures	36/36 psi F/R

ELECTRICAL

Battery	12V, 66 Ah
Earth	Negative
Generator	90A Alternator
Fuses	34
Headlights	
type	2 x Halogen H4
dip	110 W total
main	230 W total

GUARANTEE

Duration ..12 months, unlimited mileage

MAINTENANCE

Free service	at 600 miles
Schedule	every 12,000 miles

DO-IT-YOURSELF

Sump	6.5 litres 15W/50, 20W/50
Transaxle	3.8 litres SAE 75W, 90
Coolant	16 litres
Chassis lube	None
Contact breaker gap	Contactless electronic ignition
Spark plug gap	0.7±0.1 mm
Spark plug type	Bosch W145T3D or Beru 145/14/3A
Tappets	Hydraulic

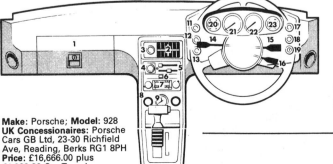

1. Locker	13. Rear fog lamps
2. Fresh air vents	14. Indicators/dip/flash
3. Air control	15. Wash/wipe
4. Heater fan	16. Cruise control
5. Heater slides	17. Rear wipe
6. Central warning unit	18. Rear screen heater
7. Radio/cassette player	19. Ignition
8. Hazard flashers	20. Water Temp/fuel gauges
9. Clock	21. Speedometer
10. Electric window switches	22. Tachometer
11. Lights	23. Oil pressure/battery gauge
12. Fog lamps	

Make: Porsche; **Model:** 928
UK Concessionaires: Porsche Cars GB Ltd, 23-30 Richfield Ave, Reading, Berks RG1 8PH
Price: £16,666.00 plus £1,388.83 Car Tax plus £1,444.39 VAT equals £19,499.22 total

★★★★	excellent	★★★	good	★★	average
★	poor	★	bad		

characteristics which, of course, remain at higher speeds. Indeed, even at the very highest cruising speeds, road noise usually dominates that from engine or wind.

The latter can be low on a still day or with a following wind — especially if you keep speeds down to 70 or 80 mph — but may become noticeable at higher speeds in blowy conditions, though never reaching excessive levels.

FINISH

★★
★★

Not all our testers found the 928's distinctive styling to their taste, but none could deny the immaculate finishing of the curvaceous body panels and the metallic paintwork.

The story is much the same inside the car; the rather loud check pattern of the seats' cloth inserts was disliked by some, but all recognised the nicely integrated interior styling, the tasteful blending of leather and plastic trim panels, the high standard of detail finish, and the 'quality' feel of all the switchgear. Having said which, we were a little disappointed to observe in our test car a few un-Porsche-like creaks and rattles over bumpy surfaces.

EQUIPMENT

★★
★★

A glance at the equipment blob chart opposite serves to show that even by the elevated standards of its price range, the 928 is exceptionally well equipped. Only a sliding roof is missing, though this, and an electrically adjustable driver's seat, are both available on other markets.

The only extra cost option on our test car was the passenger side door mirror; even the air conditioning and stereo radio/cassette (with four speakers and front/rear balance control) are standard, while other items not covered by the comparison chart include an excellent cruise control system with re-set facility, provision for adjusting the headlamp beam from the driver's seat, and door mirrors that are not only electrically adjustable, but also incorporate electric de-icer elements.

There are many other thoughtful touches, as typified by the illuminated vanity mirror, a tiny torch built into the ignition key, and door armrests which can be extended for extra comfort and which simultaneously give access to a hidden pocket below.

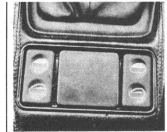

Above: electric window switches on the console behind the gear lever. Below: the lower stalk is for the standard cruise control system

IN SERVICE

So tightly packed is the Porsche's engine bay that it could be a mechanic's nightmare if the 928 was like other cars. Fortunately, however, the 928 is out of the ordinary not only in having hydraulic tappets and electronic ignition, so eliminating two of the usual service adjustments, but also in requiring a service only every 12,000 miles. It does not even require an intermediate oil change, while gearbox oil is changed every 50,000 miles. There are no chassis lubrication points.

In addition to the usual 12-month unlimited mileage guarantee, the Porsche carries a 6-year long life guarantee against the rusting through of its under-body assembly — a testament to Porsche's unusually thorough anti-rust techniques which include galvanised steel for the body and many aluminium panels.

The spare wheel of the 928 has the Goodrich space-saving collapsible tyre, and is stored with its compressor and the jack under the luggage compartment floor. These tyres do not comply with existing UK regulations and, pending a successful outcome of Porsche's attempt to have the regulations amended, owners are provided with a one-year free membership of the Car Recovery Service Club.

With an underbonnet layout like this it is just as well that the hydraulic tappets require no adjustment. Injection and ignition are all electronic

The Rivals

PORSCHE 928 £19,499

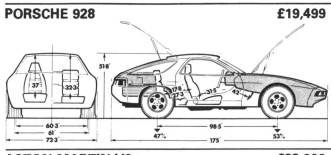

ASTON MARTIN V8 £23,999

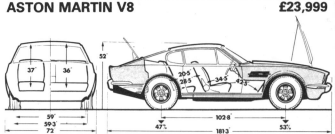

BMW 633CSi £15,379

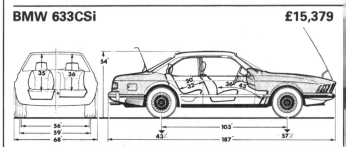

FERRARI 308 GT4 £15,250

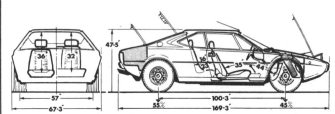

JAGUAR XJS £15,149

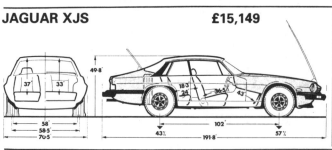

MERCEDES 450SLC £18,250

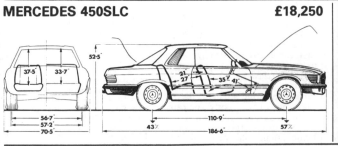

Other possible rivals include the De Tomaso Longchamps (£19,363), Ferrari 400GT (£27,000), Lotus Eclat or Elite (from £10,130), Maserati Kyalami (£21,996)

Comparisons

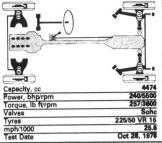

Capacity, cc	4474
Power, bhp/rpm	240/5500
Torque, lb ft/rpm	257/3600
Valves	Sohc
Tyres	225/50 VR 16
mph/1000	25.6
Test Date	Oct 28, 1976

Porsche's all-new luxury sports car hasn't the mind-blowing performance you might expect, but it's no sluggard. Refined engine and low wind noise, but potential refinement let down by excessive tyre roar. Very high road-holding and excellent handling in all but the most extreme conditions, with mediocre ride. Excellent brakes. Beautifully made and lavishly equipped. Very spacious for two, but cramped rear seat.

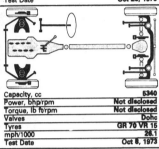

Capacity, cc	5340
Power, bhp/rpm	Not disclosed
Torque, lb ft/rpm	Not disclosed
Valves	Dohc
Tyres	GR 70 VR 15
mph/1000	26.1
Test Date	Oct 8, 1973

Quite a bit more expensive than the Porsche, the Aston is considerably faster. One of the world's most exciting cars, it has superb handling, excellent power steering, impressive brakes, and reasonable rear passenger space. Less refined than the Porsche or Jaguar but it is perhaps the most exhilarating to drive of all the cars in this group. Now also available in convertible form (for export only at present).

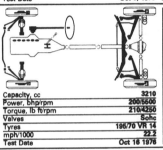

Capacity, cc	3210
Power, bhp/rpm	200/5500
Torque, lb ft/rpm	210/4250
Valves	Sohc
Tyres	195/70 VR 14
mph/1000	22.2
Test Date	Oct 16 1976

A worthy successor to the 3.0 CSi Coupe. Outstanding features include superb roadholding and handling; good performance for its size (though overshadowed in this company) coupled with a very good fuel consumption, a lovely gearchange, comfortable seats, beautiful instruments, well-planned controls, huge boot. With these plus points the flaws — poor rear seat space and ventilation — seem insignificant.

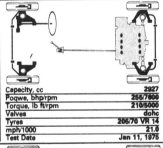

Capacity, cc	2927
Poqwe, bhp/rpm	255/7800
Torque, lb ft/rpm	210/5000
Valves	dohc
Tyres	205/70 VR 14
mph/1000	21.0
Test Date	Jan 11, 1975

Mid-engined coupe powered by 255 bhp V8 giving outstanding performance but heavy fuel consumption. Mediocre gearbox. Nominally a 2 + 2 but tiny rear seats not suitable for adults and the boot is small. Roadholding exceptional, but handling less precise and responsive than that of 246 Dino. Visibility good, but heating and ventilation rather disappointing.

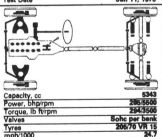

Capacity, cc	5343
Power, bhp/rpm	285/5500
Torque, lb ft/rpm	294/3500
Valves	Sohc per bank
Tyres	205/70 VR 15
mph/1000	24.7
Test Date	Feb 21, 1976

In true Jaguar tradition, the XJ-S combines exceptional performance and refinement at a very competitive price. The styling may not be to everyone's taste and the rear seat accommodation is cramped for so large a car. But if you can afford the fuel bills, the XJ-S is without doubt one of the world's most desirable vehicles. Although faster than the E-type, it's no replacement for Jaguar's classic two-seater.

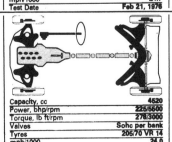

Capacity, cc	4520
Power, bhp/rpm	225/5600
Torque, lb ft/rpm	278/3000
Valves	Sohc per bank
Tyres	205/70 VR 14
mph/1000	24.0
Test Date	May 1, 1976

A magnificent motor car, and one of our favourites. Typically Mercedes, which means an exceptionally high standard of finish allied to engineering that is second to none. Performance is more than adequate while the automatic transmission sets new standards. A limited slip diff would improve already good roadholding and handling by increasing traction.

PERFORMANCE

	Porsche	Aston	BMW	Ferrari	Jaguar	Mercedes**
Max speed, mph	140†	154.8	133.8	150†	155†	134†
Max in 4th	119	136	—	123	—	
3rd	91	112	103	91	116	—
2nd	65	77	65	65	84	96
1st	44	47	38	45	50	60
0-60 mph, secs	7.0	5.7	7.8	6.4	6.7	8.5
30-50 mph in 4th, secs	5.4	5.5	8.5	5.1	6.6	3.3[1]
50-70 mph in top, secs	7.9	6.7	8.5	7.2	6.9	4.4[1]
Weights, cwt	28.9	34.7	29.0	25.3	33.4	33.0
Turning circle, ft*	34.1	38.6	32.5	39.8	34.2	34.3
50ft circle, turns	1.05	1.15	1.0	1.3	1.1	1.0
Boot capacity, cu ft	7.3	8.9	12.5	5.0	8.4	8.9

†Estimated **Automatic [1]in Kickdown *mean of left and right

COSTS AND SERVICE

	Porsche	Aston	BMW	Ferrari	Jaguar	Mercedes
Price, inc VAT & tax, £	19,499	23,999	15,379	15,250	15,149	18,250
Insurance group	8	7	7	7	7	7
Overall mpg	14.9	13.2	20.6	14.1	12.8	15.1
Touring mpg	‡	14.7	‡	18.7	14.4	‡
Fuel grade (stars)	2	4	4	4	4	4
Tank capacity, gals	18.9	25	15	17.2	20	19.8
Service interval, miles	12,000	5,000	5,000	3,000	6,000	5,000
No of dealers	18	13	143	15	350	100
Set brake pads (front) £*	52.83	47.97	16.93	14.31	20.88	13.46
Complete clutch £*	324.77	199.58	102.84	117.24	68.85	N/A
Complete exhaust £*	604.52	218.40	135.94	224.53	420.77	294.73
Front wing panel £*	220.37	344.49	249.74	137.84	84.13	125.09
Oil filter, £*	10.51	4.22	2.20	4.10	5.89	2.56
Starter Motor, £*	214.22	90.72	90.87§	166.80	67.87	82.57§
Windscreen, £*	266.87**	213.26**	80.78**	118.80**	44.28**	161.47**

*inc VAT but not labour charges **Laminated §Exchange ‡Injected

STANDARD EQUIPMENT

	Porsche	Aston	BMW	Ferrari	Jaguar	Mercedes
Adjustable steering	●	●			●	
Air conditioning	●	●				
Alloy wheels	●	●	●	●	●	
Central door locking	●	●			●	●
Cigar lighter	●	●	●	●	●	●
Clock	●	●	●	●	●	●
Cloth trim	●†	Leather	●	●	Leather	§
Dipping mirror	●	●	●	●	●	●
Electric window lifters	●	●	●	●	●	●
Fresh air vents	●	●	●	●	●	●
Hazard flashers	●	●	●	●	●	●
Headlamp washers	●					
Head restraints	●		●	●		●
Heated rear window	●	●	●	●	●	●
Intermit flick wipe	●		●	●	●	●
Laminated screen	●	●	●	●	●	●
Locker	●	●	●	●	●	●
Petrol filler lock	●				●	●
Power steering	●	●	●		●	●
Radio	●	●				
Rear central armrest	●		●	●	●	
Rear courtesy light						
Rear fog light	●		●			●
Rear wash/wipe	●					
Rev counter	●	●	●	●	●	●
Reverse lights	●	●	●	●	●	●
Seat belts — front	●	●	●	●	●	●
— rear						
Seat recline	●	●	●	●	●	●
Sliding roof						
Tape player	●	●			●	
Tinted glass	●	●	●	●	●	●
Vanity mirror	●	●	●	●	●	●

† Combination cloth and leather §Leather or cloth option

Porsche 928 automatic

A near faultless ideal

Porsche 928

Front-engine, rear-drive Porsche luxury grand touring 2 + 2 with water-cooled light alloy V8 introduced March 1977. Available with five-speed Porsche manual or three-speed Daimler-Benz automatic gearbox, in either case fitted in unit with rear drive. Elected Car of the Year for 1978.

MANUFACTURER:
*Dr.Ing.h.c.F. Porsche AG,
Porschestrasse 42,
Stuttgart-Zuffenhausen,
West Germany*

U.K. CONCESSIONAIRES:
*Porsche Cars Great Britain Ltd.,
Richfield Avenue,
Reading,
Berkshire. (RG1 8PH)*

BY SUPER-CAR standards — it is just a super-car, going by its performance — it isn't very big; only 14ft 7in. long, if a little portly at 6ft wide. People move over politely for it, yet it is not conspicuous. It has a quite large engine which is only modestly tuned by the very high standards of its maker. In Britain, where its already high price is pushed higher by the value of the Deutschmark, it costs a notable £19,499. In spite of the price, now that we have put it through the rigours of an *Autocar* Road Test, we can only echo the international approval it received when voted 1978 Car of the Year — a singular achievement for a sporting car. The Porsche 928 combines performance, practicality and the safest of road manners to a degree unmatched by any other super-car.

Above: Photographed at Chantilly during its spell abroad, the 928 shows off its remarkably compact and efficient shape.
Note the especially enlarged wheel openings which make such a feature of exposed brake discs — and which probably help in their effective cooling
Right: V8 engine is more than a little buried under its induction system; you can just see the black plastic covers at front of block enclosing what is claimed to be the longest toothed belt camshaft drive in production. Extra electric fan and air conditioning heat exchanger can be seen nearer camera, and cross tube which is part of vacuum-worked headlamp raising system.

Although it appeared 16 months after the first front-engined Porsche (the 924), the 928 is actually the first front-engine design from Zuffenhausen (or rather Weissach, Porsche's remarkable design and research centre a little way out of Stuttgart). Thoughts about it began early in the decade when it became obvious that future needs to improve comfort and refinement would force Porsche to depart from their traditional preference for air-cooled engines variously placed behind the driver. The oil crisis of 1973 and the link with Volkswagen-Audi put the 924 idea ahead, with its use of some VW components along similar lines to the then stillborn 928.

When it did come out in March 1977, the similarities were clear, but the parts were very different, with nothing major in common with any other Porsche, VW-engined or otherwise. The front-mounted engine was an all-aluminium-alloy vee-8 with one toothed-belt-driven overhead camshaft per bank working through hydraulic tappets — a far cry from normal European super-car practice — and pistons coated with iron or chromium (depending on the piston supplier) running directly in linerless aluminium alloy bores. With a 95x78.8mm bore and stroke, the water-cooled engine displaced 4,474 c.c. and with a modest 8.5-to-1 compression ratio and Bosch K-Jetronic fuel injection it livered 240 bhp at 5,500 rpm on -octane fuel, with maximum rque of 257 lb. ft. at 3,600 rpm.

To provide a fairly high polar oment of inertia, and cut down the sident nose-heaviness and erefore understeer of normal nt-engine cars, the transmission, hether Porsche's own specially signed five-speed manual box or a adaptation of the Daimler-Benz ree-speed automatic (originally und in the 350 and 450 ercedes), was put ahead of and in iit with the final drive, transaxle yle, with the battery trigger-mounted behind. It was ined to the engine and clutch by a in, 1in. diameter propeller shaft inning inside a 4in. diameter, ⅛in. alled tube containing two steady earings. To counter the extra rotary ertia of the shaft as far as earchanging was concerned, the ecessary high torque clutch llowed racing practice in being a elatively small diameter (7in.) twin late type. A common complaint bout high power road cars with anual boxes is that clutch pedal ffort is often too high. The twin late clutch helped here, and was ided by the adoption of a elper-sprung release arrangement reduce pedal effort to around 3lb. Going by brief experience of a manual 928 we sampled just before his went to press, this feature does ust what it is meant to do — a small ut real advance.

Suspension is conventional in ront with double wishbones. At the ear, a form of double wishbone eometry is used too. There is in fact nly a bottom wishbone, which akes brake and accelerating torque oads as well as helping the all-jointed single top link locate the wheel laterally. The bottom vishbone has its inboard pivot axis nclined outwards at the front, like a semi-trailing arm, to provide a neasure of anti-squat. And at the ront body pivot, it has a sort of double joint. The give of this in a corner under braking and decelerating forces — which, on what Porsche, in the land of Mercedes and BMW semi-trailing arm rear ends, call "normal" rear suspension, produces an oversteer-nducing toe-out — makes the outside rear wheel toe-in slightly. This deliberate understeering self-steer at the rear thus counters the usual accidental oversteering self-steer in the case where the driver who has entered a corner unintentionally too fast lifts off, or, worse, brakes.

Performance
Very fast yet smooth

Even with the losses inherent with conventional automatic transmission, the 928 goes magnificently, combining real speed with excellent mechanical refinement. From a standstill on a dry, well-surfaced road, there is no wheelspin, thanks mainly of course to the inhibiting effect of the torque converter stall point — the car just takes off to reach 50 mph in 6.3sec, 60 in 8.0, 90 and the quarter-mile

in 16.2, 100 in 20.1 and 120 in just over half a minute. It is near-perfectly geared for maximum speed — something Porsche among undergearing German makers are almost alone in arranging — the 138 mph recorded on the Continent in perfect conditions corresponding to 5,400 rpm, just below peak power. It is interesting to note that Porsche's claim for the manual box car, of a minimum of 143 mph, means just the other side of peak, which given the speed and greater losses of the automatic is what would be expected.

The automatic has ideal ratios, with change points at 5,300 (59 mph) and 5,800 (102 mph), so that it is near impossible to beat it by selecting higher change speeds; experiments were inconclusive here showing little advantage in over-riding. The selector is a conventional one, with the "standard" mistake of no safety stop to be released when changing from Drive to Neutral; you can therefore go into Neutral inadvertently, which is not a good thing on such a powerful car, even if a 6,300 rpm rev limiter is fitted. For our maximum speeds in 1 and 2 incidentally we went to the rev limiter and ignored the red line, which is at about 6,100. One good point about the selector is that it does not make the other common mistake, of putting a stop between Drive and 2, so that changing down manually too is perfectly easy. It is only nearer the top end of the rev range that one might want to use the over-ride, except of course when seeking engine braking or wishing to

be as smooth as possible through a roundabout. The kickdown near the top end is surprisingly slow for a Daimler Benz box. Elsewhere it works beautifully; the accelerator which always needs a rather high effort must be shoved quite hard to get kickdown, but the box generally performs the down-change very neatly. It also part throttle downchanges very well, and its upward changes are smooth too.

It makes sense to mention noise here, because mechanically as far as the engine and transmission are concerned, this is the quiet Porsche. It actually has two voices. In town it is most softly spoken, and on a smooth, fine-textured surface you glide along in a quietness which many saloons only equal. From about 50 mph onwards the engine makes itself more obvious, until with the foot down hard it utters a tigerish growl — still not obtrusively but it is obviously then a sports car power unit. Interestingly, in spite of the hydraulic tappets we noted what sounded like a cam follower tapping period at around 50 — subdued, but there.

There isn't much wind noise, but as you might expect with such squat, very low profile tyres — they are Pirelli's superb 50 per cent aspect ratio 225/VR 16in. P7s — road noise is very much at the mercy of road surface. Any coarse surface provokes a roar which although not at all uncomfortable dominates any other noise. The car is also sensitive to bump thump to a high degree. The noise seemed always to come mostly from behind one, suggesting that the open hatchback layout acts

The 928's natural attitude ultimately is understeer, accompanied by tolerable roll; here it has been provoked into oversteer, which requires a marked upset. Unlike all rear-engined road-going Porsches, breakaway is not violent, and can be caught easily

as it must do rather as an acoustic amplifier.

Our only criticism of the car's otherwise faultless induction and electronic ignition is that on several occasions, on both the automatic and manual cars, we found the engine slow to start, needing a lot of turns before it would fire. There seemed no pattern to this; some cold starts were poor, some hot were. Most of the time however it started perfectly.

Economy
Typical Porsche leanness

Regular readers of *Autocar* must be tired of reading the usual reminder that since our test mileage includes a significant proportion of flat-out performance testing, the overall consumption — here 14.6mpg — is worse than many owners will achieve. It applies as much as anywhere to the 928 automatic. Three-up, with a week's luggage plus the considerable camera gear of our photographer, Peter Cramer, we used the car to visit the Paris Motor Show — and in spite of the mixture of fast cruising and slow traffic driving that such a trip involves, we returned an easy 15.7 mpg, which is good for this size of engine. Most owners should get between our overall if they are always pressing on — something which the car undeniably invites — and up to 18 mpg if they are gentler-footed. The 19-gallon tank therefore gives a good range of between 250 and 350 miles. There is, amongst many others, a warning lamp for low fuel which Porsche say comes on when about 2.4 gallons are left. We found it lit first with 3 gallons remaining. The tank has an oddly cheap-looking, all-plastic filler cap; it fills easily, without blowback or serious delay.

Oil consumption worked out at just over 1,100 miles per pint, which seems acceptable, although one might hope that more miles of use will improve it further.

Road behaviour
Very well mannered

The steering is nicely geared, with just three turns lock to lock for usefully tight turning circles. The test car incidentally had such closely adjusted lock stops that the turning circles measured to left and right where within an inch of each other — a most unusual detail. It is power-assisted, not something you find on other Porsches, but an understandable thing when you start putting even an all-alloy 4½-litre V8 in the front instead of the back. There is the right amount of assistance at low speeds — which can be felt diminishing (as it is intended to) as the speed rises. For a modern assisted rack set up, it is surprisingly low on feel. Your hands are masked from too much road shock, arguably to too great an extent if one is to be hyper-critical; one does feel bad wheel disturbances, such as when running over a pot hole — the wheel does move then — but not much. There is as well a little slop about the straight ahead, but this is something only the very fussy will perceive — and even then it is so little that it doesn't matter.

For overall the Porsche's steering is very good. The point is that, with its near ideal weight distribution — for stability that is (classic Porsches are ideally weighted for traction and braking, but not so ideal for cornering or straight stability) — it is such an obedient, predictable car that one can easily under-estimate its very high abilities. A lot of credit must of course be given to those very expensive tyres (a careless piece of parking damage can mean a ruined sidewall and a £182 write-off, for just *one* tyre). They hang on to absurd limits, and combined with the drama-free way the car simply understeers ultimately, it is easy to dismiss the 928 as almost dull in a corner. And then you think about how fast you are going through the corner. It is remarkable just how quickly the car will turn, without any fuss. It is possible to break the back away with what Porsche call its ''Weissach axle'', if you lift off in a bend — but you've got to be going very quickly, and to be pretty violent — and even then the resulting wriggle is easily caught.

The car has anti-roll bars front and rear, not too stiff, so that there is enough roll to give the driver confidence and seat-of-the-pants feel. The same goes for braking; the car has anti-dive front suspension, but not too much, so that achieving its best stop of 0.98g with the fronts in the locking point is not difficult. It is never over-sensitive in any way. Traditional Porsche afficionados may claim that Weissach have taken the fun out of Porsche driving — there is no risk of abrupt rear end breakaway which cannot be held to salt the thrill of advancing one's cornering speed — but the 928 is just as much fun as a 911. It just does it all much more subtly.

To conclude remarks about the brakes, they are superb. One

Three-quarter rear emphasizes the tidy absence of visible outside bumpers. ''Bodywork'' reforms after a minor bump, but it is likely that paint on it doesn't; we suspect that separate black plastic facings might be more practical

Right: Headlamps pop up fairly smartly, staying up when switched off but still on sidelamps. Headlamp flashing is arranged via additional fixed lamps below

wonders how much the very handsome, wide-eyed wheels help in keeping the fade performance good, which it certainly is. Few cars have such nakedly obvious discs seen through the wheels as the 928 — a piece of functional design that makes the car look all the more what it is — ideally functional. The handbrake performance gains too from the excellent weight distribution, with its exemplary 0.4g response and easy holding on 1-in-3. Our only minor criticism of the braking performance is a minor one — when braking at all firmly in ordinary driving, the steering seems to lose castor, and almost to ''walk about''. This is a tiny quirk,

seemingly of little importance, because after a few days' familiarity with the car you don't notice it.

Ride depends on speed to a surprising degree. In town, you notice jars produced by sharp bumps, and are not impressed, especially when one-up. With two or three in the car, there is a natural improvement, but at slow speeds the ride is still not very good. At higher speeds the car is predictably much better, leaving nothing to complain about. Considering the obvious stiffness of the tyre sidewalls, it is remarkable how well the car does ride. Overall, the 928 is an almost unapproachable combination of ride and handling.

Behind the wheel
Such fascinating detail

All that stuff about German ingenuity has been heard time and time again, but that doesn't mean is dead. Far from it; Teutonic cleverness is alive and well, and, as ever, one of the places where it lives is around Stuttgart. We canno think of anyone else who pivots no just the steering column but the entire instrument nacelle too. so th when you adjust steering wheel angle, the instruments move as we There are dozens of other features which delight one. Switch on and clear red or green lettering appears in the previously blank faces of rev counter and speedometer — the warning lamp system which tells yo whether tail or stop lamp bulbs are working, or if you have low washer fluid, low coolant, low brake fluid, low brake pressure, low oil pressure worn brake pads, handbrake on, parking lamps on, in addition to the other usual warnings. A full set of instruments are included, and to help you find your way about a strange 928 at night, the ignition key incorporates a tiny but entirely effective torch so that you can find the key hole, and then, when you switch on, there is always a light in the instrument nacelle, and the lamps control switch is always subtl lit. Our only criticism of the warning light words is that in spite of the heavy hooding of the nacelle, they can be quite difficult to perceive in bright daylight. Like Citroen, Porsche use a central warning lamp however to draw your attention to any specific warning. If it is a minor thing, like a stop lamp bulb, you car press a button in mid-facia to cancel the warning for the time being; it wi come on again when you next switc on the ignition, as a gentle reminde If the fault is serious, like low brake fluid, or a faulty brake circuit, the warning cannot be extinguished.

We mention this warning lamp system first, because it is the first thing that impresses you on getting in. On early acquaintance one is also struck by the way the car encloses you; even the tall driver tends at first to feel a little sunk in the car. Shorte persons might be glad of some seat height adjustment, not provided on the test car. No one had any complaints about pedal layout, but we all felt that the electric window switches were too far back on the centre console. The seats are very comfortable, and hold one well enough for road purposes; for the really hard cornering rate which the car is capable of, something even more locating would be appreciated.

The view out is not seriously restricted in any direction, though the heavy pillaring has to be borne in mind in town, for fear of not seeing a pedestrian. You feel that it is a car in which it would almost be pleasant to suffer a roll-over accident; strong pillars and very fine, well padded leather and velour upholstery — but opinions varied about the crazy-chess-board-patterned velour.

The passenger, especially if female, appreciates the clever vanity

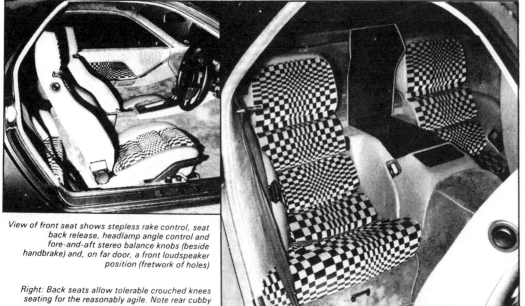

View of front seat shows stepless rake control, seat back release, headlamp angle control and fore-and-aft stereo balance knobs (beside handbrake) and, on far door, a front loudspeaker position (fretwork of holes)

Right: Back seats allow tolerable crouched knees seating for the reasonably agile. Note rear cubby

Below: Driver's armrest carries remote control for both outside mirrors — button behind heater outlets with changeover switch (left or right mirror between). Note duct for side window demister

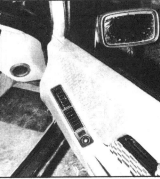

Boot space (above) is carpeted, its contents ncealable with additional cover (not shown) and prevented from flying forward between seats by elastic mesh. Seat backs can be individually folded forward, whereupon they ck into place — releasing the locks is rather awkward.

Right: Very elaborate tool kit

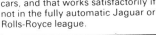

Below: Armrest pulls out to make a better rest and expose useful map pocket

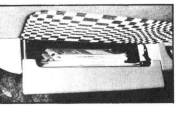

Below: Space Saver spare under boot floor and its electric pump

rror, which lights up like a shaving ss as you swing it down from its e place in the roof, instead of in e visors. The armrests swing out to cover useful door pockets, and come even better armrests in the ocess. It is surprisingly mfortable curled up in the back at, at any rate if you are three-up; e of us travelled most of the way m Calais to Paris without more an a good stretch at a fuel stop and er changing places. The back seat ssenger is encouraged to lean ck, when he or she finds that the ar glass stretches over the head, to ow a delightful view straight up — easing in mountains or as one of put it "for aeroplane spotting".

The heater is an excellent air-blender which provides proper and rapid temperature control. It is partly combined with air conditioning on British specification cars, and that works satisfactorily if not in the fully automatic Jaguar or Rolls-Royce league.

Living with the 928

Controls all work well, although we thought the indicator stalk a little heavy, like, in different ways, the throttle and brake pedals. A good cruise control is fitted. There is elaborate screen washing available — four-jet main system plus a concentrated wash fluid system which clears the more resistant screen rubbish. The headlamps have Porsche's high-pressure jet wash system, and there is a big rear wiper. With such elaborate arrangements in front, we found it odd that there is no rear wash combined with the wiper. The electric mirrors on the doors work delightfully, and are heated like a rear window glass to prevent icing up. Once, the joystick control tended to stick, so that the left mirror ran away to the extremes of its movement, but this fault cleared itself up.

Boot space is generous, and you can fold the back seats forward individually if wished. The car is fitted with near-silent remote locking of the doors, worked either from inside by rotary knobs below the sill pips or from outside when you turn the key — enormously convenient. Not so much so is the tailgate which is only opened with the key. The horn is easily sounded, by pressing any part of the steering wheel crash pad — ideal in an emergency. The headlamps pop up tolerably quickly when wanted and give a very good spread and range of light; a knob beside the driving seat allows you to adjust their beam height as you drive.

A remarkable Blaupunkt AM/stereo FM-cum-cassette player wireless is standard, which self-seeks. It works well, but is not ideal if you want to switch from one chosen station to another which is to the left of it on the dial. One must keep dabbing the self-seek knob until the system has ranged over the entire dial to where you want. A simple knob tuner would be a very welcome additional feature. There is an incredible tool kit and the usual Goodrich Spacesaver spare under the boot floor, with the also usual Porsche electric inflation pump. Porsche Great Britain continue to seek a waiver of our blanket tyre regulations about mixing radial and bias-belt tyres to make the use of this legal here; in the meantime, an owner is automatically enrolled into the Car Recovery Club for a year, just in case.

The car has deformable polyurethane front and back ends instead of normal bumpers. This is neat but we wonder how cheap and practical. The deformability of the ends of the car do not get over the fact that if, as happened to the test car, someone unknown bumps into you whilst parked, the paint surface is damaged and must be repaired. Plain matt black bumpers, MGB or Volvo style, are perhaps less trouble.

The Porsche 928 range

It isn't much of a range really — just a choice of two equally (we believe after a short trial in the manual car of which a Test Extra will follow later) magnificent motor cars equally priced with either automatic or manual five-speed boxes. As far as Britain is concerned, there are no extras fitted to the test car, which gives some idea of just how complete a machine the 928 is.

Entire instrument console moves with steering column for angular adjustment. Switches on left (from top) control lamps, front and rear fog lamps; those on right, rear window wiper and ignition lock. Instruments (from left) are temperature/fuel gauges, all-electronic trip speedometer and revcounter, and oil pressure/battery volts. Horn is sounded from any part of crash pad. Centre console (from top) contains air-conditioning control, Bosch self-seeking stereo wireless cum cassette player below heater controls, safety belt warning lamp, switch, ashtray with cigar lighter

Porsche 928 (A) £19,499

Front engine, rear drive

Capacity
4.474 c.c.

Power
240 bhp (DIN) at 5,500 rpm

Weight
3,347lb/1,518kg

Road Test
None previously published

Aston Martin V8 (A) £22,999

Front engine, rear drive

Capacity
5,340 c.c.

Power
Not quoted

Weight
3,970lb/1,800kg

Road Test
14 October, 1978

Jaguar XJ-S (A) £15,149

Front engine, rear drive

Capacity
5,343 c.c.

Power
285 bhp (DIN) at 5,500 rpm

Weight
3,870lb/1,750kg

Road Test
28 May, 1977

Maserati Khamsin (A) £24,563

Front engine, rear drive

Capacity
4,930 c.c.

Power
320 bhp (DIN) at 5,500 rpm

Weight
3,019lb/1,640kg

Road Test
17 May 1975

Mercedes-Benz 450 SLC(A) £16,840

Front engine, rear drive

Capacity
4,520 c.c.

Power
225 bhp (DIN) at 5,000 rpm

Weight
3,685lb/1,670kg

Road Test
11 October 1975

Porsche Carrera 3.0 Sportomatic (A) £14,000

Rear engine, rear drive

Capacity
2,956 c.c

Power
200 bhp (DIN) at 6,000 rpm

Weight
2,475lb/1,122kg

Test Extra
24 January 1976

MPH & MPG

Maximum speed (mph)

Aston Martin V8 (A)	146
Jaguar XJ-S (A)	142
Porsche Carrera 3.0 (A)	141
Porsche 928 (A)	138
Mercedes 450SLC (A)	136
Maserati Khamsin (A)	130

Acceleration 0-60 (sec)

Aston Martin V8 (A)	7.2
Porsche Carrera 3.0 (A)	7.3
Jaguar XJ-S (A)	7.5
Maserati Khamsin (A)	7.5
Porsche 928(A)	8.0
Mercedes 450 SLC	9.0

Overall mpg

Porsche Carrera 3.0 (A)	21.0
Maserati Khamsin (A)	15.1
Porsche 928 (A)	14.6
Mercedes 450 SLC	14.1
Jaguar XJ-S (A)	14.0
Aston Martin V8 (A)	13.0

Obviously for sheer performance, it has to be the Aston Martin, not surprisingly in view of its muscle-y engine. The Porsche, by virtue of its price, which in this company does not seem too high, nevertheless finds itself in heavy competition, in all senses of the word. For quietness and almost incredible refinement, there is still nothing to touch the way the Jaguar combines such qualities with sheer sweet performance. We have included the 911 variant of Porsche because it is the nearest comparable model with any sort of automatic box, and to give some scale in the Porsche world to the 928's position. As can be seen, it holds its own very well indeed, lying close to its rivals in speed and, as usual for a Porsche well up the field in economy.

ON THE ROAD

Again, this is a company of equals, or nearly so. The Citroen-steered and braked Maserati is not an easy car to drive, because of the deliberate peculiarities of the Citroen parts — variable ratio steering and rather abrupt brakes. We look forward to the day when Modena runs out of Citroen bits and goes over to conventional systems here. The Carrera is probably the most entertaining of the six, and equally the most tricky if you are ever unfortunate enough to go over its very high cornering limit; but its combination of traction, braking and cornering is nevertheless hard to beat. It's just that it bites if you do try to beat it, where all the others forgive. The Mercedes is another essay in very high quality engineering which is very rewarding to drive, and which makes a fascinating comparison in attitudes between Weissach and Unterturkheim — two very different ways of attacking a near similar problem.

The Aston is equally worthy in a totally honest and still very exciting way. Its great strength apart from its sheer speed is its remarkable handling and steering, which are both superb in a more masculine way than for the others. But you always come back to the Jaguar, which does everything so very serenely, in ride, handling and refinement. How does the Porsche stand up here? Without any hesitation one has to say at head level; it steers no better but no worse, but its grip on those P7s is probably that much better. It has nothing to be ashamed of, apart perhaps from the road noise, which is a reasonable price to pay for such roadholding. And, typically Porsche, it is apart from its brother, the most handily sized of the lot.

SIZE & SPACE

Legroom front/rear (in)

(Seats fully back)

Aston Martin V8 (A)	43/31
Mercedes 450SLC (A)	41/33
Jaguar XJ-S (A)	42/30
Porsche Carrera 3.0 (A)	43/28
Porsche 928 (A)	41/27
Maserati Khamsin (A)	43/10

The Porsche 928 stands well up here because of its good front seat legroom range, which is exceptional; for once none of *Autocar's* taller staffmen had to have the seat right back. This gives it a mildly exaggerated position in comparison with the others, since although as mentioned in the test one can be tolerably comfortable in the back, it isn't really a full four seater (and nor do its makers claim it to be so). It is however, a very practical car for its compact overall dimensions. Naturally the bigger cars score in some cases in boot space, especially the very roomy Mercedes; near enough the same goes for the Aston, and for the Jaguar. Naturally the Porsche Carrera is well down the field, since it is the smallest of the group, which is one reason why it is so quick.

VERDICT

A difficult one this as usual it depends what you want. The Aston Martin for only another £500 is a lot of very fine car, which undeniably goes. The Mercedes will be valued for its character by those who like that sort of thing, and for its room. The Khamsin is for the specialist, a fascinating and tantalising car, perhaps the most beautiful to look at here, if that matters to you. The Carrera, or rather its current equivalent is for pure excitement — a demon of a car which is irresistible for some.

If refinement matters, then you cannot deny the XJ-S is leader here. But the Porsche 928 is undeniably a pattern maker in its sheer functionalism, its performance combined with economy, and its near perfect road manners. Its detail engineering isn't just a gimmick; and it is a never-ceasing source of satisfaction. You could call the 928 the grown-up super-car. There is no nonsense about it — and no boredom either.

HOW THE PORSCHE 928 AUTOMATIC PERFORMS

MAXIMUM SPEEDS

Gear	mph	kph	rpm
Top (mean)	138	222	5,400
(best)	138	222	5,400
2nd	110	177	6,300
1st	70	113	6,300

TEST CONDITIONS

Wind: 10-20 mph
Temperature: 16 deg C (61 deg F)
Barometer: 29.6in. Hg (1003 mbar)
Humidity: 85 per cent
Surface: dry asphalt and concrete
Test distance: 1,228 miles

Figures taken at 3,600 miles by our own staff at the Motor Industry Research Association proving ground at Nuneaton, and on the Continent

All Autocar test results are subject to world copywright and may not be reproduced in whole or part without the Editor's written permission

ACCELERATION

FROM REST

True mph	Time (sec)	Speedo mph
30	3.1	31
40	4.6	41
50	6.3	51
60	8.0	60
70	10.2	69
80	13.0	80
90	16.2	90
100	20.1	100
110	25.9	110
120	34.4	120

Standing ¼-mile: 16.2 sec, 90 mph
Standing km: 29.3 sec, 115 mph

IN EACH GEAR

mph	Top	2nd	1st
0-20	—	—	1.8
10-30	—	—	2.4
20-40	—	—	2.8
30-50	—	—	2.9
40-60	—	—	3.2
50-70	—	5.1	3.8
60-80	—	5.3	—
70-90	—	5.8	—
80-100	—	6.6	—
90-110	11.2	9.5	—
100-120	12.6	—	—

FUEL CONSUMPTION

Overall mpg:
14.6 (19.4 litres / 100km)

Constant Speed:
Maker's figures used.

mph	mpg	mph	mpg
30	31.4	70	20.2
40	30.7	80	16.6
50	29.7	90	16.4
60	27.4	100	16.0

Autocar formula: Hard 13.1 mpg
Driving Average 16.1 mpg
and conditions Gentle 19.0 mpg
Grade of fuel: Regular, 2-star (91 RM)
Fuel tank: 19.1 Imp. galls (86 litres)
Mileage recorder reads 0.8 per cent short

Official fuel consumption figures
(ECE laboratory test conditions; not necessarily related to Autocar figures)
Urban cycle: 13.2 mpg
Steady 56 mph: 29.1 mpg
Steady 75 mph: 16.7 mpg

OIL CONSUMPTION

(SAE 20W/50) 1,100 miles / pint

BRAKING

Fade *(from 90 mph in neutral)*
Pedal load for 0.5g stops in lb

	start/end		start/end
1	40-30-25	6	40-50-45
2	40-30-40	7	50-50-40
3	25-45	8	50-50-40
4	30-50-40	9	50-45-50
5	40-40-45	10	50-50-60

Response *(from 30 mph in neutral)*

Load	g	Distance
20lb	0.20	151ft
40lb	0.43	70ft
60lb	0.72	42ft
70lb	0.84	35.8ft
80lb	0.98	30.7ft
Handbrake	0.40	75ft

Max. gradient: 1 in 3

WEIGHT

Kerb, 29.9cwt / 3,347lb / 1,518kg
Distribution F/R, 52.1 / 47.9
Test, 33.3cwt / 3,726lb / 1,690kg
Max. payload 926lb / 420kg

DIMENSIONS

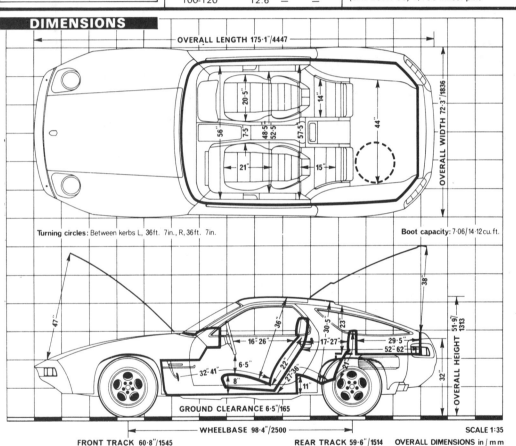

OVERALL LENGTH 175·1"/4447
OVERALL WIDTH 72·3"/1836
44"
20·5" 14"
56 7·5 48·5 52·5 57·5
21" 15"

Turning circles: Between kerbs L, 36ft. 7in., R, 36ft. 7in.
Boot capacity: 7·06/14·12 cu. ft.

47" 36" 38" 30·5" 23"
16" 26" 17"-27" 29·5" 52"-62"
6·5" 51·9"/1313
32·41" 27-36" 11" 32"
8" OVERALL HEIGHT
GROUND CLEARANCE 6·5"/165
WHEELBASE 98·4"/2500
SCALE 1:35
FRONT TRACK 60·8"/1545 REAR TRACK 59·6"/1514 OVERALL DIMENSIONS in /mm

PRICES

Basic	£16,666.00
Special Car Tax	£1,388.83
VAT	£1,444.39
Total (in GB)	**£19,499.22**
Seat Belts	Standard
Licence	£50.00
Delivery charge (London)	£30.00
Number plates	approx. £15.00
Total on the Road (exc. insurance)	**£19,594.22**

EXTRAS (inc. VAT)
*Passenger door mirror £63.18
Fitted to test car

TOTAL AS TESTED ON THE ROAD £19,657.40

Insurance On application

SERVICE & PARTS

Interval	
Change	**12,000**
Engine oil	Yes
Oil filter	Yes
Gearbox oil	Yes
Spark plugs	Yes
Air cleaner	Yes
Total cost	**£69.64**

(Assuming labour at £6.50/hour)

PARTS COST (including VAT)

Brake pads (2 wheels) —front	£48.92
Brake pads (2 wheels) —rear	£43.89
Exhaust complete (stainless steel)	£559.74
Tyre — each (typical)	£181.74
Windscreen (laminated, tinted)	£247.10
Headlamp unit	£51.97
Front wing	£204.05
Rear bumper	£359.43

WARRANTY

12 months / unlimited mileage plus 6-year underbody rusting-through conditional guarantee.

SPECIFICATION

ENGINE

Head/block	Front, rear drive, Aluminium alloy
Cylinders	8, in 90-deg vee
Main bearings	5
Cooling	Water
Fan	Viscous + electric, linerless
Bore, mm (in.)	95.0 (3.74); bored, linerless
Stroke, mm (in.)	78.9 (3.11)
Capacity, cc (in³)	4,474 (272.97)
Valve gear	Ohc, hydraulic tappets
Camshaft drive	Toothed belt
Compression ratio	8.5-to-1
Ignition	Breakerless
Induction	Bosch K-Jetronic
Max power	240 bhp (DIN) at 5,500 rpm
Max torque	257 lb ft at 3,600 rpm

TRANSMISSION

Type	Daimler-Benz three-speed automatic epicyclic with torque converter, transaxle

Gear	Ratio	mph/1000rpm
Top	1.0-2.0	25.64
2nd	1.400-2.920	17.56
1st	2.306-4.612	11.10
Final drive gear	Hypoid bevel	
Ratio	2.750-to-1	

SUSPENSION

Front — location	Independent, double wishbone
springs	Coil
dampers	Telescopic
anti-roll bar	Yes
Rear — location	Independent, semi-trailing arm
springs	Coil
dampers	Telescopic
anti-roll bar	Yes

STEERING:

Type	Rack and pinion
Power assistance	Hydraulic
Wheel diameter	15.8 in.
Turns lock to lock	3.0

BRAKES:

Circuits	Twin, split diagonally
Front	11.1 in. dia. disc
Rear	11.38 in. dia. disc
Servo	Vacuum
Handbrake	Side lever, rear drum within disc

WHEELS:

Type	Light alloy
Rim width	7in.
Tyres —make	Pirelli
—type	P7 radial tubeless
—size	225/50 VR 16in.
—pressures	F36; R36psi (normal driving)

EQUIPMENT

Battery	12 volt 66 Ah
Alternator	90 amp
Headlamps	120/110 watt
Reversing lamp	Standard
Hazard warning	Standard
Electric fuses	34
Screen wipers	3-speed, intermittent
Screen washer	Electric
Interior heater	Air blending
Air conditioning	Standard
Interior trim	Velour and leather seats, vinyl headlining
Floor covering	Carpet
Jack	Screw
Jacking points	4, under sills
Windscreen	Laminated, tinted
Underbody protection	Paint, galvanising, bitumastic, wax, treated box sections

PORSCHE 928 AUTOMATIC

*Porsche's best
is an automatic success*

ROAD & TRACK
R&T
ROAD TEST

PHOTOS BY JOHN DINKEL

PORSCHE PUSHERS FAMILIAR with the marque since its inception might be shocked the first time they slip behind the wheel of a 928 and discover a shift lever that moves only fore and aft. But they shouldn't be surprised because the sporty, luxurious and expensive 928 is a perfect candidate for clutchless driving. Two-pedal driving isn't new to Porsches—911s listed Sportomatic as an option from 1968 through 1977 and the 924 can be ordered with a 3-speed automatic. The 911 transmission was a semi-automatic design, a combination of torque converter, automatic clutch and manual 4-speed gearbox. Porsche could have gone fully automatic with the 911 but decided its typical customers wouldn't want to be totally weaned from gearbox stirring. This obviously isn't the case with the 924 or the upmarket 928, which is competing in the same price market as the Mercedes-Benz 450SL and SLC, Jaguar XJS and Lotus Elite, all of which offer fully automatic transmissions as standard equipment or as an option. Buyers of such machinery are very often willing to trade some sportiness for the extra convenience and driving ease an automatic offers.

A 928 automatic makes sense from a financial as well as a marketing standpoint. The clutchless transmission is a no-cost option, but when you're laying out $28,500, Porsche can afford to be a little lax with the profit margin. The same option in the lower-price 924 will set you back around $400.

Rather than design and tool for an all new automatic, Porsche struck a deal with crosstown rival, Mercedes-Benz. Porsche is buying the innards of the 450SEL 6.9's automatic transmission, a reinforced version of the torque converter plus 3-speed automatic used on other S-class Mercedes. These components are placed in a cast housing of Porsche design, the Mercedes case being unusable because the 928's rear transaxle has the gearbox in union with the final drive. It's not quite that simple, of course, and the usual modifications such as plumbing changes and matching the transmission upshift and downshift points to the

torque and horsepower characteristics of the 928's 4.5-liter V-8 have been made.

More important to the average 928 owner than design details is how the transmission functions. Our immediate reaction was one of mild disappointment. Mercedes-Benz uses a superb gated shifter that allows stick shift-style driving for those so inclined. We expected no less from a car as sporty as the 928. Instead we were greeted by a T-handle lever not unlike that found on many American cars.

But the proof is in the driving and here the Porsche shifter works nearly as well as the M-B design. The driver of a 928 automatic has complete freedom to downshift from Drive to 2nd without going through a detent lockout. Slap the handle and you've got 2nd gear in an instant. For 99 percent of all your driving this is the most important downshift. There are few times under less than all-out racing conditions that a driver needs such control over a 2-1 downshift. And because the transmission is calibrated to pull redline in 1st gear with the lever in the Drive slot, there's nothing gained by leaving the transmission in Low during wide-open-throttle acceleration. Left in Drive, the transmission shifts out of 2nd at 5250 rpm; we couldn't improve upon the acceleration times by leaving the lever in 2nd to the 6000-rpm redline. The only time the Porsche shifter isn't as precise as the M-B is during a shift from 2nd to Drive. A ham-fisted 928 driver could push the lever from 2nd directly into Neutral; that's virtually impossible with the Mercedes design.

Under all driving conditions the 3-speed automatic is as good as it is in the S-class Mercedes. Constant readers will know that means it's excellent. Upshifts are precise, smooth and crisp. Ditto for downshifts. There's no pussyfooting around waiting for a gear to engage as with some automatics. Pull the lever or step on the throttle and you get a higher or lower gear RIGHT NOW.

Surely there are some drawbacks to the automatic? Very few. Off the mark the 3650-lb (curb weight) 928 is a little sluggish, feeling as if the transmission has a loose torque converter. And it doesn't really reach its stride until around 3500 rpm. Then the V-8 rushes toward its redline with the same relish as the 5-speed model. For the convenience of automatic shifting the 928 owner gets a Porsche that's 1.0 sec slower in the quarter mile and 1.3 sec slower from 0-60 mph, but still appreciably quicker than any of its competitors except the 12-cylinder Jaguar XJS. When you compare performance figures for the automatic and 5-speed 928, it's obvious that it's the low-end acceleration that suffers. The automatic is 1.3 sec slower to 30 mph, a deficit that remains virtually constant up to 100 mph.

There are few other changes of note in the automatic 928 other than tires. Automatic 928s get Dunlop SP Sport 215/60VR-15 radials instead of 225/50VR-16 Pirelli P7s, but wheel width remains at 7.0 in. The reason is that P7s are in short supply and Porsche reasoned that the buyer of a 2-pedal 928 would be less interested in all-out performance than his 5-speed counterpart. The Dunlops don't offer the sheer cornering power of the Pirellis and aren't as good in the rain, but they achieved stopping distances as short as the P7s during our simulated panic stops without the moderate rear locking we encountered with the Pirellis.

We drove the 928 in New York City and the surrounding areas and tested at Pocono International Raceway because an automatic 928 wasn't available on the west coast. It was quite a treat to renew our acquaintance with the marvelously balanced handling and wonderfully precise assisted steering we commented on in our test last April. And the rough, broken, frost-heaved, pot-holed roads of New York, New Jersey and Pennsylvania gave new insight into the incredible ride comfort Porsche has designed into a car that handles so well.

For 1979 Porsche expects 75 percent of 928 sales to be 5-speeds. The long-range forecast is a 50/50 split, but some Porsche marketeers have looked at Mercedes-Benz sales and predicted production might eventually be biased more toward the automatic. We have no reason to doubt those projections because the Porsche 928 takes to automatic like Goodyear racing tires take to cornering.

The 928's usual Pirelli P7s are replaced with Dunlop SP Sports when the automatic transmission is ordered.

PHOTO BY LESLIE DINKEL

PRICE
List price, all POE	$28,500
Price as tested	$28,600

GENERAL
Curb weight, lb	3650
Weight distribution (with driver), front/rear, %	48/52
Wheelbase, in.	98.4
Track, front/rear	60.8/59.6
Length	175.7
Width	72.3
Height	51.7
Fuel capacity, U.S. gal.	22.4

CHASSIS & BODY
Body/frame....unit steel with aluminum doors, hood, front fenders
Brake system .... vented discs; 11.1-in. front, 11.4-in. rear, vacuum assisted
Wheels .... forged alloy, 15 x 7J
Tires .... Dunlop SP Sport, 215/60VR-15
Steering type .... rack & pinion, power assisted
Turns, lock-to-lock 3.1
Suspension, front/rear: upper A-arms, lower trailing arms, coil springs, tube shocks, anti-roll bar/upper transverse links, lower trailing arms, coil springs, tube shocks, anti-roll bar

ENGINE & DRIVETRAIN
Type	sohc V-8
Bore x stroke, mm	95.0 x 78.9
Displacement, cc/cu in.	4474/273
Compression ratio	8.5:1
Bhp @ rpm, net	219 @ 5250
Torque @ rpm, lb-ft	254 @ 3600
Fuel requirement	unleaded, 87-oct
Transmission	automatic; torque converter with 3-sp planetary gearbox
Gear ratios: 3rd (1.00)	2.75:1
2nd (1.46)	4.02:1
1st (2.31)	6.35:1
1st (2.31) x 2.0)	12.71:1
Final drive ratio	2.75:1

CALCULATED DATA
Lb/bhp (test weight)	17.1

Mph/1000 rpm (3rd gear)	27.9
Engine revs/mi (60 mph)	2150
R&T steering index	0.98
Brake swept area, sq in./ton	235

ROAD TEST RESULTS

ACCELERATION
Time to distance, sec:
0-100 ft	3.6
0-500 ft	9.4
0-1320 ft (¼ mi)	16.6
Speed at end of ¼ mi, mph	91.5

Time to speed, sec:
0-30 mph	3.8
0-50 mph	6.7
0-60 mph	8.3
0-80 mph	13.0
0-100 mph	20.1

SPEEDS IN GEARS
3rd gear (4800 rpm)	133
2nd (6000)	115
1st (6000)	68

FUEL ECONOMY
Normal driving, mpg	15.0

BRAKES
Minimum stopping distances, ft:
From 60 mph	139
From 80 mph	248
Control in panic stop ....very good
Pedal effort for 0.5g stop, lb 20
Fade: percent increase in pedal effort to maintain 0.5g deceleration in 6 stops from 60 mph ....nil
Overall brake rating ....excellent

HANDLING
Speed on 100-ft radius, mph	33.7
Lateral acceleration, g	0.760
Speed thru 700-ft slalom, mph	55.3

INTERIOR NOISE
All noise readings in dBA:
Constant 30 mph	66
50 mph	69
70 mph	72

SPEEDOMETER ERROR
30 mph indicated is actually	29.5
60 mph	60.0
70 mph	70.0

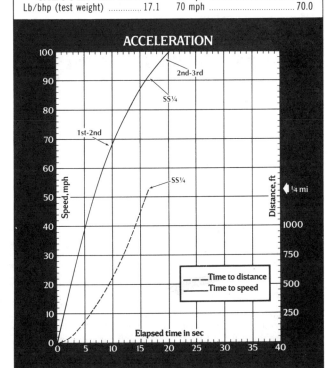

ACCELERATION

Road Test

PORSCHE 928S

At last, the 928 that goes like a Porsche should. A number of small improvements, enthralling performance and impressive economy make the £25,000 928 S truly desirable

FOR DYED-in-the-wool Porsche fanatics — most owners and would-be owners are — the 928 was a bitter pill to swallow. A supercar yes; a car that would buffer Porsche from the increasingly repressive legislation to which all sports car manufacturers can fall prey; a car to shake the likes of Mercedes-Benz, Jaguar and BMW; even a Car of the Year. But with its front-mounted 90 deg V8 driving the rear wheels via a transaxle, a car not only far removed from the rear-engined, air-cooled flat-six 911 concept but the product of a compromised design philosophy which rejected the acknowledged dynamic advantages of a mid-engine layout for what some would call the soft option in

pursuit of greater interior space and practicality.

Porsche, rightly we think, saw the 928 as the only long-term option for the supercar's survival and rejected the argument that mid-engined was necessarily best. After all, its Pirelli P7-shod Turbo handled and cornered as well as any mid-engined rival, and that was a car with a fundamentally unsound chassis configuration. At Porsche, development could triumph over design.

There was nothing much wrong with the 928 anyway. It performed effectively in its intended role and posed a far more potent challenge to its formidable class rivals than the initially

disappointing 924 did in the sporting 2-litre ranks.

And despite the 'soft' tune of its low compression 4.5-litre V8 which endowed the 32cwt car with only relatively modest performance; despite minor shortcomings in its dynamic make-up, the 928 bore all the hallmarks of Porsche quality and thoroughness plus a host of detail niceties. Few doubted such proud perfectionists as Porsche would realise the potential of its design or successfully iron out the initial bugs and thus turn the 928 into the magnificent motor car it could so easily be.

The car that succeeds on both counts is now available in the UK: it is called the 928S and we test it here. Its credentials are formidable. With a top speed in the region of 155 mph and acceleration to match, it joins the elite ranks of the world's fastest production cars, while its overall fuel consumption of 16.0 mpg makes it more economical than any rival of comparable performance and weight. If other supercar makers are to justify their existence in the face of dwindling energy resources they will need to follow the lead taken by Porsche who, with the 924 Turbo and the 928S, have shown the world that high performance doesn't have to be synonymous with a high thirst.

In the Porsche tradition, the 'S' suffix signifies more power and, in the case of the 928, visual changes and a more

comprehensive specification too. Externally, the 928S differs from its plainer 928 stablemate by the adoption of a front air-dam, with two small rectangular slots for brake cooling, and a rear lip spoiler made of polyurethene (said to give a lower drag coefficient of 0.38), new 16in forged alloy wheels (wearing 225/50 section P7s rather than the 215/60 section P6s now fitted as standard to the 928) and a discreet side rubbing strip to protect the alloy doors and front wings. Otherwise, the 928's front engine/rear-wheel drive layout is left much as before, with its five-speed gearbox mounted at the rear in unit with the final drive, and all-independent suspension by double wishbones at the front and lower wishbones with upper transverse links at the rear. While all four wheels are still braked by ventilated discs, the

Above: wrap-around facia cocoons passengers and is superbly detailed and finished.
Below: three-way electrically-powered front seats are almost beyond criticism.
Bottom: the rear seats are only really suitable for children over long distances.

discs themselves are thicker in the S and are used in conjunction with redesigned calipers and larger pads.

The most significant changes, however, are under the bonnet where the 928's all-alloy water-cooled V8 receives a small increase in capacity from 4,474cc to 4,664cc (achieved by stretching the bore of the linerless cylinders from 95 to 97mm) and, in line with all 1980 928s, a higher 10:1 compression ratio (requiring the use of 4 instead of 2-star petrol) and revised camshaft profiles. These changes boost the power output by 25 per cent to 300 bhp (DIN) at 5900 rpm while maximum torque is up by 10.3 per cent from 257 lb ft at 3600 rpm to 283.4 lb ft at 4500 rpm. The 4.5-litre 928's maximum torque is increased from 257 lb ft to 280 lb ft at 3600 rpm. Bosch K-Jetronic fuel injection is retained.

The interior changes are more subtle but include the adoption of a thermostatically controlled heating and air-conditioning system, a new four-spoke steering wheel, the standardisation of electrically powered seats with height, reach and backrest adjustment. A neat cassette holder residing under the centre armrest is standard, as are the heated and electrically-powered remote-control door mirrors. In common with the ordinary 928, Porsche's excellent three-speed automatic transmission is available as an option to the five-speed manual gearbox.

At £25,250 — £3,423 more than the ordinary 928, but £2,700 less than the top-of-the-range 3.3 Turbo — the 928S is marginally cheaper than such as the Aston Martin V8 (£29,998) and the Maserati Kyalami (£25,539), though it is comfortably undercut by Jaguar's XJS (£19,157) and Mercedes' 450 SLC (£21,861). Ferrari's desirable mid-engined 308 GT4 is also cheaper at £17,534 but is about to go out of production and be replaced by the Mondial 8.

On balance, though, the 928S is very competitively priced — more so than the ordinary 928, as, unlike its less powerful stablemate, it offers an unrivalled blend of performance,

economy, refinement, grip, finish and equipment. Porsche must be congratulated for exploiting the 928's potential and improving its weak areas — notably poor road noise suppression, an indifferent ride and slightly suspect high speed stability. It is a sophisticated and mature supercar and although it does not provide the thrills and excitement of the best 911s, its new-found urgency and aggression make a welcome counterpoint to its underlying smoothness and cold efficiency. The balance is more satisfying than before; whether it will convert 911 die-hards, only time and relative sales will tell. That it will win new friends seems certain.

If the original 928's unexceptional performance prompted unfavourable comparisons with the 911, the boot is firmly on the other foot with the 928S. Of the other models we've tested from the current Porsche range, only the equally powerful but appreciably lighter 3.3 Turbo is any faster; and that's no disgrace as the Turbo is the fastest-accelerating production car *Motor* has ever tested.

Make no mistake, the 928S is a very rapid car, capable of sprinting from a standstill to 60 mph in just 6.2 sec and to 100 mph in an equally stunning 14.8 sec. With beautifully controlled wheelspinning starts these figures were easily achieved and repeatable, matching Porsche's claims to within a few tenths of a second. Our car went on to reach 120 mph in 22.1 sec and covered the standing ¼-mile in 14.2 sec. For reference, our original 928 test car (slightly less powerful than the current versions remember) recorded 0-60, 0-100, and 0-120 mph and standing ¼-mile times of 7.0, 17.8, 31.3 and 15.2 sec respectively. These figures put the 928S at the head of our selected rivals, though the manual version of the Aston Martin V8 would have acceleration of the same order.

Unfortunately, we were unable to measure the Porsche's top speed accurately but on a number of occasions we achieved over 150 mph with some more to come. With this in mind, Porsche's claim of 156 mph seems believeable. Of course, a top speed of close on 160 mph is purely academic in this country, but it does at least provide a measure of the new car's dramatically superior top end performance (the original 928 was all-out at 140 mph) and serves to underline the car's much improved stability at such speeds — though one tester who has driven the BMW M1, an obvious home market rival for the 928S, at 150 mph + judged the mid-engined Bavarian supercar the more stable of the two.

If we praised the original 928's

4.5-litre V8 for its smoothness, refinement and, above all, its outstanding flexibility, the 4.7-litre version is even more impressive. The more powerful unit is, if anything, even smoother throughout the rev range, just as flexible in the low and mid-ranges, yet far more urgent in character above about 3500 rpm, revving freely and strongly to its 6,000 rpm 'red-line'. The fourth gear acceleration times illustrate the differences perfectly. Over the 30-50, 50-70 and 70-90 mph increments, the 928 and 928S are fairly evenly matched returning 5.4/5.2, 5.2/5.2 and 5.6/4.9 sec times respectively. But over the 80-100 and 100-120 mph increments, the 928S asserts its power advantage in no uncertain terms, returning 5.1 and 7.2 sec respectively against the 928's 6.4 and 14.0 sec.

As with most Bosch K-Jetronic installations, starting and warm-up are remarkably fuss-free. The 4.7-litre engine gives a crisp V8 bark at high revs without the mild top end harshness that afflicts the smaller unit, though at low revs it can seem slightly throbby and the idle is lumpy.

It almost goes without saying that a car of the Porsche's performance cannot be driven as hard for as long as, say, a 2-litre family saloon without running the gauntlet of the law. But the 928S was driven hard in our hands yet still returned an impressive overall fuel consumption of 16.0 mpg. This is yet

another demonstration of the value of Porsche's engine modifications, especially when you remember that the much slower 928 returned 14.9 mpg and that the consumption spread of our selected rivals ranges from 10.4 mpg for the automatic Aston to 15.1 mpg for the Mercedes. Assuming a touring consumption of 19.0 mpg, the 18.9 gallon tank affords a range of nearly 360 miles.

While few of our testers complained about the quality of the Porsche's gearchange which, although strongly biased towards the 2nd/3rd plane, is quick and positive, they were less keen about the gate pattern which places the top four forward gears in a conventional H pattern with first over to the left and back (with reverse opposite) so requiring a dog-leg movement for the first-to-second change — a movement which is awkward and can become tiresome in traffic. As in the ordinary 928, the clutch has a long travel — and must be fully depressed for clean changes — but is light and progressive, though prone to judder if you try to pull away with too few revs.

The spacing of the gearbox ratios is excellent, 6000 rpm allowing 44, 65, 91 and 119 mph maxima in the intermediates. And with the very long-legged fifth giving 26.5 mph/1000 rpm, 70 mph corresponds to just 2700 rpm.

Only revised rear tyre pressures (36 psi front/44 psi rear instead of 36 psi all round) and *forged* as opposed to cast alloy wheels serve to distinguish the chassis specification of the 928S from the original 928 — the current 928 wears narrower-section P6s on one inch smaller diameter (15in) rims, though P7s are still optional at extra cost. These small changes along, we suspect, with a few undisclosed running improvements have maintained the 928's stunning grip in the dry and tipped the handling balance towards

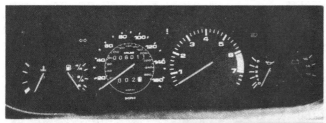

mild initial understeer, especially in tight bends.

More positive benefits of the changes, though we are reluctant to attribute them solely to the increased rear tyre pressures, are even more perceived feel from the already excellent power-assisted rack and pinion steering and, more importantly, a reduced tendency for the wide tyres to follow longitudinal ridges, white lines and road cambers. Although the steering isn't particularly high-geared, the sheer bite of the P7s means that even the smallest of steering inputs is answered by a swift and accurate response: it doesn't make the car feel nervous or twitchy, just superbly agile.

While, in normal driving on dry roads, the handling is biased towards mild understeer, the determined driver can use the extra power of the S to balance the car's attitude through a fast tight bend and, if conditions permit, power past the apex on a few degrees of easily-held opposite lock. Mid-corner stability and poise is excellent too, the Porsche-Weissach rear toe-in axle geometry ensuring that there is no instant oversteer should you lift off the throttle; nor do bumps exert even the slightest influence over the driver's chosen line. In the wet, the P7s retain enough of their grip for the 928S to be driven quickly and safely though, obviously, with so much power on tap a delicate touch is required and if tail slides are provoked, it isn't wise to let them get too pronounced.

As you would expect with 11in discs all round, the 928S has immensely powerful braking; even during the hardest of our driving (including repeated quick stops from around 130 mph at MIRA) there was no evidence of fade, the pedal always remaining firm and progressive under the foot and requiring moderate pressure.

In other respects, the 928S is very similar to the ordinary 928, details of which have been well chronicled in these pages. Viewed as a pure two-seater, the 928S is extremely spacious, with excellent leg, head and shoulder room, the split rear backrests folding forward to give a large luggage space. Access to the luggage platform is by the large, self-supporting tailgate. In its intended role as a 2+2, however, the rear 'bucket' seats, although fine for children, are unsuitable for adults on long journeys as the seats themselves are cramped and both rear leg and head room are very limited.

In the finest Porsche tradition these seats are superbly shaped and proportioned, providing ideal support for even our largest testers. With three-way electrically-powered adjustments for reach, height and backrest angle, the seats can also be finely tailored — in conjunction with the adjustable steering/instrument pod in the driver's case — to give an excellent driving position for drivers of widely varying shapes and sizes though a few tall testers complained that when the

Top: clean, clear and beautifully callibrated. Above: handbrake is mounted to the right of the driver's seat along with the power-seat controls, headlamp height adjuster and front/rear speaker balance control

cushion was adjusted to give adequate thigh support and was a comfortable distance from the pedals, the steering wheel, which lacks telescopic adjustment, was virtually out of reach. Visibility, however, remains poor in confined spaces, even tall drivers finding it difficult to judge the width of the 928's invisible (from the driver's seat) bulbous nose when parking and the wide central pillars necessitate caution at angled road junctions. The door mirrors, wipers (both front and rear) and lights (which can be adjusted from within the car) are all first class.

Although improved in the 928S, poor suppression of road noise remains the chink in this Porsche's armour. Bump thump is ever-present over poor roads and tyre roar on coarse surfaces, while seldom obtrusive, is more insistent than you might expect in a £25,000 car. Both characteristics serve to make the ride sound worse than it really is. In fact, the ride of the 928S is really quite good for a taut-handling supercar, firm yet pliant around town, absorbent and well-damped at speed.

The standard air conditioning is incapable of providing cool air at face level when heated air is required in the footwells. In cold weather this leads to stuffiness. Equally unsatisfactory is the tendency for the inside of the car to mist up requiring too frequent use of the noisy fan-boost 'demist' facility.

The instruments, among the most clearly calibrated and cleanly styled around, are perfectly positioned and totally reflection-free. So that they are never obscured by the rim of the adjustable steering wheel, the whole instrument pod moves up and down with the steering as an assembly. The major controls and column stalks are well positioned and feel satisfyingly precise in their actions.

Cast in the traditional Porsche mould, the build quality and finish of the 928S are immaculate both inside and out with superb paintwork, precision panel fits and an interior as remarkable for its tasteful blend of materials and colours as its air of relaxed efficiency and impressive attention to detail. With only an electric sunroof missing from the comprehensive specification, the 928S is extremely well equipped, even by the elevated standards of the class.

PERFORMANCE

CONDITIONS
Weather	Wind 5-15 mph
Temperature	44°F
Barometer	30.2 in Hg
Surface	Dry tarmacadam

MAXIMUM SPEEDS
	mph	kph
Banked Circuit	155 (see text)	249
Best ¼ mile Terminal Speed:		
at ½ mile	98	158
at kilometre		
at mile		

Speed in gears (at 6000 rpm):
	mph	kph
1st	44	71
2nd	65	104
3rd	91	146
4th	119	191

ACCELERATION FROM REST
mph	sec	kph	sec
0-30	2.4	0-40	1.9
0-40	3.3	0-60	3.1
0-50	4.9	0-80	4.6
0-60	6.2	0-100	6.5
0-70	7.8	0-120	9.0
0-80	9.7	0-140	11.8
0-90	12.0	0-160	14.7
0-100	14.8	0-180	18.6
0-110	17.9		
0-120	22.1		
Stand'g ¼	14.2	Stand'g km	25.8

ACCELERATION IN TOP
mph	sec	kph	sec
20-40	7.6	40-60	5.2
30-50	7.7	60-80	4.3
40-60	7.6	80-100	5.3
50-70	7.3	100-120	5.2
60-80	7.6	120-140	5.0
70-90	8.4	140-160	6.5
80-100	8.7		
90-110	10.2		
100-120	10.6		

ACCELERATION IN 4TH
mph	sec	kph	sec
20-40	5.2	40-60	3.8
30-50	5.2	60-80	2.7
40-60	5.3	80-100	3.3
50-70	5.2	100-120	3.6
60-80	5.0	120-140	2.8
70-90	4.9	140-160	2.6

80-100	5.1	160-180	4.2
90-110	5.7		
100-120	7.2		

FUEL CONSUMPTION
Touring*	19.0 mpg / 14.9 litres/100 km
Overall	16.0 mpg / 17.6 litres/100 km
Govt tests	14.2 mpg (urban) / 28.5 mpg (56 mph) / 22.6 mpg (75 mph)
Fuel grade	98 octane / 4 star rating
Tank capacity	18.9 galls / 80 litres
Max range	360 miles / 579 km
Test distance	933 miles / 1502 km

*Consumption midway between 30 mph and maximum less 5 per cent for acceleration.

NOISE
	dBA	Motor rating*
30 mph	63	9.5
50 mph	68	14
70 mph	70	16
Max revs in 2nd	78	

*A rating where 1 = 30 dBA and 100 = 96 dBA, and where double the number means double the loudness

SPEEDOMETER (mph)
Speedo	30	40	50	60	70	80	90	100
True mph	30	40	50	60	70	80	90	100

Distance recorder: accurate

WEIGHT
	cwt	kg
Unladen weight*	32.3	1640
Weight as tested	36.4	1849

With fuel for approx 50 miles

Performance tests carried out by Motor's staff at the Motor Industry Research Association proving ground, Lindley.

Test Data: World Copyright reserved; no unauthorised reproduction in whole or in part.

GENERAL SPECIFICATION

ENGINE
Cylinders	V8
Capacity	4664 cc (285 cu in)
Bore/stroke	97.0/78.9 mm (3.82/3.11 in)
Cooling	Water
Block	Alloy
Head	Alloy
Valves	Sohc per bank
Cam drive	Belts
Compression	10.0:1
Carburetter	Bosch K-Jetronic injection
Bearings	5 main
Max power	300 bhp (DIN) at 5500 rpm
Max torque	283.4 lb ft (DIN) at 4500 rpm

TRANSMISSION
Type	5-speed manual
Clutch dia	7.8 in
Actuation	Hydraulic

Internal ratios and mph/1000 rpm
Top	1.00:1	26.5
4th	1.34:1	19.8
3rd	1.82:1	15.2
2nd	2.47:1	10.8
1st	3.60:1	7.4
Rev	3.16:1	
Final drive	2.75:1	

BODY/CHASSIS
Construction	Steel monocoque, alloy doors, bonnet, front wings
Protection	Galvanised steel body, underbody protection: 6-year long-life guarantee

SUSPENSION
Front	Double wishbones, strut type dampers with co-axial coil springs, anti-roll bar
Rear	Independent, lower wishbone, upper transverse link (Porsche-Weissach patent geometry) coil springs, telescopic dampers, anti-roll bar

STEERING
Type	Rack and pinion
Assistance	Yes

BRAKES
Front	11.0 in ventilated discs
Rear	11.0 in ventilated discs
Park	On rear (drum in disc)
Servo	Yes
Circuit	Split diagonally
Rear valve	Yes
Adjustment	Automatic

WHEELS/TYRES
Type	7J x 16 Alloy
Tyres	Pirelli P7 225/50 VR
Pressures	36/44 psi F/R

ELECTRICAL
Battery	12V, 66 Ah
Earth	Negative
Generator	90A alternator
Fuses	34
Headlights type	2 x Halogen H4
dip	110 W total
main	230 W total

Make: Porsche
Model: 928 S
Maker: Dr Ing h. c. F. Porsche AG, Stuttgart-Zuffenhausen, West Germany
Concessionaires: Porsche Cars Great Britain Ltd, Richfield Avenue, Reading, RG1 8PH. Tel: 0734 595411
Price: £20,268.00 plus 1,689.00 car tax and £3,293.55 VAT equals £25,250.55

The Rivals

Another possible rival for the 928 S would be the £31,781 Bristol 412

PORSCHE 928 S — £25,251

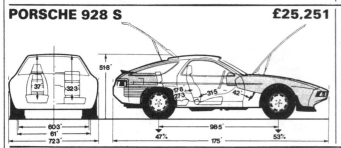

Power, bhp/rpm	300/5900
Torque, lb ft/rpm	283.4/4500
Tyres	225/50 VR 16
Weight, cwt	32.3
Max speed, mph	155†
0-60 mph, sec	6.2
30-50 mph, sec	5.2
Overall mpg	16.0
Touring mpg	19.0
Fuel grade, stars	4
Boot capacity, cu ft	7.3
Test Date	April 12, 1980
†Estimated	

High performance version of Porsche's front engine/transaxle 928 supercar. Larger 4.7-litre V8 engine gives stunning acceleration and flexibility and a top speed in the region of 155 mph with 16.0 mpg economy. Poor suppression of road noise remains its Achilles heel though both handling and ride have been subtly improved. Gearchange is quick and positive but has an awkward gate pattern. A very fast but still smooth and sophisticated supercar.

ASTON MARTIN V8 — £29,998

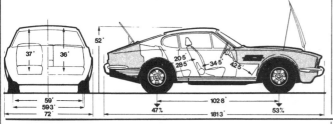

Power, bhp/rpm	Not available
Torque, lb ft/rpm	Not available
Tyres	225/70 VR 15
Weight, cwt	34.8
Max speed, mph	145†
0-60 mph, sec	7.5
30-50 mph in kickdown, sec	2.3
Overall mpg	10.7
Touring mpg	14.6
Fuel grade, stars	4
Boot capacity, cu ft	8.9
Original Test date	Oct 21, 1978
†Estimated	

A superb motor car, and now it is superbly made. Recent revisions have made vast improvement to interior, and overall quality is noticeably better. Otherwise as before: excellent handling, astounding performance, powerful and progressive brakes, ride reasonable at low speeds, good at high speed. Very expensive and rather thirsty, but if you can afford it, it's worth it. Even faster manual version is the same price.

FERRARI 308 GT4 — £17,534

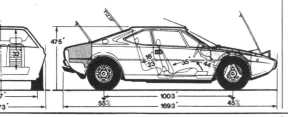

Power, bhp/rpm	255/7600
Torque, lb ft/rpm	210/5000
Tyres	205/70 VR 15
Weight, cwt	25.3
Max speed, mph	150†
0-60 mph, sec	6.4
30-50 mph in 4th, sec	5.1
Overall mpg	14.1
Touring mpg	18.7
Fuel grade, stars	4
Boot capacity, cu ft	5.0
Test Date	Jan 11, 1975
†Estimated	

Mid-engine coupé powered by 255 bhp V8 giving outstanding performance but heavy fuel consumption. Mediocre gearchange. Nominally a 2 + 2 but tiny rear seats not suitable for adults and the boot is small. Roadholding exceptional, but handling less precise and responsive than that of 246 Dino which remains one of our all time favourite supercars. Visibility good, but heating and ventilation disappointing. Although production has ceased, the replacement Mondial is not yet available.

JAGUAR XJS — £19,157

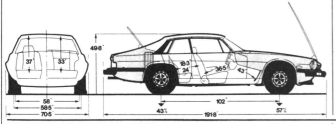

Power, bhp/rpm	285/5500
Torque, lb ft/rpm	294/3500
Tyres	205/70 VR 15
Weight, cwt	33.4
Max speed, mph	155
0-60 mph, sec	6.7
30-50 mph in 4th, sec	6.6
Overall mpg	12.8
Touring mpg	14.4
Fuel grade, stars	4
Boot capacity, cu ft	8.4
Test Date	Feb 21, 1976

In true Jaguar tradition, the XJ-S combines exceptional performance and refinement at a very competitive price. The styling may not be to everyone's taste and the rear seat accommodation is cramped for so large a car. But if you can afford the fuel bills, the XJ-S is without doubt one of the world's most desirable vehicles. We've only tested the manual but it's available in auto form.

MASERATI KYALAMI — £25,539

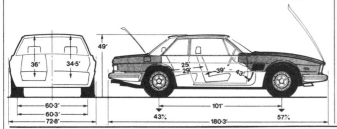

Power, bhp/rpm	270/6000
Torque, lb ft/rpm	289/3800
Tyres	205/70 VR 15
Weight, cwt	33.3
Max speed, mph	147†
0-60 mph, sec	7.6
30-50 mph in 4th, sec	6.2
Overall mpg	11.6
Touring mpg	14.7
Fuel grade, stars	4
Boot capacity, cu ft	8.9
Test Date	July 22, 1978
†Estimated	

Notchback 2 plus 2 has De Tomaso-derived body, but the engineering is pure Maserati. Not as quick as some rivals, but more thirsty. Excellent high speed cruiser, handling good until limit is approached, but ride only fair. Engine less refined than those of many rivals, sounding strained at high revs; gearchange slow. Powerful, progressive brakes. Interior finish leaves much to be desired. A disappointment — not in the same league as the Aston or Porsche.

MERCEDES-BENZ 450 SLC — £21,861

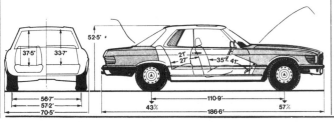

Power, bhp/rpm	225/5000
Torque, lb ft/rpm	278/3000
Tyres	205/70 VR 14
Weight, cwt	33.0
Max speed, mph	134†
0-60 mph, sec	8.5
30-50 mph in 4th, sec	3.3
Overall mpg	15.1
Touring mpg	—
Fuel grade, stars	4
Boot capacity, cu ft	8.9
Test Date	May 1, 1978
†Estimated	

A magnificent motor car, and one of our favourites. Typical Mercedes, which means an exceptionally high standard of finish allied to engineering that is second to none. Performance is more than adequate while the automatic transmission sets new standards. A limited slip diff would improve roadholding and handling by increasing traction. The 5.0-litre lightweight version has been sold on the Continent for some time and will soon be available here.

The Deutsche Mark Economy Run:
928 vs. 450 SLC

The only thing ludicrous about this is the title

by Ro McGonegal

PHOTOS BY DON GREEN

What we're talking about here is hedonism, plain and simple. In Des Moines or Shreveport, it means you're top banana. In Westchester or Marin, it's called keeping up. In LA, even the low-rollers have one or the other. It doesn't matter that these icons have doubled and tripled in price since their introductions (the 928 in '77, the SLC in '72); it only matters that people are still clamoring to get one, regardless of cost.

Here in Angel City, where the envelopment by *hedone* is even more powerful than that of the smog, this single fact is apparent. We are assailed by it unrelentingly—something that does not occur in Savannah or Reno. Even though half of the 928 and SLC population here is rented, that fact is as plain as the sign on the Hollywood Hills. To be seen behind the wheel of either speaks in clear terms that you have indeed made the grade; your intentions and your credit go unquestioned. You become a sliver of that flimsy elitism, so it doesn't matter that your face has not been seen before, because you're holding your credential by its leather-lined steering wheel.

But certainly there must be more to this obsession than preferential treatment by mustachioed parking-lot maitre d's. We know what the beast is, but we don't know how it got that way, how it has come to mean what it does. Unquestionably, the two cars are supreme beings in their narrow field, and undoubtedly they are symbols of status, but underneath the images are two wonderfully made machines. They are paradigms of active and passive safety. They are made the way all cars should be made.

Before all else, they have been built to consider good visibility, readable instruments, placement and design of controls, seating design and comfort, and ventilation to be highest priorities. This is the stuff that keeps drivers at their freshest and most alert, so that they

may find their way *around* the trouble before it starts. This all imparts, as we discovered, a feeling most important. That feeling is called control.

We know that both cars will hold four people in completely understated comfort. At 4.5 liters, engine size is identical. Although a Porsche buyer might order up his 928 with a manual transmission, we took ours with an automatic to more closely align it with the SLC's equipment. But the similarity ends here. Ride quality, cornering power, interior appointments, level of engine response and degree of people response are remarkably different.

Given these differences, we find the cars approaching a Y-split in the road: one is heading left, the other right. They will ford the same crossing, but each will do so indigenous to its heritage. And so their forebears are worth investigation.

Since the word Porsche is synonymous with powerful, no-nonsense, air-cooled engines, the people in Weissach knew they would have a credibility gap to fill with the production of the 928. Although the 911 will most probably endure until public acceptance wanes (highly unlikely), or the EPA deems it

unfit for public consumption (highly likely), it will continue to be produced for the U.S. market. But in the long run, Porsche feels that the 911's days are limited. The reasons for this are safety and purity.

The rear-engine car was designed before intense government and public concern for the well-being of its occupants. According to Porsche, a car with an aft-mounted engine does not constitute enough of a crush zone for adequate crash protection. Besides this, a rear-mounted, air-cooled engine produces more noise than a front-mounted, water-cooled engine does.

Further investigation tempted them with another feature from the past: move the engine amidships, as in the 914 series. But this also proved unacceptable because the design precluded +2 seating and the sufficient interior storage space they wanted in the 928. That settled it: the new car would be front-engine, using a water-cooled V-8 (with cylinders arranged at a 90-degree angle). It was ascertained that the hoodline of the 928 could slope away almost as abruptly as that of the 911 and it could match the fenderline angle at the same time, making the front of the car lower than that of the 911. While the 4.5-liter engine remained in front, the transmission would be located in the rear as part of a transaxle unit, thus allowing the preferred equal front/rear weight bias.

The rear suspension is one of the marvels of modern automotive history. It is known as the Weissach axle (a patented device named for the Porsche de-

velopment center but devilishly transformed into an acronym: Working Elastics Integrated for a Systematic Stabilizing Alignment CHange). The Weissach combats the natural forces of physics as well as the inadequacies of soft suspension bushings.

In practice, the axle minimizes the tendency of the rear tires to tuck under during hard braking or abrupt deceleration while negotiating a curve. Anyone who has experienced oversteer (the trailing-throttle variety) knows the sweaty-palm feeling. A test rig was fitted with a separate steering device for the rear wheels. Using this, Porsche engineers were able to determine when and where the dread toe-in change began and devised the system around this evidence. They used high-rigidity rubber bushings (a must for street use), a twin transverse-link axle, coil springs over shock absorbers, and a twin torsion bar unit located under the rear seats. Just a little something to keep you out of trouble when you need it.

We don't mean to belabor the genius involved; we only mean to produce evidence for the future. Porsche and Mercedes, though relatively small auto makers on the world scale, want to produce cars for as long as possible. They tend to thrive on betterment of the breed, not in producing as many vehicles as they can. They are frugal people, and as such, they realize better amortization of high initial investments through extended car-model life.

The 450SLC's sheet metal has been around for nearly 10 years; that of the Porsche 911 for more than 20. Both

configurations are still considered mature and refined and completely unaffected by short-term styling fads. In a sense, they are timeless, and each example provides a peek at its heritage as well as its future. And so the 928's form was dictated by three criteria: a good drag coefficient (.39); a "timeless," long-run exterior; and the dutiful retention of the Porsche silhouette.

Development for the 928 started in 1971, one year prior to the debut of the Mercedes 450SLC series. It was introduced to the world in August 1977. With minor adjustments, the 928 will retain its present form through the decade. (Through ironic but practical circumstance, the 1971 350SL convertible was used as an early staging ground for 928 development. It was fitted with the Porsche V-8 and the first-stage transaxle. Porsche probably did this because the wheelbase and other dimensions of

the 350 were close to what they wanted for their own creation, but the fact remains.)

From the 350 came the 450SL and, one year later, the hardtop SLC body. It incorporated a longer wheelbase (97 inches vs. 111 for the Slick One), room for two, maybe three people in the back, a substantial trunk, dirt-shedding lower body and taillights, and the encyclopedia of ergonomics. These features have remained unchanged since their inception and will continue through the first part of next year. At that time, the new 450SLC will be introduced in the U.S.; it will be a tucked-in, folded-over and laid-back version of the car you see here, looking only as *it* could look and expecting another 10 years of ungrudging acceptance.

It is the beginning of life for one car and the end of part of a life for another; but is it really a matter of new

vs. old? And is there any way on earth these cars are worth the down payment on a house?

To find the truth, we decided to take the Top Bananas out of their cushy LA environment and put them on *The Road.* We would leave Los Angeles and head north to make our night stop and base of operation in the drive-through burg of Lone Pine. Lone Pine has the distinction of being directly adjacent to the highest point in California and the lowest point in the continental United States. The summit is more than 14,000 feet, to the top of Mt. Whitney; the cellar is 100 miles to the east, in that lovely heat-rippled sink known as Death Valley. To get to the depths of the Land of the Dead we had to traverse one mountain range and then another. In the interim there were slim sections of roadway with 300-degree turns and little room for oversteer error; if you went too far astray, you'd find yourself all the way down wrapped up in a $40,000 ball.

The roads that connect the mountain ranges, however, are as flat and straight as the Kansas Turnpike, and they invite you to drive as fast as you want for as long as you dare. Even nature complied: the temperature started at 50° F. at night and soared to more than double that during the daytime. And there was wind. Great, booming gusts of it blew east from the saline flats that covered the valley floor. Sometimes the only way to tell if it was fierce was to watch the undergrowth bend to it. Other times it was so laden with talc you could see it coming for miles. Then,

seemingly multiplying in speed, it would slam into our sides, the movable force meeting the movable object.

Now, sit back, close your eyes, and slowly inject your feelings with what it's like to be alone in desolation. In a matter of minutes, your awareness is at full pitch. Then every half-hour or so tantalize yourself with a camper that sails silently by, a desert gossamer that ceases to exist as soon as it is out of sight. My good friend Don Green and I have a revelation: we realize there is no better place than this to feel these cars. Since the space we are occupying is miniscule compared to the natural landscape, the distractions of noise, concrete, humanity and ego are almost totally erased. It's like being able to write when you are alone, after the rest of the office has gone home: the power of concentration is so high it becomes the wonderful distraction, and the only sound you hear is your own. All the better to experience you, my two beauties.

The smell and feel of leather and the intangibles of ambience are waiting inside. The SLC softly says "sedan." Using only the dashboard for reference, we could well be in an SEL. The steering wheel is large, almost clumsy looking, and you feel as if you need hands the size of Mean Joe's to make it look right. But it's connected to a wonderfully stable steering system that gives great road feel and requires just the right amount of effort to operate. The SLC can turn its full radius in a little over 38 feet. This is because it has a wheelbase that is a foot longer than that of the 928.

The next obvious thoughts are related directly to the wide and very firm seats, seats that other drivers found better for driving than for riding shotgun. They, as in all Mercedes, can be fitted to your contour by pulling a handle and turning a knob. The steering-wheel angle must be magically correct for every driver, since there is no provision for adjustment. You use the seat's mechanics to do that. And since the steering wheel does not move, the unmistakable gauges are never obstructed from your view. The instruments are as easy to comprehend as the words in a primary reader, and they should be. They've been around in the same basic form for more than 20 years.

With your hands on the steering wheel and your arms bent at 60 degrees, the center rest as well as the padded window sill are at a perfectly comfortable height. There are no sharp edges anywhere, nor is there anything else so outstanding as to detract from your concentration on the road. Everything blends like the smoothness of Black Forest cake, and the taste pleasantly lingers. All controls, save for the climate control panel, are close to steering wheel-stuck fingers. Without question, the ventilation system is the easiest accessory in the world to use, and it can be operated without the driver having to take his eyes from the road. Plink two switches and it's working. It may be a little loud when the "high" button is engaged, but it is effective almost immediately.

The 928 (say *nine-two-eight*) is altogether different. You don't sit up on those leather buckets; you slide down and into them, into a completely new environment. The Porsche seats tend to resemble a body pod: they spell out *sport*, not *sedan*, rather quickly. Since you sit low, there is a provision, at a $625 premium, that enables you to fool with the 6-way power seat. This is one thing the Benz doesn't offer, but we found the 450's more conventional bucket easier to live with on the long run. In the 928, some people complained that the angle of the seat bottom didn't match the plane of the seatback and that they were sitting with their legs slightly to one side at a back-bothering angle, but this was not apparent to me.

If the power seat won't get you where you want to be, then move the dashboard. Directly beneath the wheel module is a flap that pushes easily forward. The steering column and instrument pod move up and down in a 3-inch arc as one unit, so the gauges are never hidden from view. The leather smell is stronger in the 928 than in the 450, and because there are only two major seats, the interior is cozier and more intimate than that of the Mercedes. The ambience is much more compelling, expounding not only subdued comfort,

928

450SLC

928

450SLC

but, more important, a much higher level of performance. The gauges are bold high-tech pieces, white numbers on a somber black field given meaning by the sweep of red chisel-point needles. None of Porsche's racing heritage has been lost here.

You can actuate any of the minor controls without taking your hands from the steering wheel, and both right- and left-hand outside mirrors can be positioned electronically. Steering input is as direct as that of the SLC, requiring little effort but transmitting a great deal of road feel back to the operator. Our 928 was equipped with optional 16-inch Pirelli P7 tires and alloy wheels ($740 extra, and a deal at that), which lay about twice as much rubber on the tarmac as the Mercedes' 70-series Michelins. Twice as much contact makes for

a commensurate amount of feedback, but, then, the Porsche has a different purpose than the Mercedes.

While it may seem ridiculous to even offer an automatic transmission with the 928, it makes good economic sense to Porsche marketing people. They expect to sell as many automatics as manuals this year because to some buyers the 928 will be strictly for tooling around instead of getting down to business. In town, the transmission tends to hang in 2nd a lot; to make it shift you must either maintain speed and lift your throttle foot, or be forced to get into the gas when it isn't safe to do so. This creates a motorboat effect, the droning resonance of an engine hooked to a sloppy-shifting transmission. It also tends to pull fuel mileage down to curb level. But under power, the 3-speed bangs off shifts like a drag-race car (the automatic is a recased 6.9 Mercedes unit, modified for use with the transaxle and fitted with Porsche's own gear ratios).

The SLC is open to the same criticism because it has the same tendencies, but the transmission shifts sooner. If the gear change is a normal upshift, you are permeated by its smoothness: there's no snap, no jerk, only a continual flow, as if there's a river of fluid running through it. Full-throttle upshifts—the kind you need when you try an escape out the bathroom window of the Beverly Hills Hotel—come on a little faster, but with nowhere near the abandonment exhibited by the 928.

Handling characteristics are similar but not matching. Both cars use suspension systems that are designed for maximum safety with minimal driver input. They can flat save your ass and you won't even know it. In the city, ride quality has authority and maybe it even borders on harsh, but at cruising speed, the sinew becomes supple. Road-holding power becomes evident, but it is different in both automobiles. On a good day, the SLC will outweigh the 928 by at least 350 pounds; it has more glass above its beltline, and its tires are much narrower than those on the 928. At moderate speed, those tires and suspension transmit road-surface idiosyncracies to the driver in a continuum. They are always there and you are glad they are because this is the kind of

feedback that makes driving fun. Only the most severe dips or bumps will change the expression on your face; everything else is for the pure feel of it.

The 928 goes this rapture one better. Groveling around town is not the 928's forte. In those confines, it feels sluggish and heavy, but still smooth. It gives you the idea that the faster it goes, the better it will feel. Muscles will unknot, and kneecaps will stop popping if you just get her up to speed, and when equipped with an automatic, this is probably the biggest difference between it and the SLC.

On the desert floor we were able to make the engines ring while passing over some fairly large moguls (otherwise known as *whoop-dee-doos)*, the kind that play havoc with the camber change on all four wheels. Literally, both cars were a hair from being airborne and both exhibited a tendency to wiggle for a half-second after touchdown. This was the one and only time either displayed incorrigibility. The head-splitter came during one of those long, don't-take-your-brain-off-the-road-for-a-second, decreasing-radius turns. I had simply steered the 928 around this monstrous jughandle. But the following day, I was in the 450 following Green around the same curve at the same speed, and I had to ease off v-e-r-y slowly for fear of losing it. Another driver might have machoed-it out, but I could guarantee adrenalin seepage. I let out a howl. Later, I told Don what had happened and he laughed. The same thing had happened to him; he hadn't told me because he wanted me to experience that rarest of rushes, the chill of impending doom.

Power for both Teutons is pumped from overhead-cam aluminum-alloy fuel-injected V-8s that displace 275 cubic inches. The 928 engine produces about 60 more horsepower (on paper, at least) and reaches a peak of 220 when the rpms go to 5500. The SLC makes its 160 horses at a meager 4200 rpm. Torque for both engines is nearly the same (255 pounds-feet, Porsche; 230, Mercedes), but the Mercedes' comes on at a very usable 2500 rpm. The 928's doesn't show until 1500 rpms later, and since most city flogging is done between 2000 and 3000 revs, the heavier car has the obvious tractability advantage.

The V-8 in the SLC spins silently, almost turbine-like, and it meshes with the automatic transmission the same way; indeed, the loudest thing you'll hear from the 450 is the thermostatic fan, which stays silent most of the time anyway. The tip of the muffler is so far to the rear and the insulation in the car is so good that the exhaust note is undetectable.

But the Porsche engine had a real rump in its idle, and the exhaust exited on the driver's side, fluting a good deal of expectation in its tune. Leaning on

mirrors, and if we happened to catch them side-glancing, they'd snap eyes front like their names had been called on the first day of summer camp.

But the best response in the world is mine. It is near dusk and Green is plodding through his picture-taking ritual. Green is always talking about the right light, the low, even light, and how important it is. And I have always nodded, thinking I was sure I knew what he was telling me. But here on this windy bluff overlooking the valley floor, sitting on a pile of these weird claret-colored cinders, I have a small revelation. I realize for the first time what he's been saying all along. These two cars are different. It's the light, which has turned silvery. It draws attention only to the strongest of the 928's character lines, and it diminishes all that is unimportant.

Green has almost finished now and he's in the 928, moving it out and away from its closeness to the SLC. The taillights are glowing and the engine is running.

The title of this story suggests a comparison, which I feel reasonably sure of having offered. If there is a winner, then we must leave that to your requirements and subjectivity. Perhaps because these cars are so outstanding, a choice would have to be predicated on minutia. The Porsche offers a 6-way seat, electrically operated mirrors, and even an air-conditioned glove box. The Mercedes counters with armrests big enough to be used as tables, a real back seat and a real trunk. Then you can wrestle with each marque and everything it implies. Maybe the fat P7 radials will be the decider. Do you see what I mean?

As for the economy part, well, as Elvis once said, " . . . that was just a lie." As you can see by the chart, these beauties aren't all that bad, but they do like to drink when they're having a good time. No, their economy is found in design, in metalwork that will never become tiresome, and in accessories that will always delight the passengers. It's marked by prudent exteriors that are wrapped around spacious interiors, and by economy of motion.

Is the 450SLC worth $43,726? Is the 928 worth $39,880?

Who knows?

But when you can ride for 200 miles, get out of a car and then get right back in for another 200 and feel refreshed while doing it, then, yes, either car is worth the money. When you can take a two-tonner and flash it through street rabble the same way you would a Civic and be able to do it with enough moxie and smoothness in braking, acceleration and evasive action to make you sing, then, yes, they're worth the money. Had I the wherewithal, I'd own both. But I don't. My time in these preferred stocks is up and I'm glad. My anonymity is too precious. 〔MT〕

the throttle induces a momentary lag, and then the engine works out right to redline in what seems like half the time of the SLC's acceleration. But there's a price to pay for the fury: the alloy engine is durable but somewhat delicate. Its pistons travel in a sleeveless cylinder block that will not tolerate inordinate heat buildup. If the oil level (and probably coolant level) drops below two quarts, a sensor will read this and shut off the ignition. The car will stop dead. Fresh oil will revive it as quickly as a shot of amphetamine, but when this happens late at night, or in a section of lightly traveled desert, there's matter for concern. So you prevent this by checking the dipstick periodically, just like any knowledgeable car owner *would* do.

The way the populace responds to these mega-cars is patterned, and their reaction depends on whether you're in the car or not. If you're close and they know you've something to do with this rich guy's ride, they most likely start in about the old days, or what a nice car, or what do these cost nowadays? If you're out of sight and it's nighttime, they may decide to leave a sign. The 928 was key-laced in Lone Pine, and the SLC was scarred in a similar incident in Hollywood. So much for the demographics of miscreants.

But the real people chose to verbally ignore the SLC and to concentrate on the 928. Some thought it was beautiful, while others simply lamented the passing of the air-cooled engine. When we were moving, occupants of other cars would sneak looks in their rearview

PORSCHE 928S...

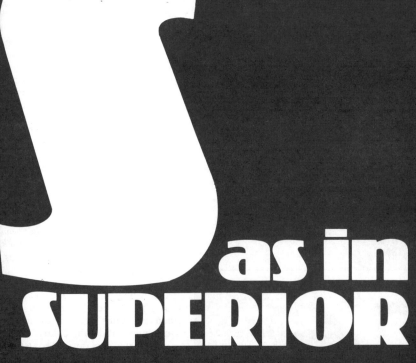

S as in SUPERIOR

More than just a better 928, the S model is different and superior enough to stand distinctly apart and above. It's a true total-performance machine with acceleration, flexibility, handling, steering and braking that mean it's as much a sports car as a Grand Tourer as a luxury coupe — a rich and rare combination, in praise of which superlatives are the rule.

THE PORSCHE 928S is a fascinating car, if for no other reason than that it's many things to many people. You could question a group of people who have driven, ridden or merely ogled the 928S, and you'd get as many different good reasons for owning it.

Considering the near-$68,000 price as a mere formality, one could buy the 928S not just because it's a prestigious Porsche, but rather because it's the best Porsche. Others might be seduced, responsively, by its quality construction, its once-a-year servicing, its flawless finish, its lavish equipment level, its assured appreciation. Some might be won by its lines — its un-beautiful but undeniably special lines ... tough, chunky and somehow purposefully mean; with muscles even in its eyebrows so to speak. Some might well find it endearing because it is uncommonly easy to drive, with controls almost as supple as Japanese cars' but with purely European feel and precision. And so the list would go and grow, reason by reason.

And what of the driver-buyer? His reasons are best of all. Above everything else, beyond its many other attractions, the 928S is a car for driving, for enjoying, for taking your breath away with the sheer brilliance of its dynamics in every respect. Every respect.

It's a total package, the 928S — a finely honed and beautifully balanced combination of remarkable acceleration, flexibility, braking, handling, roadholding, stability, steering and ride — each interwoven with the others to give an endless chain of performance that has no weakest link.

I'm heading towards Sydney, along the Bell's Line of Road across the Blue Mountains, alone in the Porsche and motoring rather faster than the speed advisory signs suggest. Time and again there's a flashing realisation that I'm approaching corners faster than ever. That's enough to provoke the lightest caress of the brake pedal, or just a sucking intake of breath and a quickening heartbeat, not to check the speed so much as to make some self-assuring gesture that I mean to do it, that I can do it. So I turn the wheel, just turn the wheel, and the Porsche goes round the corner, and exits, accelerating as hard as it can, and my breath lets go with a gasp and I'm thinking: Jeez! that was fast for me and the car wasn't even trying.

Another time, on a damp road, at relatively moderate velocities, I play with the 928S in safety. Lesson one was that in the wet it's easy to generate power-oversteer with the throttle, and, indeed, not difficult to provoke lots of it if you let

your right foot get the better of your brain. Even P7s can do only so much on a slick surface when over-activated by that extremely healthy engine.

What the wet session mainly proved was just how predictable the 928S is, and how finely controllable it remains when pushed beyond the point of its mild-understeer/neutral handling normality. The understeer increases somewhat, without approaching ploughing, if the 928S is thrust into slow corners on a trailing throttle. Through open corners, however, the oversteer is available upon request. With familiarity and skill the Porsche can be set up to hang the tail out seemingly as wide and as long as you like, and you can have much more fun with it than is perhaps usual among cars of its performance potential and price. But the speed and grip are so great that discretion is the better part ...

I don't know where the limit lies in the dry, and don't really care because it's so far above normal levels that it's quite academic. I do know that on a favourite long, winding climb, with a clear road and a spare confidence-cushioning lane on the outside, I'm able to let the Porsche have its head in third. It sees 6000 rpm up the short straights and gets through the turns with the otherwise mute P7s howling magnificently as they yield so little and so precisely to the tremendous loads while the car creeps bodily outwards. Even then it takes only small, almost instinctive, touches on the wheel and throttle to keep the 928S pointed and going where it's meant to. And as we crest that grand climb, the Porsche and me, I know that we were really trying and that I just didn't want to get any closer to my limit, let alone the car's, not at those sorts of cornering speeds.

The S engine is a magic thing. Absolutely superb, nothing less. The specifications tell you that it's a water-cooled, petrol-injected, front-mounted 90-degree V8 with single overhead cams, 97 × 78.9 mm bore and stroke, 221 kW maximum power and 385 Nm maximum torque. What the specs don't tell, what they simply can't convey, is the wonderful smoothness and liveliness of the engine. It's one of the all-time Greats.

It goes of course. The acceleration figures bear that out, even though the test car wasn't quite as quick at the top-end as factory figures and some overseas tests show. It was a few points slower for the 0-400 m, for instance, and we wondered whether the explanation might be that the Australian edition is slightly different to meet the ADR exhaust emission standards. But the local agents say it's exactly the same as the European model.

The 928S proves that it's a mistake to associate the V8 configuration with the relatively slow-revving engines from Detroit. Zuffenhausen's answer is a high revver. It develops maximum torque at 4500 rpm, which is two to three times the speed at which most US V8s do it, and is in fact farther up the rev scale than most of their maximum power points, or even their maximum revs. That specification, combined with the 5900 rpm power peak, might suggest that the S engine is all top-end, with not much to offer below middling revs. Wrong.

The Porsche is outstandingly flexible. Considering the car's speed and acceleration potentials, the tractability is phenomenal. The engine pulls like the proverbial train, albeit rather more excitingly, with never a hint of wayward temperament. It can be allowed to drop to less than 500 rpm in fifth gear, and will then draw away with aristocratic disdain for the task. You could drive round Australia in fifth. Admittedly the initial acceleration in top gear is fairly leisurely, but the faster it goes the quicker it becomes.

That effect is even more pronounced in third and fourth. Flatten the pedal while idling along and the car responds like the adrenalin pump that it is, becoming quicker and quicker until the acceleration rate dips. You think that that was good and you expect it to continue tapering off. Instead, the engine takes a fresh breath and surges ahead with an awesome vigour. Again, the faster you go, the quicker it becomes. Fan-bloody-tastic! Who needs a turbo? Not when you've got this engine under you, you don't.

In third the acceleration continues quickening until you reach the 140 km/h – 6000 rpm red line marks. In fourth the mind-bending surge doesn't begin to abate until you're beyond 160 km/h (5000+ rpm) when air resistance finally gets the edge.

Though the 928S accelerates impressively enough, the way in which it happens is even more remarkable. It's just as though you were opening a tap. For all its rapidity the acceleration is exceptionally smooth. It pushes you deeply into the seat, for sure, yet it doesn't have the savage shoulder-thumping punch of a good, say, Falcon GT or Monaro 350. The differences include the engine — which spins so eagerly that heaven only knows where it would desist if there wasn't a rev-limiter at 6500. The close-ratio five-speed gearbox abets the smoothness too, for when you take the Porsche up to the red line and snap it through to the next cog, the revs drop only to the 4000-or-so mark, and the power just keeps on coming.

A third factor is that the rear suspension keeps the wheels planted on the road, and the way the big Pirellis bite the bitumen. Even so, with all that torque underfoot, and the dragstrip starting area slick from a recent race meeting, it proved easy to waste time making smoke at the line. The most effective technique was to drop the clutch at about 3000 rpm to squirt the car away from the start, easing the pedal slightly to minimise wheelspin, then planting it a few metres out to send the S on its way like a wild thing, but running straight as a die.

Like the engine, the transmission deserves high praise, though in this case with a couple of qualifications. Curiously, the shift lever is unexpectedly sloppy from side to side, yet the shift action is as positive as you could wish for. The shift pattern is a mixture too. It has the $\frac{R\ 2\ 4}{1\ 3\ 5}$ layout long favoured in Porsche's five-speeders, but now abandoned in the 924.

Though the 928S will start from rest in second gear without any fuss, we always used first, as doubtless do most drivers. The catch here is that to reach the First/Reverse plane, the lever must be pushed through a detent, which is a bit tiresome in stop-start conditions. Also, there's no lock-out between First and Reverse, meaning that drivers used to conventional $\frac{1\ 3\ 5}{2\ 4\ R}$ systems may absent-mindedly move the lever far-left and forward when preparing to depart. That can be embarrassing at least.

Initially the First-Second shift feels a bit long and a little slow in normal driving conditions, because it seems natural to guide the lever through the dog-leg. But when running the performance figures we found it takes only a single throw, as fast as you can move it, to send the lever home.

Few cars have steering as good as the 928S's, and it's difficult to imagine how any could be better. In the Porsche it's a power-assisted rack and pinion system. The power assistance takes care of the load and ensures that the S is easy to manoeuvre even when parking. The assistance also enables the use of a reasonably quick (17.75:1) steering ratio which translates to three turns lock to lock for the turning circle which, at 10.9 m diameter, is about average for a car of this size.

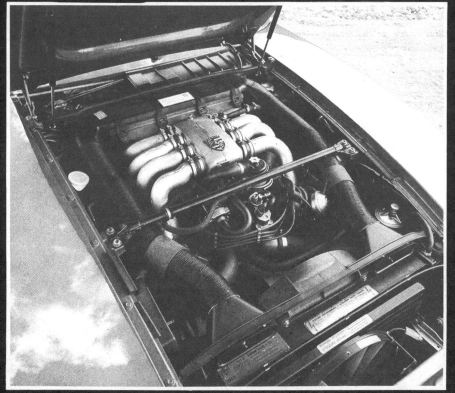

The 928S engine is a wondrous thing with brilliant performance, amazing flexibility and thrifty fuel economy.

The important thing about the power assistance is that it bestows its benefits without detriment to the steering's feel and precision. There's a two-way traffic in the steering ... your hands' control commands are transmitted directly to the front wheels without losing anything along the way and you, in turn, get messages from the wheels to tell you what they're doing, even to the extent of some slight kickback up the column on rough roads. As a steering system, it really is the best of both worlds.

Then there's the brakes. Ah, yes, the brakes.

I'm motoring comfortably (which, in the 928S, means comfortably quickly), just using fifth and occasionally fourth, darting through the twisty bits with never more than an eighth or so turn this way or that, mostly keeping the speedo needle tidy, near vertical. Cruising **vivace.** *Dive into another corner and, Hell's Bells, a sign ...* **Flagman Ahead — Prepare To Stop.** *One's allowed the blink of an eye to prepare because the sign is on the exit not the approach of course, much too close to the man who is signalling STOP of course, because the immediate*

foreground is full of a huge truck stretched right across the road of course. And in that instant I just know that there's no chance of stopping of course. But I try, meaning that I lean on the brake pedal as hard as I know how, half expecting the wheels to lock at front or back or both ends, and the Porsche simply clamps itself to the road, slows mightily and stops — centimetres from the wide-eyed flaggie. Metres to spare. I suggest that he move the sign up, not necessarily up the road either; others might come round the corner as fast but not stop as quickly.

The 928S's brakes don't only work magnificently, they also feel superb. They're light enough for m'lady round town, without being at all over-servoed and too sensitive, yet are immensely powerful when you need them so. You then have to push on the pedal as though you're serious, with a deliberate effort to prove you mean business, and the brakes respond in kind. The handbrake is excellent also. Its right-hand lever affords plenty of purchase and is as effective as a low-speed brake as it is for holding securely on the steepest grades.

The 928S's refinement is also reflected

in its ride because the needs of comfort clearly have been met without unduly compromising the handling and roadholding. Thus the 928S rides very comfortably, not softly and spongily absorbing every little rut or ripple but ironing them out in a way that confirms the suspension is firmly controlled, without being harsh. Indeed, lack of harshness confirms the suspension's efficacy, because the result could so easily be otherwise due to the tyre's very low profile (and relatively stiff) design being compounded by the unusually high recommended inflation pressures; higher at the rear than front incidentally. The ride remains relatively good on very rough roads, though the firmness shows through of course, sometimes enough to induce obscure creaks in the otherwise tremendously tight, solid-feeling body.

The noise aspect isn't as clear-cut as the other issues in the 928S. Whereas the engine, transmission, suspension, brakes and ride are always near or at the excellent level, the *car* isn't consistently quiet. The engine is just noisy enough that its throatily virile growl registers on your senses without becoming obtrusive

---

SPECIFICATIONS

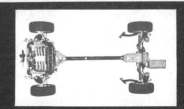

MAKE	Porsche
MODEL	928S
BODY TYPE	2 + 2 coupe

ENGINE:

Cylinders	Eight, 90-degree V, front-mounted
Valves	SOHC
Intake	Petrol injection
Compression ratio	10 to 1
Bore × stroke	97 × 78.9 mm
Capacity	4.664 litres
Power at 5900 rpm	221 kW
Torque at 4500 rpm	385 Nm

TRANSMISSION:

Type: Manual 5-speed transaxle, rear-mounted, dry twin-plate clutch

RATIOS:

	Gearbox	Overall	km/h per 1000 rpm
First	3.601:1	9.902:1	11.7
Second	2.466:1	6.781:1	17.1
Third	1.819:1	5.002:1	23.3
Fourth	1.343:1	3.693:1	31.5
Fifth	1.000:1	2.750:1	42.4
Final drive	2.750:1		

CHASSIS:

Construction: Unitary steel chassis body; aluminium doors, bonnet, front guards.

SUSPENSION:

Front: Unequal length, non-parallel wishbones, coil springs, anti-roll bar.
Rear: Porsche-Weissach semi-trailing arms, upper control arms, coil springs, anti-roll bar.
Dampers: Telescopic

STEERING:

Type	Power assisted rack and pinion
Turns l to l	3.0
Turning circle	10.9 m

BRAKES:

Type	Power-assisted discs

DIMENSIONS:

Wheelbase	2500 mm
Track, front	1549 mm
Track, rear	1521 mm
Length	4447 mm
Width	1836 mm
Height	1282 mm
Kerb mass (weight)	1530 kg
FUEL TANK	86 litres

TYRES: Pirelli Cinturato P7 225/50VR16
Pressure, front/rear | 248/303 kPa (36/44 psi)

PERFORMANCE

TEST CONDITIONS:

Weather	Fine, mild
Surface	Castlereagh Dragway
Load	Two people
Fuel	Super

SPEEDOMETER ERROR:

Indicated km/h	50	70	90	110	130
Actual km/h	50	70	90	109	128

MAXIMUM SPEEDS IN GEARS:

First	70 km/h (6000 rpm)
Second	102 km/h (6000 rpm)
Third	140 km/h (6000 rpm)
Fourth	190 km/h (6000 rpm)
Fifth	250 km/h (5900 rpm)

ACCELERATION:

Through the gears:

0-50 km/h	2.4 sec
0-60 km/h	3.1 sec
0-70 km/h	3.8 sec
0-80 km/h	4.5 sec
0-90 km/h	5.5 sec
0-100 km/h	6.8 sec
0-110 km/h	7.9 sec
0-120 km/h	9.1 sec
0-130 km/h	10.5 sec
0-140 km/h	12.5 sec
0-150 km/h	14.3 sec
0-160 km/h	16.0 sec

In the gears:	Second	Third	Fourth	Fifth
30-60 km/h	2.7	4.0	5.9	8.5 sec
40-70 km/h	2.6	3.6	5.6	8.3
50-80 km/h	2.5	3.7	5.5	8.2
60-90 km/h	2.3	4.0	5.3	7.8
70-100 km/h	2.1	3.9	5.2	7.6
80-110 km/h		3.9	5.2	7.6
90-120 km/h		3.6	5.4	7.4
100-130 km/h		3.3	5.5	7.6
110-140 km/h		3.2	5.3	8.4

STANDING START (0—400m): 14.8 secs

Right: Wondered what it looks like with the headlights up? The "headlight flasher" actually flashes the driving lights.

Below: The lines aren't exactly beautiful but are impressively aggressively purposeful.

Below right: The 928S making its mark(s) at Castlereagh dragstrip.

even on a long hard run. There's very little other mechanical noises either, and even when you're deep into three-figure speeds the car scarcely ruffles the wind and you can continue to talk to each other just like this . . . on fine road surfaces anway. On coarse bitumen there's a lot of tyre noise, so much in fact that the first time it happened (changing from hot-mix to coarse metal surface) we thought a fault had developed. But no, it's a characteristic of the tyres and car. When it's there, the sound ranges from a grumble to a whine according to the road texture and might well prove wearisome over a period.

The 928S's accommodation is strictly first class. The front seats are superb, that word again, for their shape and upholstery give commendable comfort with commanding security. The test car's buckets were manually adjustable and there was no hardship in that, but electrically-adjustable versions are a factory-fitted option at about $931 each. Steering wheel height is adjustable (with the column and instrument binnacle moving in concert), to help optimise the driving position, but some may be disappointed, if not slightly discomforted, that wheel reach can't be altered to suit.

The deeply bucketed rear seats are strictly occasional even for small adults; indeed the legroom is marginal even for some pre-teeners. The use of ordinary rear belts, rather than the inertia-reel type, adds conviction to the assumption that rear accommodation rates fairly low among Porsche's priorities. In fact the best thing about the rear seats is that they fold (individually) to extend the rear floor length.

The equipment level leaves little to be desired, or bought. Leather trim is standard; it looks rich and smells sensuous. Automatic air conditioning (cold and hot) is provided, likewise a cruise control system, and a fine sound system. There's not a lot of instrumentation — speedo, tacho and the principal gauges — but what there is is excellent. Not so pleasing is the use of a left-hand turn indicator stalk. Someone ought to tell Porsche (and other European makers) that there are times when one needs to indicate and change gear at the same time.

Detail touches include a tailor-made cassette holder on the centre tunnel, bins within the door armrests, electrically adjustable exterior mirrors with demisting elements that coincide with the rear window demister switch, and a self-lit vanity mirror behind the passenger's sun visor. One of the two knobs next to the hand-brake lever adjusts the balance between the front and rear speakers, while the other enables you to adjust the headlight beam to compensate for heavily-laden tail-down attitude. Apart from the electric chairs, the only other listed options are metallic paint, a $466 alarm system and an $1861 sunroof.

Nothing else is available or needed to add to the 928S. It's very very close to an ideal Grand Tourer, with degrees of performance, refinement and sheer desirability that few can match and none can better. It's not quite a perfect car, however. There are some minor blemishes — the turn indicator stalk's position, the lack of remote hatchback lid release, absence of Reverse lock-out, the sometime road noise and a few others.

One would have to be unduly critical not to forgive Porsche most of those small trespasses. In a sense, it's reassuring to have found them for the oversights add to the 928S's icing in their own way. They help humanise the car, spice its character, enable it to be criticised on some points at least. Without them the 928S might be too impersonal, might be too close to perfection. As it is, the 928S is a marvellous car . . . a car so good that it's sometimes hard to believe but always easy to enjoy. □

Porsche 928
Automatic
Better than ever

No ugly additions mar the 928's very smooth lines. Bumpering lies behind deformable polyurethane front and rear mouldings. Finish is superb

UNTIL RECENTLY Porsche were in the fortunate position of having their normally aspirated 928 and 911 engines running in a pretty low state of tune. All that was needed to provide a significant improvement in fuel efficiency and mid range performance was a good increase in compression ratio, accompanied by a change to four star fuel.

Even so it says something for the inherent combustion efficiency of both the 928 and 911 power units that they are able to accept significant increases in compression ratio without any fundamental modifications.

The 928 power unit is a markedly oversquare (95 x 78.9 mm) 4,474 c.c., all aluminium V8. Slightly domed pistons account for the rise in compression ratio from 8.5 to 10.0 to 1. Other alterations introduced in 1980 specification engines were double valve springs, and a lighter camshaft. Detail changes to the Bosch K-Jetronic fuel injection include a new "capsule valve" in the fuel distribution head to give initially richer mixture on snap throttle opening, and a modified air weighing mechanism giving better flow characteristics.

According to Porsche, peak power remains unchanged with 240 bhp being produced at 5,250 rpm instead of at 5,500 rpm, however as expected there is a very worthwhile increase in torque from 257 lb ft, to 280 lb ft peaking at the same 3,600 rpm. All 928 Automatics are now fitted with the higher torque capacity Daimler Benz based transaxle from the 928S, plus the shorter

propshaft and attendant tubular casing that this requires.

The final most obvious change is in tyres. Gone are the previous ultra low profile 225/50VR P7s on 16 in. diameter rims (these are still a standard fitment on the 928S) in favour of slightly narrower and taller sidewalled (though closely similar in diameter) 215/60VR P6s on 15 in. diameter rims. There have been very minor changes to the front wishbone suspension geometry on 81 models. A tubular 22.5 mm dia rear anti roll bar replaces the previous solid 20 mm stabilizers, and the brakes now feature stiffer calipers.

Our road test car tipped the scales at 29.9 cwt, remarkably within 5lb of the original test car.

Performance
Better than ever

When the 928 first appeared we were surprised by the similarity in acceleration and outright performance between the automatic and manual versions. Credit for this must go to the engine's huge torque output. Now this has been

increased the car goes even better in the mid range. With a complete lack of fuss (and no wheelspin getting away on MIRA's damp surface) the latest 928 went to 30, 60, 100, and 120 mph in 2.9, 7.2, 18.4 and 31.5 sec, a useful improvement over the earlier car which recorded 3.1, 8.0, 20.1 and 34.4 sec to the same speeds. In spite of rather unfavourable testing conditions the gains in the mid range were small but clear, with 0.2 sec shaved off between 20-40 and 30-50 mph in low, 0.7 sec from 50-70 and 60-80 in intermediate, and 1.2 sec when accelerating from 90-110 mph in top gear.

On the road this translates into a car with the most delicious immediacy of overtaking response. It simply bounds forward to overtake a slow moving lorry or a line of traffic. Given the right conditions the 928 bowls happily along at 120 mph, stable and at ease. On this particular example the rev limiter cut in at 6,300 rpm giving maxima in the lower two ratios of 70, and 110 mph. Normal full throttle upchanges occurred smoothly at 5,700 rpm (63 and 100 mph), while kickdown

was available commandably close to these speeds, from Intermediate to Low from 65 mph downwards, and from Top to Intermediate lower than 95 mph.

As we have previously discovered particularly with very torquey power units there is nothing whatever to be gained in acceleration from rest by overriding the automatic change points and revving the engine to the limit. On full or part throttle, gearshifts are smooth. However when seeking a kick down change the Daimler Benz based gearbox responds rather slowly. Where we must once more take issue with the Porsche (and most other) selector arrangements is that there is no safely stop to inhibit the free movement of the T handle selector between Intermediate, Drive, and Neutral with potentially damaging consequences to the engine if the lever is pushed clumsily too far forward when changing up manually. In other respects the selector arrangement is excellent allowing free movement for a downchange from Drive to Intermediate. A stop has to be overriden when going for Low.

As we have come to expect of Bosch fuel injected engines, start up was always immediate and driveability during the warm up period utterly quirk free. Unfortunately we were unable to take this particular Porsche abroad for maximum speed testing. However we feel safe estimating it to be marginally faster than its predecessor which did a comfortable and impressively stable 138 mph.

Porsche 928 Automatic
The 928 first appeared in March 1977. Elected Car of the Year for 1978. High compression engine and stronger automatic transmission introduced in the Autumn of 1979 together with even higher performance 928S. Other recent changes to the 928 include a change from P7 to P6 tyres, and revised front suspension geometry.

PRODUCED BY:
Dr. Ing. H.D.F. Porsche AG
Porschestrasse 42
Stuttgart-Zuffenhausen
D-7000, West Germany

SOLD IN THE UK BY:
Porsche Cars Great Britain Ltd
Richfield Avenue
Reading
Berks
RG1 8PH

Despite a greater than usual percentage of the test mileage being on urban and city centre roads, the 928 showed a useful improvement in fuel consumption over its predecessor (down from 14.6 to 15.9 mpg overall). On one occasion we bettered 17 mpg whilst most interim checks showed the car was doing better than 16 mpg, giving a touring range of close on 300 miles before the fuel warning light starts to light. One particularly pleasing point is that one wastes little time at the filling station because the 928 brims straight to the filler neck without delay. Oil consumption was measured at 700 miles per pint.

Noise
Marginally less

The slightly narrower P6 tyres now fitted have resulted in a small reduction in ultimate grip. The 928 can well afford this for the slight improvement in levels of transmitted road noise, not that the 928 is a particularly quiet grand touring car in this respect even now. Pattern noise (the continuous roar of varying intensity one usually hears in a wide tyred car) is very evident particularly at high cruising speeds and on coarse concrete surfaces. Above 90 mph road induced noise dominates and one has to turn the radio up a little to maintain clarity. As in previous 928s and oddly enough the latest 911SC we also noticed a mildly irritating low frequency boom through the bodyshell at any speed over 80 mph. Tyre thump over potholes and unmade surfaces is now tolerably well subdued — certainly not a source of irritation. The Porsche's V8 remains a source of delight. It is almost inaudible at tickover and at high cruising speeds. On full throttle it emits a most pleasing low pitched growl — always muted but purposeful. Excellent door sealing and the 928's cleanly sculptured external shape keep wind noise at an extremely low level at any feasible cruising speed.

Road behaviour
Impressive

Once one acclimatises to the 928's width, it is a disarmingly manoeuvrable car, capable of generating high levels of grip, despite the slight downgrading tyre width. The power steering has an ideal 3 turns from lock to lock. The degree of assistance diminishes with speed, and at all speeds its above averagely heavy weighting particularly suits a car of this performance. It is impressively free from kickback, at some expense in feel suggested one tester. Most of us soon grew used to its slight deadness, and certainly the car responds beautifully to small steering inputs. Cornering roll is also very well controlled. This plus its extremely well behaved Weissach axle semi trailing arm rear end allows the car to be hurtled through the country lanes with the greatest confidence. Traction is superb out of slow corners and when driving briskly the impression is of how well the car hugs the road. As with any powerful car with such good traction, handling balance depends to some extent on driving style. In slow and medium speed corners the 928 displays some gentle understeer. Use too much throttle and the excess driving torque goes into pushing the rear end out of line (not into wheelspin as in lesser cars). The car responds to correction with great neatness. In faster corners the 928 barely understeers at all. It simply goes round — we would say on rails but for its one real on limit handling quirk, seemingly more noticeable now the car is running on narrower tyres. Back off suddenly when cornering in extremes and the rear end breaks away quite sharply and is inclined to want to go on sliding pendulously.

These are test track tactics, and only likely to surface in a tightening bend entered much too fast. Normally the 928 is beautifully mannered — able to cover large cross country distances fast and without fuss. Considering the car's pleasingly positive handling response, ride quality is a good compromise; closely controlled though not uncomfortable at town speeds, becoming more supple as speeds increase. Long undulations are beautifully absorbed as are the smaller ripples, once one is moving at a reasonable pace. In contrast transverse ridges taken at slow speeds occasionally produce a quite sharp reaction in the car, plus an unexpectedly loud thump.

Ventilated discs are fitted front and rear. Braking from all speeds feels pleasantly "un-servoed"

with pedal efforts increasing in line with retardation. Fade resistance is truly excellent with little variation in pedal pressures during repeated and hard usage. Previous 928s exhibited a tendency to "walk about" under heavy braking from high speeds. The combination of narrower, taller sidewalled tyres, and revised front suspension geometry appears to have effected a complete cure because even on uneven surfaces the new car brakes straight and true.

Behind the wheel
Luxurious yet workmanlike

The 928 is at its best on a long trip, where the car caters beautifully for the driver's needs. We have yet to hear one complaint of discomfort. The high quality cloth faced seats are firm but give superb overall support. Longitudinal adjustment is sufficient for drivers of well over 6ft, and back rest movement is of the infinitely adjustable micro type.

Once more we must compliment Porsche on the clever way the entire instrument binnacle, also the stalk controls, move with the steering column as it is adjusted for rake. Instrumentation is complete. The speedometer and rev counter are flanked on the left by a combined fuel contents and water temperature dial, and on the right by a matching dial containing oil pressure and battery condition gauges. Also contained within the normally black faced dials are a full set of fluid level warning signals. The appropriate lettering also lights if the brake pads need replacement. Round the cowl's outer rim are easily reached rotating switches for hazard warning, heated rear window, side, rear fog and head lights. Under its bottom edge are turnwheels to control instrument lighting and intermittent wipe speed. Stalk controls follow the ISO pattern with indicators and headlamp flash on the left (the electrically driven headlamps rise promptly, and the right hand one working the powerful three speed wipers and four jet screen wash (this automatically brings the high pressure headlamp wash into action when the headlamps are working). A smaller right hand stalk works the cruise control — push forward to set, pull back to cancel (or touch the brakes) and pull down to return to the speed last selected.

Climbing in the 928 for the first time one is aware of the superb trim quality, then of its high waist line, sloping away bonnet and rather thick padded screen pillars. The taller driver is not likely

The entire instrument binnacle moves with the steering column when adjusted for rake. Rotating switches on left control main lights, plus front and rear fog lights; those on the right, the heated rear window, hazard warning lights. Instruments are from left, the combined water temperature/fuel gauge, speedometer (with press to reset trip), revcounter, and dial containing oil pressure and battery volts gauges. Left-hand stalk is for indicators, dip/main beam. Its opposite (also hidden) works the wipe/wash. Cruise control stalk is visible on right. Centre console neatly contains two of six ventilation outlets, heater controls, Panasonic self-seeking radio, clock (hidden), T handle gear selector plus rocker switches for electric windows and rear window wipe

Adjacent to the handbrake is headlamp level control. Smaller knob controls speaker balance. Front seats are superbly comfortable if somewhat low. Rear seat passengers are not so well catered for. Door armrests contain window demist vents, electric mirror switch (driver's door) plus lidded pockets

HOW THE PORSCHE 928 (A) PERFORMS

ACCELERATION

FROM REST

True mph	Time (sec)	Speedo mph
30	2.9	30
40	4.4	41
50	5.7	51
60	7.2	61
70	9.2	72
80	11.7	82
90	14.6	93
100	18.4	103
110	24.2	114
120	31.5	124

Standing ¼-mile: 15.3 sec, 93 mph
Standing km: 28.1 sec, 118 mph

IN EACH GEAR

mph	Top	2nd	1st
0-20	–	–	1.9
10-30	–	–	2.4
20-40	–	–	2.6
30-50	–	–	2.7
40-60	–	–	2.9
50-70	–	4.4	3.8
60-80	–	4.6	–
70-90	–	5.3	–
80-100	–	6.7	–
90-110	10.0	10.3	–
100-120	12.9	–	–

TEST CONDITIONS:
Wind: 10-18 mph
Temperature: 40 deg C (40 deg F)
Barometer: 29.7 in. Hg (1,006 mbar)
Humidity: 100 per cent
Surface: damp asphalt and concrete
Test distance: 669 miles

MAXIMUM SPEEDS

Gear	mph	kph	rpm
Top (mean)	140	225	5,450
(best)	140	225	5,450
2nd	110	177	6,300
1st	70	113	6,300

FUEL CONSUMPTION

Overall mpg: 15.9 (17.9 litres/100km)

Official fuel consumption figures
(ECS laboratory test conditions; not necessarily related to Autocar figures)
Urban cycle: 18.8 mpg
Steady 56 mph: 23.0 mpg
Steady 75 mph: 29.1 mpg

OIL CONSUMPTION

(SAE 20/50) 700 miles/pint

WEIGHT

Kerb, 29.9 cwt/3,342 lb/1,518 kg
(Distribution F/R, 51.3/48.7)
Test, 32.6 cwt/3,652 lb/1,658 kg
Max. payload 925 lb/420 kg

PRICES

Basic	£17,520
Special Car Tax	£1,460
VAT	£2,847
Total (in GB)	**£21,827**
Seat Belts	Standard
Licence	£70.00
Delivery charge (London)	£100.00
Number plates	£15.00

Total on the Road (exc. insurance)	£22,012.00
EXTRAS (inc. VAT)	
Limited slip diff.	350.08
Electric sunroof	698.91
TOTAL AS TESTED ON THE ROAD	**£22,012.00**
Insurance	Group 8

DIMENSIONS

Length: 175.1 in.
Width: 72.3 in.
Height: 51.9 in.

Boot capacity: 14.12 cu. ft.
Turning circle:
between kerbs: L 36 ft. 7 in. R 36 ft. 7 in.

SPECIFICATION

ENGINE
Head/block	Front; Rear drive Aluminium alloy
Cylinders	8 in 90° Vee, linerless alloy block
Main bearings	5
Cooling	Water
Fan	Viscous + Electric
Bore, mm (in.)	95.0 (3.74)
Stroke, mm (in.)	78.9 (3.11)
Capacity, cc (in³)	4,474 (273)
Valve gear	Ohc hydraulic tappets
Camshaft drive	Toothed belt
Compression ratio	10-to-1
Ignition	Breakerless
Injection	Bosch K-Jetronic
Max power	240 bhp (DIN) at 5,250 rpm
Max torque	280 lb ft at 3,600 rpm

TRANSMISSION
Type	Daimler Benz three speed automatic

Gear	Ratio	mph/1000rpm
Top	1.000	25.64
2nd	1.400	17.56
1st	2.306	11.10

Final drive gear	Hypoid bevel
Ratio	2.75 to 1

SUSPENSION
Front – location	Double wishbone
springs	Coil
dampers	Telescopic
anti-roll bar	Yes
Rear – location	Semi-trailing
springs	Coil
dampers	Telescopic
anti-roll bar	Yes

STEERING
Type	Rack and pinion
Power assistance	Yes
Wheel diameter	15.8 in.
Turns lock to lock	3.0

BRAKES
Circuits	Twin split diagonally
Front	11.1 in. dia. disc
Rear	11.4 in. dia. disc
Servo	Vacuum
Handbrake	Side lever, rear drum within disc

WHEELS
Type	Alloy
Rim width	7in. × 15
Tyres – make	Pirelli P6
– type	Radial, tubeless
– size	215/60VR-15
– pressures	F 36 R 36 psi (normal driving)

EQUIPMENT
Battery	12V 66Ah
Alternator	90A
Headlamps	110W 230W
Reversing lamp	Standard
Electric fuses	34
Screen wipers	3-speed + intermittent
Screen washer	Electric
Interior heater	Water valve
Air conditioning	Standard
Interior trim	Cloth seats, vinyl headlining
Floor covering	Carpet
Jack	Screw
Jacking points	4, under sills
Windscreen	Laminated/tinted
Underbody protection	Paint system/ Bitumastic wax/ Galvanised

Inlet air trunking runs front to back on both inner wings. Engine is topped by eight cast inlet pipes. Daily checks are straightforward. The distributor is accessible but little else is simple to reach

to allow the apparently low seating position to inhibit him for long. For somebody not so tall, an electric seat height adjustment is available as an option. The only serious blind spot is to the threequarter rear and caused by the relatively thick B post. The view rearwards is excellent thanks to the deep hatch window.

Air conditioning is standard and works well. The Porsche 928 water valve/air blending heating and ventilation system offers good temperature control, however we felt directional control to be somewhat vague in not allowing sufficient flow to the footwell area. The four speed fan is commendably quiet on the first two speeds and is effective in boosting flow.

Living with the 928

It is the details one appreciates. Both electric door mirrors are heated, the passenger's side sun visor contains an illuminated mirror, a knob on the driver's side sill adjusts headlight beam level, and the ignition key contains a press button operated light to assist the driver in locating the lock at night. There are the sun visors for the rear seat passengers. A self seeking Panasonic MW/LW/FM stereo radio cassette player is standard, and the test car's worked exceptionally well. Unless the seats are adjusted well forward, rear seat passengers will find rear seat legroom extremely limited. In contrast oddments space is surprisingly generous with a decent glovebox, a shelf below, lidded door pockets, and a lockable cubbyhole between the rear seats. The rear seat backs fold flat to provide reasonable flat floored load space.

Minor criticisms are that the rear hatch can only be opened with the key, and we still wonder why in a car of this nature Porsche could not find room for a normal spare wheel. As it is the collapsable Goodrich spacesaver is technically illegal in this country, and a time consuming operation to dig out from under the rear floor, pump up (with the electric pump provided), and fit – then there is always the problem of finding room for the punctured assembly when the car is already loaded with luggage. To overcome the afforementioned illegality Porsche provide owners with one year's "free" membership of the Car Recovery Club.

One is always impressed by the very high level of finish Porsche manage to obtain both inside and out. Pride of ownership can only be further encouraged by the company's 7 year anti corrosion warranty. As with other models in the Porsche range service intervals are at 12,000 mile intervals.

The engine bay is positively crammed with engine and ancillaries – a beautiful sight, also a slightly forbidding one for anybody attempting to locate a minor fault should such a thing occur. The oil and water are simple to check, and a very comprehensive set of tools are clipped to a panel at the back of the load bay. A screw in towing eye is included.

The Porsche 928 range

The 928 and more powerful 928S cost £21,827 and £25,251 respectively. Automatic transmission is a no cost option.

Rear seats fold flat individually. Stowed under the left-hand rear floor is the wheel changing equipment; jack, wheelbrace, Goodrich spacesaver assembly, electric pump, and warning triangle plus a box of spare bulbs. A pretty comprehensive tool kit is provided

Porsche 928 (A) £21,827

front engine,
rear drive

Capacity
4,474 c.c.

Power
240 bhp (DIN)
at 5,500 rpm

Weight
3,342 lb/1,518 kg

Autotest
18 April 1981

Jaguar XJS £19,763

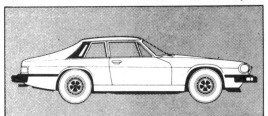

front engine,
rear drive

Capacity
5,343 c.c.

Power
296 bhp (DIN)
at 5,400 rpm

Weight
3,890 lb/1,767 kg

Autotest
24 January 1981

BMW 635Csi (A) £18,950

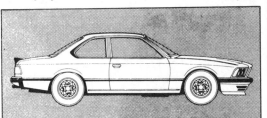

front engine,
rear drive

Capacity
3,453 c.c.

Power
218 bhp (DIN)
at 5,300 rpm

Weight
3,447 lb/1,564 kg

Autotest
635Csi manual
26 January 1979

Aston Martin V8 (A) £34,498

Front engine,
rear drive

Capacity
5,340 c.c.

Power
Not quoted

Weight
3,970 lb/1,800 kg

Autotest
14 October 1978

Maserati Khamsin (A) £29,900

Front engine,
rear drive

Capacity
4,930 c.c.

Power
320 bhp (DIN)
at 5,500 rpm

Weight
3,019 lb/1,640 kg

Autotest
17 May 1975

Mercedes Benz 380 SLC £21,531

Front engine,
rear drive

Capacity
3,818 c.c.

Power
218 bhp (DIN)
at 5,500 rpm

Autotest
None so far

MPH & MPG

Maximum speed (mph)

Jaguar XJS	151
Aston Martin V8 (A)	146
Porsche 928 (A)	140
*BMW 635Csi (A)	140
†Mercedes 380 SLC	136
Maserati Khamsin (A)	130

Acceleration 0-60 (sec)

Jaguar XJS	6.6
Aston Martin V8 (A)	7.2
Porsche 928 (A)	7.2
Maserati Khamsin (A)	7.5
*BMW 635Csi (A)	8.5
†Mercedes 380 SLC	9.0

Overall mpg

BMW 635Csi (A)	17.5
Porsche 928 (A)	15.9
Maserati Khamsin (A)	15.1
Jaguar XJS	14.3
†Mercedes 380 SLC	14.1
Aston Martin V8 (A)	13.0

*Figures for manual 635Csi
†Figures for earlier 450 SLC

We have no reason whatever to doubt Mercedes' claim that the latest 380 series engine and model range is faster than the recently discontinued 450s. Improvements were needed because by present day standards the figures for the 450 model show how much it lags in performance and economy, being easily beaten on all counts by most of the cars here. After languishing a shade behind the voracious Aston, Jaguar are back on top with the high compression engined XJS. It now tops the performance league for GT Automatics. Porsche have gained performance *and* economy in the latest high compression engine 928 but if you are looking for plenty of performance and the best possible economy the BMW will take a lot of beating. Low overall gearing and a rev limited engine severely limited the road test Khamsin Automatic's top speed. The Aston and Maserati are probably the least mechanically refined, which is where the Jaguar wins yet again.

ON THE ROAD

Least likeable handling characteristics are to be found in the BMW. Its semi-trailing arm rear suspension invites rather sudden oversteer (with or without power) especially if the roads are slippery. The Maserati is fundamentally better behaved but its suspension is pretty stiff and unyielding, also most will find the Khamsin's very high geared (2 turns) Citroen SM inspired power steering difficult to get used to.
By contrast the Porsche and Mercedes are almost viceless, the P6 shod 928 being perhaps just the more preferable (certainly for the press on type) for its superb roll free handling response and sheer grip. If it's ride refinement you are after the Jaguar

has no peer followed (we think) by the Mercedes, Aston and Porsche, then rather soft BMW and over-hard Maserati. The XJS sticks to the road well, and behaves beautifully if pushed to the limit — but is still a just less "chuckable" car than the deDion rear axled Aston — a car that steers particularly nicely, better than the Jaguar whose steering remains a shade overlight for our taste. Jaguar, Porsche, and Mercedes have excellent heating and ventilation. Aston and BMW retain pure water valve systems, the former being relatively efficient, and the latter more or less uncontrollable.

SIZE & SPACE

Legroom front/rear (in.)

(seats fully back)

BMW 635Csi (A)	42½/32
Aston Martin V8 (A)	43/31
Mercedes Benz 380 SLC	41/33†
Jaguar XJS	42/30
Porsche 928 (A)	42/27
Maserati Khamsin (A)	43/10

†Mercedes 450 SLC figures

As long-distance tourers the first four are not only the roomiest, but have the distinct advantage of using a normal size spare wheel. The Porsche has a spacesaver (strictly speaking illegal in this country) while the Maserati has an equally inconvenient extra narrow spare. The latter two are hatchbacks with just that bit more load versatility. The others have good size boots. The Mercedes, BMW and Aston provide quite reasonable accommodation for four, while as the dimensions suggest the Jaguar and Porsche are cramped in the back. Rear seat room in the Maserati is strictly for two small children, or one adult sitting across the car.

VERDICT

The Aston is much liked for its predictable handling and sheer mid-range muscle. It remains an expensive and thirsty car by any standards — not that the others could be called frugal! BMW's 3.5-litre straight six is a mechanical delight. Not much can beat the 635Csi for its combination of refinement and fuel efficiency — even if the car still has questionable handling characteristics. Likewise the Maserati's unusual steering and braking might mar the car for some. It is a superb looker but a car you are likely to have to *live for*. The latest 928 goes better and is more frugal. It's a beautifully made no nonsense grand tourer that handles well, and probably grips better than any car here, plus it has a 7-year anti-corrosion warranty. Those looking for a "softer" car might consider the Mercedes — a good handling machine, also beautifully built.
Beating all these for top speed and sheer refinement is the V12 Jaguar. It has the best ride, lacks nothing in handling or grip, and looks good value for money. You just need the purse to run it.

PHOTOS BY JOHN DINKEL

PORSCHE 928

*More mileage and a new handling package for the
1981 version of Porsche's big V-8 GT*

STEADY REFINEMENT AND one surprise are probably the best way to characterize the 1981 928, flagship of the Porsche fleet as we know it in North America. This ongoing process of refinement, typical for Porsche, has gone on in an atmosphere of adversity recently. Last year was a tough one for the automobile industry, with all market segments suffering losses. For Porsche the major problem was with the "bread-and-butter" 924; the 928, with a dropoff only from 1555 units in 1980 to 1466 in 1981, was almost immune to the industry sickness. The pattern continues: Mention 924 sales for 1981 to Porsche executives and you'll see wrinkled brows, but the market for the 928 has firmed up and they are projecting fully 1800 sales before 1981 is out.

First introduced in Europe in 1977, the 928 is what Porsche planners deemed in the early Seventies the right formula for a luxury sports-GT car of the Eighties and beyond. It was a big departure—and a huge investment—for the small West German maker of thoroughbred sports cars. Porsche was abandoning its traditional formula of rear-engine cars with air cooling and relatively small displacement for a front-engine car with a big water-cooled V-8. The 928's development had started well before the first big oil shock in 1973; had it begun, say, in 1974 Porsche might have taken a different approach to its conception.

As it turned out, in today's context the 928 is a relatively big,

heavy and thirsty automobile. Going into 1981 it remains essentially unchanged, though since its 1977 introduction it has undergone numerous detail changes and improvements. A unit steel body-chassis with extensive aluminum panelwork is the platform. Power comes from a 4474-cc aluminum V-8 at the front, driving the rear wheels through a rear-mounted transaxle with either 5-speed manual or 3-speed automatic innards. The 928's suspension, like that of all Porsches, is all-independent, its brakes vented discs all around and Porsche fits it with a choice of high-performance tires. On the creature-comforts side, the 928 boasts a list of convenience and ergonomic features excelled by hardly any other maker.

The 928 is what you might call the Ultimate GT Car. There are GTs and sports cars that, at least superficially, seem to be more exotic (see elsewhere in this *Guide*). Porsche itself builds a faster car, the 930 Turbo; but that car is no longer available in America. In reality, though, it's the 928 that has everything and does everything that counts, whether you compare it with other luxury GTs or with all-out sports cars like the Turbo.

One of the 1981 changes—adding an air pump to the 1981 engine—might sound like a backward step, but actually isn't. Last year Porsche engineers made some pretty extensive underhood modifications, mainly to improve fuel economy: a 3-way catalytic converter with oxygen sensor to replace the former 2-way converter, a half-point increase in compression ratio to 9.0:1, electronic Bosch L-Jetronic fuel injection instead of the mechanical K-Jetronic system used before, and revised ignition timing. This year's change once again illustrates how Porsche fails to follow the leader. Instead of feeding air to the exhaust ports as do most engine air pumps, the 928's pumps it directly into the catalyst's oxidation portion, improving catalyst effectiveness and helping Porsche meet tightened 1981 emission limits with no loss of power.

EPA fuel-economy figures for the 928 are also up for 1981, by 1 mpg. This is not the result of the engine changes, but rather of detail weight reductions throughout the car that include a couple of tubular transmission shafts replacing solid ones. See what is meant by refinement?

We again tested an automatic 928 for the *Guide*, and it is that car for which all data in the accompanying panel is listed. But we also drove a manual-gearbox 1981 model equipped with what Porsche calls a Competition Package. The exterior photos here are of the car with this new option, which we will call CP for brevity.

Available as a no-extra-cost alternative to the excellent standard 5-speed manual gearbox, the Mercedes-built automatic transmission is essentially that formerly used in the other Stutt-gart carmaker's most powerful models. Though Mercedes has gone on to 4-speed units, Porsche continues with this excellent 3-speed, specially tailored to Porsche ideas about how an automatic transmission should perform.

The Mercedes automatic is one of the best 3-speeds around, but Porsche has made a few changes of questionable value. One is the selector lever. Mercedes uses a superb gated shifter that allows almost stick-shift-style driving for those so inclined. Porsche, whose selector linkage serves a rear- rather than front-mounted transmission, chose a T-handle with pushbutton release for selecting the driving ranges other than those most frequently used. Though it is not quite as nice as the Mercedes gated arrangement, it is still quite manageable.

Another difference is Porsche's shift calibration. Upshifts come relatively late in gentle driving, so that one gets the feeling the box should shift before it does. And the torque converter, a "loose" one in engineer's parlance, allows such high engine speeds in moving off from rest that the engine sounds as if it were struggling. But this is merely a subjective impression. In hard driving the shift points come at high speeds too, and this is very purposeful, for the unit lets the engine rev all the way to its 6000-rpm redline in 1st gear and to its power peak of 5500 rpm in 2nd. So there's no need to shift manually to get best acceleration. That acceleration is strong: the test car went from rest to 60 mph in just 8.1 seconds and covered the quarter-mile in 16.2 sec.

The 1981 news of greatest interest is availability of an $1100 Competition Package, including front and rear spoilers, 16 x 7J forged alloy wheels, 225/50VR-16 Pirelli P7 or Goodyear NGT radial tires, sports shocks, a leather-covered 3-spoke steering wheel similar in design to that of the 930 Turbo's, and sports seats with more lateral support by way of deeper side bolsters.

. . . as are front and rear spoilers. Car looks like a European 928S.

Sports seats with wide bolsters are part of the Competition Package . . .

AT A GLANCE			
	Porsche 928	Ferrari 308 GTSi	Mercedes-Benz 380SL
Curb weight, lb	3370	3250	3495
Engine	V-8	V-8	V-8
Transmission	3-sp A	5-sp M	4-sp A
0-60 mph, sec	8.1	7.9	11.5
Standing ¼ mi, sec	16.2	16.1	18.6
Speed at end of ¼ mi, mph	89.5	88.0	74.0
Stopping distance from 60 mph, ft	138	154	155
Interior noise at 50 mph, dBA	72	76	69
Lateral acceleration, g	0.811	0.810	0.700
Slalom speed, mph	59.7	60.6	54.2
Fuel economy, mpg	est 18.0	11.5	17.5

In other markets Porsche includes this equipment in the 928S, which has a 4664-cc version of the V-8 with 60 bhp more than the standard 4.5-liter. Because of the cost of "federalizing" an additional engine and the fuel-economy penalty the more powerful unit would entail, Porsche decided against offering the S as such—and against calling something less than a true S an S.

Other than the CP and the engine air pump, things are pretty much unchanged with the 928 for 1981. Leather upholstery remains standard, as are air conditioning, central locking and power steering. Porsche continues to omit a stereo system from the standard-equipment list, however; the 928 buyer can order a radio-tape unit with digital display at $795 extra. Other options come mighty expensive too—electrically adjustable seats (not available with the CP) cost $660 per, and a right-side electrically adjustable and heated mirror lists for $110.

One of the 928's competitors, however, doesn't even offer a remotely adjusted right-hand outside mirror. And it is details like this—most of which are standard, not optional—that make the 928 cockpit such a tour de force of innovative and practical ergonomic ideas. One such item is the instrument pod, which moves up and down with the adjustable steering column so that it is never obscured by the steering-wheel rim. Another is the warning lights it contains: they remain invisible except when functioning. Yet another is the control for those outside mirrors, which allows adjustment of either from a hemispherical 4-way switch on the driver's door.

In part because of such things, the 928 is the most comfortable and ergonomically satisfactory Porsche ever built. But there is one hitch. It is that with the 928's amorphous body shape and the driver's low vantage point inside, it is very difficult to judge where the car's corners might be for maneuvering in or into tight places.

The 928's comprehensive heating/ventilation/air-conditioning system works very well generally, although there is one drawback to its operation in the ventilation mode. The two middle dash air outlets deliver air only in the a/c mode, and most of our drivers found the adjustable vents in the doors inadequate. For most 928 owners this is probably an academic point, as our experience indicates that they'll use the a/c instead of trying to save fuel by using ventilation only. For us, however, this is a significant fault.

Another possibly academic point concerns access to the rear seats. Maybe some 928 owners will value the stylish but barely usable +2 seating for children, pets or the occasional short-distance rider, but it cannot be considered a place for grown folks. Porsche, however, has taken it very seriously, providing grab handles, an ashtray and lighter, a shallow storage compartment, a map light and sun visors that rotate to shade the leading edge of the big rear window. We found the rear seats most useful with their backrests folded flat and the full cargo capacity available.

Rubber for lots of sticking power: Pirelli P7s, front spoiler.

The 928 was Porsche's first car with power-assisted steering, and not surprisingly it follows the general practice of other German carmakers of giving relatively little assistance, a lot of road feel and a quick ratio. Parking maneuvers are assisted just enough to do the job; then the hydraulic assist to the rack-and-pinion steering gear falls off with increasing speed to provide plenty of feel in managing the car's wonderfully balanced, capable chassis.

No other Porsche production model, in fact, has such finely balanced handling, even though the 930 Turbo feels sportier and can outdo it in terms of pure cornering power. It's the near 50/50 weight distribution that gives the 928 its edge here. And what an edge it has: almost race-car reflexes in its response to the steering wheel, as well as complete freedom from the tailheaviness that makes all the 911 variations (including the 930 Turbo) tricky to manage in extreme cornering situations. It will oversteer if the driver so commands, but it takes either a very advanced, or very foolish, driver to push it that far. Most drivers will merely enjoy the remarkable handling feel and the wide margin of safety between what they'll wager and what it can do.

With its standard suspension, the 928 also rides remarkably well—especially considering the 50-section tires. But the same can't be said of the ride with the CP. You can feel and hear the heavy-duty suspension working through the wide Pirelli P7s; every road irregularity comes through more clearly, the tires feed more noise into the structure and there's an overall stiffness characterized by a lack of body roll when steering is cranked in quickly. In all, the CP-equipped 928 has an even tauter, crisper feel than the already taut, crisp 928. Just what the CP brings in the way of added cornering power we did not have the opportunity to measure, but because its tires and wheels are the same as those of our test car we expect little change in the skidpad figure. The major improvement with the CP is in its transient cornering behavior.

Despite this clearly sportier handling, though, and the fact that we'd have no qualms about recommending such a package for the 911, it's questionable how many 928 buyers would readily accept the way the package compromises the car's luxury image. For the prospective 928 owner who is interested, we strongly suggest a test drive in a CP-equipped car before taking the plunge.

Under most conditions the 928's big vented disc brakes do just what is asked of them, but in simulating an emergency stop from 80 mph we found that the rear wheels tended to lock, requiring considerable attention from the driver to get the car stopped in minimum distance. Applying that attention, we got the 928 stopped in just 248 ft from 80 mph. And from 60 mph it took just 138 ft to halt the Porsche. So the stopping capability is there; it just takes a bit more care to extract it than you would expect with a Porsche.

It's already pretty close to 1982 model time. From what we know now, it appears that next year will be another evolutionary one for the 928. The 928 is now the only Porsche sold in America with a "dogleg" shift from 1st to 2nd gear, that is, with 1st out of the H, to the left and back. It will remain so for 1982, but a reverse lockout has been added to make absolutely sure nobody gets into reverse by mistake. The standard-equipment list grows longer too, gaining a fuel-consumption gauge, power driver's seat, automatic air conditioning, a heavy-duty battery and the larger brakes from the European S model.

Allow us a distinction now. The 928 is not the best *sports car* Porsche has ever built. That distinction still goes to the 911 in its various forms, including the 930 Turbo. Rather, the 928 is the *best car* Porsche has ever built. It can be a great sports car, or a fabulously luxurious GT. It can be used for commuting or picking up the family groceries, without undue drama and, if the buyer so desires, without shifting gears. At any given time, to any given person, it can be almost any type of car. And that is what makes it Porsche's best car. Not to mention one of the world's best cars—period.

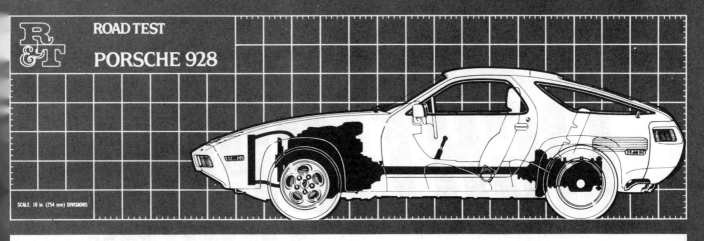

SCALE: 10 in. (254 mm) DIVISIONS

PRICE

List price, all POE $38,850
Price as tested $40,305
    Price as tested includes std equip (air cond, power-assisted strg, leather uph, cruise control), auto trans (no chg), elect. adj driver's seat ($660), AM/FM stereo/cassette ($795)

IMPORTER

Porsche-Audi Div, VW of America, 818 Sylvan Ave, Englewood Cliffs, N.J. 07632

GENERAL

Curb weight, lb/kg	3370	1528
Test weight	3550	1610
Weight dist (with driver), f/r, %		50/50
Wheelbase, in./mm	98.3	2497
Track, front/rear	60.8/59.6	1545/1515
Length	175.7	4463
Width	72.3	1836
Height	51.6	1311
Ground clearance	4.7	119
Overhang, f/r	39.7/37.7	1008/958
Trunk space, cu ft/liters	6.3 + 14.2	178 + 402
Fuel capacity, U.S. gal./liters	22.4	85

ACCOMMODATION

Seating capacity, persons		2 + 2
Head room, f/r, in./mm	36.5/927	32.0/813
Seat width, f/r	2 x 20.0/508	2 x 15.0/381
Seat back adjustment, deg		70

ENGINE

Type		sohc V-8
Bore x stroke, in./mm	3.74 x 3.11	95.0 x 78.9
Displacement, cu in./cc	273	4474
Compression ratio		9.0:1
Bhp @ rpm, SAE net/kW	220/164 @ 5500	
Equivalent mph / km/h		144/233
Torque @ rpm, lb-ft/Nm	265/359 @ 4000	
Equivalent mph / km/h		104/169
Fuel injection		Bosch L-Jetronic
Fuel requirement		unleaded, 91-oct

Exhaust-emission control equipment: 3-way catalyst, oxygen sensor

DRIVETRAIN

Transmission ....automatic; torque converter with 3-sp planetary gearbox

Gear ratios: 3rd (1.00)	2.75:1
2nd (1.46)	4.02:1
1st (2.31)	6.35:1
1st (2.0 x 2.31)	12.70:1
Final drive ratio	2.75:1

MAINTENANCE

Service intervals, mi:

Oil/filter change	15,000/30,000
Chassis lube	none
Tuneup	30,000
Warranty, mo/mi	12/unlimited

CALCULATED DATA

Lb/bhp (test weight)	16.1
Mph/1000 rpm (3rd gear)	26.0
Engine revs/mi (60 mph)	2310
Piston travel, ft/mi	1197
R&T steering index	0.98
Brake swept area, sq in./ton	251

CHASSIS & BODY

Layout	front engine/rear drive
Body/frame	unit steel with aluminum doors, hood, front fenders

Brake system .... vented discs; 11.1-in. (282-mm) front, 11.4-in. (290-mm) rear, vacuum assisted

Swept area, sq in./sq cm	440	2839
Wheels		forged alloy, 16 x 7J
Tires		Pirelli P7, 225/50VR-16
Steering type		rack & pinion, power assisted
Overall ratio		17.8:1
Turns, lock-to-lock		3.1
Turning circle, ft/m	31.5	9.7

Front suspension: upper A-arms, lower trailing arms, coil springs, tube shocks, anti-roll bar

Rear suspension: upper transverse links, lower trailing arms, coil springs, tube shocks, anti-roll bar

INSTRUMENTATION

Instruments: 85-mph speedometer, 7600-rpm tach, 999,999 odo, 999.9 trip odo, oil press., coolant temp, voltmeter, fuel level, clock

Warning lights: central warning system, oil press., brake press., fluid, pad wear; parking brake; stop lamp, tail lamp failure; coolant, windshield-washer fluid, oxygen sensor, seatbelts, hazard, high beam, directionals

RELIABILITY

Owners of earlier-model Porsches reported 11 problem areas and 4 disabling reliability areas compared to overall Owner Survey averages of 11/6. So we expect the overall reliability of the Porsche 928 to be better than average.

ROAD TEST RESULTS

ACCELERATION

Time to distance, sec:

0-100 ft	3.5
0-500 ft	9.0
0-1320 ft (¼ mi)	16.2
Speed at end of ¼ mi, mph	89.5

Time to speed, sec:

0-30 mph	3.2
0-50 mph	6.3
0-60 mph	8.1
0-80 mph	13.0
0-100 mph	21.7

SPEEDS IN GEARS

3rd gear (5000 rpm)	est 140
2nd (6000)	107
1st (6000)	68

FUEL ECONOMY

Normal driving, mpg	est 18.0
Cruising range, mi (1-gal. res)	385

HANDLING

Lateral accel, 100-ft radius, g	0.811
Speed thru 700-ft slalom, mph	59.7

BRAKES

Minimum stopping distances, ft:

From 60 mph	138
From 80 mph	248
Control in panic stop	good
Pedal effort for 0.5g stop, lb	18

Fade: percent increase in pedal effort to maintain 0.5g deceleration in 6 stops from 60 mph .... nil

Parking: hold 30% grade?	yes
Overall brake rating	very good

INTERIOR NOISE

Idle in neutral, dBA	66
Maximum, 1st gear	83
Constant 30 mph	69
50 mph	72
70 mph	73
90 mph	78

SPEEDOMETER ERROR

30 mph indicated is actually	29.0
60 mph	59.5
80 mph	80.0

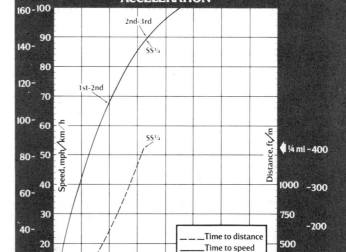

ACCELERATION

LIGHT SPEED LUXURY

A manual gearbox isn't a prerequisite for the enjoyment of a true supercar, says Paul Harrington.

TO MOST PEOPLE of early middle age, the name Porsche is synonymous with air cooled "boxer" engines hung out behind the back axle.

For years, all Porsches were like that, starting with the slightly modified Volkswagen engines of the very earliest models, progressing through the entirely redesigned units which came along with the 911 series, right up to the incredible turbocharged power plants which are still current. That the 924 series should bring about a turnaround in philosophy, came as something of a shock to enthusiasts for the marque. And indeed, successful though the 924 may have been commercially, it wasn't, and still isn't a very good car in its basic form.

The German company did much better with the 924 Turbo, and the 944 however, following the traditional teutonic route of development and refinement of a basic theme.

A far greater shock was the introduction of the Porsche 928 in 1977. Here was a world still reeling under the impact of the second "oil shock", witnessing a small, spe-

cialist manufacturer announcing a sports car powered by a gas guzzling 4.5 litre V8 engine. Many a head was shaken in disbelief, and the demise of Porsche Ag was prophecied with conviction.

Not only did Porsche survive, against all such predictions, but the company progressed, surely and steadily, to a point at which demand currently is tending to exceed supply on a world scale. While its true that the cheaper Porsches are in the greatest demand, the flagship V8 holds its own to this day.

Power simply for the sake of power is wasteful, providing only brief satisfaction periodically. When it is wrapped up in a super luxury package however, making it possible to enjoy a car whether crawling in traffic or burning up the bitumen, it has far more meaning. In the latest 928, with its bigger bore engine, Porsche has produced just such a package which cannot help but satisfy the lucky few who might be able to afford the $65,000 price tag.

There's something about the 928's prac-

ticality that is almost incongruous. How can it possibly be that such a flowing, curvaceous shape requires nothing special in terms of driving skill. You'd imagine that, as with a highly complex advanced fighter aircraft, there'd have to be an intensive conversion course to enable one to step from the mundane into this Porsche. It does tend to intimidate those unused to such vehicles. And oddly, although the car has been around for a number of years, it still attracts attention wherever its parked. In white finish, it stands out in any company, and yet, in darker colors it blends easily into the background throng of tin boxes.

People at Porsche are only too ready to explain the many advantages of ownership. Not the least of these is the seven year warranty against rust and corrosion. Sheet steel, hot galvanised on both sides, is used for the basic body shell, including the central cabin and the rear guards. The doors, front guards and engine cover are all made of alloy, while the front and rear extremities are made from polyurethane. Out of sight behind these extreme outer front and rear panels are sturdy bumpers with shock absorbing capabilities which can sustain quite reasonable impacts without permanent deformation. Under everyday parking impacts, the polyurethane can be compressed against the hidden bumpers without damage at all, springing back into place immediately. Because the body color is integral with the plastic material, seldom is there any subsequent evidence of contact. At least it avoids the age old "Darling. I had a teensy weensy little accident with the car at the supermarket this morning."

Luxury is a word which keeps on cropping up where Porsche's 928S is concerned. On the face of it, it might seem that takes precedence over even the accepted performance advantages which are implicit in the marque.

angle and cushion height. Although the left hand front seat has to be manually adjusted, there is a power option.

Window lifters are electric, centre console mounted rocker switches looking after their operation. They are placed either side of the console, with other switches between them to control the optional electrically operated sun roof and the rear screen wiper system.

Air conditioning is standard. This is of the automatic climate control type. Set the temperature required and forget it! There's a five speed fan however, if the equipment needs extra boost. The climate of the glove box is included in the deal, making it possible to store delicate bits and pieces there without fear of them melting or being damaged by heat.

Up front, in addition to the glovebox, there are lidded bins in both front doors. These double as arm rests, and, with the lids extended inwards, the arm rests become adjustable. The bins are long and deep, with enough width to accept most small things the average person might want to carry. Another bin is located in the console between the front seats, this designed especially for the storage of cassettes.

When you get around to driving the car, Porsche's designers go as far as just about anybody in providing the right tools for the job. Exterior rear vision mirrors are electrically adjusted for instance, and that's important with the fairly thick "B" pillars creating small blind spots to either rear quarter.

At no extra cost, the buyer has the choice of leather or cloth seat trim, and either a five speed manual or three speed automatic transmission. The latter is the most popular, being more in keeping with the luxury character. It's no imposition though as it compromises the performance aspect hardly at all.

Even the least ambitious driver must feel a glow of anticipation after sliding in behind the wheel. Long before the actual joy of hearing that 4.7 litre power unit gruffly bark into life, there's a whole welter of experiences, visual and tactile, to set the blood coursing faster.

Is the steering wheel a little too low? Then it's a simple matter to raise it after releasing the lock beneath the steering column shroud. That allows the complete instrument binnacle to move too, maintaining the relationship between the wheel and instrument visibility. Adjustment for the seating position is power assisted. Three two way rocker switches on the right hand side of the seat cushion facilitate changes to reach, backrest

The 928S stereo sound system is a pleasure in itself. It has an AM/FM radio and a cassette player, together with four speakers. Even flat out, there's no distortion of the excellent sound quality emanating from the equipment which has just about every feature the mobile sound nut could ever want.

Storage areas within the Porsche are many and varied. The boot is a reasonable size for a car of this type, with easy access through the gas strut supported rear hatch. A removable tonneau is featured to hide whatever's being carried, and there's an optional net available to locate small items securely. Boot space is increased measureably when the two rear seat backrests are locked down flat. This turns the complete rear compartment into a load area, just at the flick of a catch.

Once the ignition key is turned the car's check panel lights up. This monitors just about anything that might go wrong, whether it be of major or minor importance to safe driving. Once the engine is switched on, all being well, the red lights are extinguished. Should there be something of a minor nature — a rear light globe out for example — a cancel button gets rid of the warning. If the problem is a definite hazard to the vehicle's operation — brake wear or something like that — the light will stay on until the fault has been rectified. Should these things occur while on the move, an exclamation mark lights up instantly as a warning, then, either the problem is minor and the cancel button can be punched, or it's major and the car should be brought to a halt as quickly as possible. The check system encompasses oil level, brake fluid level, water level and many other things, providing a very comprehensive automatic warning system which requires no action on the part of the driver other than to turn the ignition key.

The instrument binnacle is dominated by a 260 km/h speedometer and a 7500 rpm tachometer. There's also a temperature and fuel level gauge to one side, with a battery condition and oil pressure gauge the other. Twist knobs arranged around the edge of the binnacle look after headlights, driving lights, the hazard warning and the rear screen demister. This latter switch controls three stages of screen demisting to cater for a wide range of possibilities. Steering column stalks are for the direction indicators on the left, and for the windshield wipers to the right. The wiper system has three normal speeds, together with an adjustable intermittent mode. There's also an intensive windshield washer system with its own metering pump, not to mention another which looks after the headlights. On the subject of lights, a small twist knob on the floor to the right of the driver's seat controls beam height when the car may be heavily laden.

Power for the 928 comes from one of the last V8 engine designs the world of automobiles is likely to see. It's fitting that the unit is also one of the most sophisticated production power plants around. Light and relatively compact, it's an all alloy construction with single overhead camshafts on each bank of four cylinders, driven by toothed belts. Running on a high 10:1 compression ratio, 221 kW power at 5900 rpm and 385 Nm torque at 4500 rpm are produced smoothly on 98

octane petrol. The "S" engine is a bored out version of the original 928 unit, increasing capacity from 4474cc to 4664cc, and adding 44 kW extra power with an extra 600 rpm. Only an extra 5 Nm torque come with the larger engine however, proving that higher performance in terms of maximum speed was the aim of the exercise. While the 4.5 litre engine can take the 928 to just 230 km/h, the "S" increases these outer limits to 250 km/h — a speed, incidentally, which we didn't attempt to reach on test. Well, surely 220 km/h is enough for anyone!

Bosch K-Jetronic fuel injection is fed from

an 86 litre fuel tank. On EEC testing, this gives the Porsche a range of well over 650 kilometers between fills at a steady 120 km/h. Vehicle availability meant we were unable to conduct our own economy tests during the small number of days it was in our possession.

While it might appear odd that driving nuts such as ourselves should think that way, we recommend the automatic transmission highly. Admittedly we would have preferred the five speed manual at the outset, but in view of the fact that 80 percent of 928S models sold have the auto, we went along with Porsche Australia's selection of vehicles for test. Within half an hour we were convinced.

Bear in mind that many owners use their cars mostly around town. Thus, the automatic solves many driving problems in congested conditions. In fact, we found that ratios selected made the car an even greater joy under all conditions, certainly more pleasant to drive than a five speed we borrowed for a few hours previously.

The transmission is rear mounted in unit with the final drive. Power is taken from the rear of the engine, and transmitted by a torsion shaft enclosed in a tube running the length of the car. Although there is some loss of economy when being given a little "stick" out on the open road, because of the change points designed into the power train, around town economy is, if anything, better than with the manual. This is undoubtedly due to the fact that most stick shift cars are kept in too low a gear unnecessarily.

Pirelli's low profile P7 tyres give the 928 a firm but by no means uncomfartable ride, even over quite rough surfaces. It's firmer at low speed of course, smoothing out as the vehicle gets into its stride — which is very quickly. Steering power assistance has been kept to a bare minimum, and this means there's always planty of road feel coming through the wheel. On uneven surfaces there's a continual need for steering correction in a straight line. It seems that this is a

result of the "Weissach" rear suspension geometry as much as anything. Because it has been designed to retain neutral steering characteristics under conditions when, otherwise, distinct oversteer of the traditional Porsche type, might become too strong, it does perform these functions minimally when one rear wheel or the other negotiates a bump or depression running in a straight line.

The Weissach axle uses specially designed suspension arm joints which enforce compensatory toe in and toe out wheel movements under cornering loads. These same movements are present under acceleration or deceleration.

Handling and road holding are, despite all this, entirely predictable. The car always feels responsive, no matter what the speed, and the surefootedness with which it turns into corners is quite staggering. Unlike some Porsches, it is possible to be ham fisted with a 928S and still live a long and happy life! Provoked under test conditions with an unnecessary application of power in mid corner, we found nothing more than a shift of weight bias, and a slight tucking in of the nose. And even when hitting the brakes under the same conditions, the movement of the tail outwards was in no way violent, and was certainly controlled easily.

Very high cornering forces can be used without either end breaking loose, and the normally forbidden wholesale throttle lift off has little more effect than on most normal touring cars.

Standard 928S wheels are made of cast alloy, featuring those prominent large round holes around the periphery. Our test car was equipped with the much more expensive, and much stronger forged alloy wheels which have slotted vents instead for brake cooling. It goes without saying that there are disc brakes on all four corners, all of the ventilated type, and with floating calipers. The braking system is diagonally split so that, at all times there's retardation on two diagonally opposite wheels in the event of a system failure.

Stopping power is almost unbelievable for a car on road tyres. From 100 km/h it could come to a standstill in under 40 metres, never once exceeding that mark even after four or five heavy applications in succession. Remember, the coefficients of friction between the Pirellis and the road surface have to be incredible to achieve these sort of distances where a 1450 kilogram car is concerned.

It is our belief that, in the 928S, Porsche has produced the ultimate touring car. "Touring" really is the right word too, rather "sports", for this model will always spend the majority of its life in a touring mode of one sort or another, despite its incredible performance potential. No more successful compromise can we think of than this. And yet, there are no obvious signs of compromise to be seen!

To drive a Ferrari, or a Lamborghini, one has to be prepared to compromise for the majority of the time. They're not easy to get into, and often there are allowances which have to be made in terms of interior noise, vibration, and visibility. To own either of those Italian marques, a person has to be deeply in love with their aura and what they represent. Although Porsche has a similar aura where the 928S is concerned, no demands are made on an owner other than that he has sufficient bread to lay out up front. Once he has taken delivery, despite all that Porsche represents, he can use the car in all conditions just as with any everyday sedan.

He doesn't have to be a contortionist to climb in and out. He doesn't have to send the bulk of his luggage on by train because it won't fit in the boot, and he doesn't have to turn up the stereo to drown out the clatter of camshafts and timing gears.

Our period testing the 928S, short as it was, was one we won't forget for a long time to come.

ACTION ANALYSIS

MODEL.............................Porsche 928S
COUNTRY OF ORIGIN.............. Germany
BODY TYPE...... Two Door Hatchback Coupe
SEATING CAPACITY.................... 2 + 2
PRICE (excluding on road costs)
OPTIONS FITTED
PRICE AS TESTED

ENGINE:
location.....................................Front
cylinders.......................... Vee Eight
capacity................................. 4664 cc
bore/stroke.................... 97 x 78.9 mm
block.......................................Alloy
head.......................................Alloy
valve actuation.....................SOHC x 2
induction........ Bosch K-Jetronic Injection
compression ratio...................... 10:1
power (kW/bhp)...... 221/300 at 5900 rpm
torque (Nm/ft lbs)... 385/274.9 at 4500 rpm

TRANSMISSION:
driving wheels......... .... Rear
gearbox type........ T e Speed Automatic
shift location.......... Centre Console 'T' Bar
gear ratios

1st.. 2.310
2nd.. 1.460
3rd.. 1.000
final drive ration..................... 2.750

BODY/CHASSIS:
construction........................... Unitary
material.......... Steel, Alloy, Polyurethane
kerb weight........................ 1450 kgs
O/A length........................ 4447 mm
O/A height........................ 1282 mm
wheelbase........................ 2500 mm
front track.......................... 1552 mm
rear track.......................... 1529 mm
fuel tank capacity.................. 86 litres

SUSPENSION:
front type... Independent-double wishbones
springs.................................. Coil
rear type Independent-semi trailing arm-upper
.... transverse link
springs.................................. Coil

STEERING:
type...... Rack and pinion — servo assisted.
turning circle...................... 11.5 meters

BRAKES:
actuation......... Hydraulic — Servo assisted
front type................. Disc — Ventilated
rear type................... Disc — Ventilated

WHEELS:
material..................... Forged aluminium
diameter/width.................. 16 x 7 inches

TYRES:
make/type.......................... Pirelli P7
dimensions...................... 225/50 VR16

PERFORMANCE DATA
Weather:.......................... Warm-still
Road:............................... Clean-Dry
Odometer reading....................... 6900
Speedometer error at
  60 km/h................................ 51.2
  80 km/h................................ 70
  100 km/h............................... 90
Maximum speeds in gears:
  1st.............................108 km/h
  2nd............................. 164 km/h
  3rd...................... 250 km/h claimed
Acceleration from rest to-
  60 km/h............................4.2 secs
  80 km/h............................5.8 secs
  100 km/h...........................7.3 secs
  120 km/h...........................9.9 secs
  60 to 100 km/h......................4 secs
            (3rd gear manual of "D" auto)
  400 meters...................... 15.5 secs
            terminal speed............. 150 km/h
Braking from 100 km/h to STANDSTILL
  average of four tests.......... 40 metres

61

PORSCHE 928S

More of a good thing

To some, the idea of introducing a Sport version of a car like the Porsche 928 may seem a bit redundant, like unveiling a mean version of a mad dog. The standard 928 with its fuel injected 4.5-liter sohc aluminum V-8 and highly developed chassis was already a very fast and fine handling road car; a yardstick against which the performance of other cars is measured. A machine of superlatives, it was considered by many (including several people around here) to be the best GT car in

the world, while suffering from none of the drawbacks—complex maintenance, scattered dealerships, nonexistent parts, etc—normally associated with more exotic automobiles. Hard to imagine, then, what might be done to make the 928 sportier or usefully faster.

But just as you can never be too rich or too thin, it might follow that a GT car can never be too fast or too agile. Following that pleasant logic, Porsche has replaced last year's 928 with the 1983 928S, a car with a larger engine, bigger tires and higher gearing, among other things. And another superlative has been added to Porsche's sales literature: "The fastest street legal production car sold in the U.S. is the new 928S."

Europe has always had a standard and an S version of the 928 to choose from, both making considerably more than the 220 bhp of the U.S. model. The normal 4.5-liter European version is rated at 240 DIN bhp (about 228 SAE net) and the 4.7-liter S model produces 300 DIN bhp, or about 280–285 SAE net bhp. Americans in search of something extra have had to be satisfied, until now, with ordering the optional Competition Package on the standard car. The Competition Package included a number of parts off the European S, such as a small spoiler at the base of the rear window, another spoiler under the front bumper, stiffer shocks and 7x16-in. flat-disc forged alloy wheels with 225/50VR-16 tires replacing the standard 15-in. wheels and tires.

Now the U.S. gets a genuine S model with all the options of the Competition Package and one item that was missing before—a more powerful engine. The 4.5-liter V-8 has been enlarged to 4.7 liters, just like the European S, by increasing the bore from 95.0 to 97.0 mm. The stroke remains at 78.9 mm. Compression has also been raised, for its second increase in the car's 5-year history, from 9.0:1 to 9.3:1. Despite that increase, the 928's TOP (Thermally Optimized Porsche) engine design allows it to run on unleaded regular.

Various sensors about the engine measure throttle position, engine temperature, rpm, crank position, intake air temperature, airflow and exhaust gas oxygen content. The signals are sent to a computer that, after some rapid pondering, adjusts ignition timing and the pulses of the L-Jetronic fuel injection to provide the right combination of spark and mixture. The other half of the equation is a cylinder head design with a very small squish area and a centrally located sparkplug. The goal of the TOP system, which was developed on the 944 engine, is to provide (what else?) more performance without a sacrifice in fuel economy.

Not exactly a novel goal in the automotive world these days, but Porsche has managed to increase the 928's horsepower while boosting its EPA mileage slightly. The combination of greater displacement, higher compression and computer controlled spark and fuel injection has pushed the engine from 220 to 234 bhp at the same 5500 rpm and boosted torque from 254 lb-ft at 3600 rpm to 263 lb-ft at 4000.

Fuel economy has never been the 928's long suit, and the Porsche flagship established itself back in 1978 as a relatively large, heavy (3365-lb curb weight) and thirsty GT car with an average test mileage of 16 mpg, occasionally dipping below 10 mpg around town. When Bosch L-Jetronic injection replaced the old K-Jetronic in 1980, our test car managed an 18-mpg average. Driven hard, our 1983 928S averaged 16.0 mpg, but its EPA city/highway figures are up from last year's 16/25 to 16/27, so a driver with the strength of character, or lack of imagination, to drive this car gently may do slightly better on the highway. At any rate, most 928S owners, having spent $43,000 for the fastest production car in the U.S., are not going to quibble over a few mpg, and the 22.7-gal. fuel tank gives the car plenty of range between fill-ups.

Also intended to improve fuel economy, and to take advantage of the engine's added horsepower and torque, is the 928's rear-mounted gearbox, which now has higher (lower numerical) ratios in all five speeds. The final drive ratio is also taller at 2.27:1, compared with last year's 2.75:1. With that gearing, the big V-8 with its 6100-rpm redline is loafing at only 1850 rpm at 60 mph. A new 4-speed automatic transmission also uses the same final drive ratio. Porsche formerly used a Daimler-Benz 3-speed automatic in the 928, but the 1983 S uses new 4-speed D-B internals in a transmission housing produced by Porsche. As in all previous 928s, the rear-mounted manual and automatic transmissions are both linked solidly to the engine with an enclosed driveshaft tube.

So the 928S has a larger, more powerful engine and taller gearing. Does that make it, as Porsche claims, the fastest street legal production car in the U.S.? Perhaps. Our test car turned a creditable quarter-mile time of 15.4 seconds at 92.0 mph and accelerated from 0–60 in 7.0 sec and 0–100 in 19.3 sec. The new 1984 (introduced in 1983) Corvette negotiated the quarter mile in 15.5 sec at 88.0 mph, did its 0–60 mph in 7.1 sec and 0–100 in 22.3—with an automatic transmission. What the Corvette 4-speed manual will do remains to be seen. But the Corvette and the new 4-valve Ferrari, for that matter, were not around when the 928S was introduced, and it may still best both cars in a run for all-out speed (more on that when we get our hands on the Corvette and Ferrari). It's hard to make subjective comparisons between the acceleration of the old 928 and the new 928S without a back-to-back comparison. but nearly all those who drove the car thought the 4.7-liter felt noticeably fast-

er. Yet as our Senior Editor noted, "What difference does it make if the tire marks are 10 or 12 ft long?"

Whether the car holds its own in the battle of microseconds is probably beside the point; the 928S is one of, if not *the*, fastest cars available to the American buyer and, as such, belongs to a very select group. What we do know is that the 928S produces power, and plenty of it, all the way through its 6100-rpm rev band. At low rpm it rumbles and burbles like a proper V-8, moving off the line or through slow traffic with relaxed, almost lazy torque. As the revs climb, the engine assumes a snarling note of urgency and slingshots the car down the road in true eye-opening fashion. The power delivery is a wonderful blending of traditional V-8 torque and that slightly raspy, hammers-of-hell busyness that Porsche engines have always had; the blend is controlled with the accelerator pedal and gearshift lever.

The gearshift lever, incidentally, is still shifted in a pattern that has reverse at the upper left and 1st at the lower left, straight back. The other four gears are laid out in a normal H pattern. The gearbox shifts with solid, if not gratifyingly smooth, precision, and several drivers noted it felt less balky than last year's linkage.

In keeping with our expectations from past models, the 928S's handling is delightful. It has tremendous cornering power, controlled but supple suspension, mild understeer at the limit, and power assisted steering that gives help when it's needed but doesn't interfere with road feel or driver input.

When we got down to measuring things, however, our test Porsche's handling and braking perplexed us a bit. Skidpad and slalom were, respectively, a little higher (0.818g versus 0.810) and a tad lower (58.4 mph vs 59.0) than figures recorded with the last 928 we tested. Now these differences are just tantalizingly within the ranges we'd ordinarily expect for test reproducibility: Slalom differences of 0.6 mph border on the insignificant; skidpad values differing by 0.012g can be considered pretty much a wash.

But when we did the panic stops, our distances of 156 ft from 60 mph and 280 ft from 80 were disappointingly long for a car of the 928S's character. As with earlier ones, this car exhibited

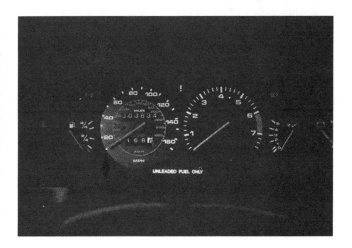

rather more rear lock sensitivity than we'd like. However, with previous 928s, it wasn't difficult for an educated right foot to extract distances some 20 ft shorter—and this was significant.

We sought reasons that might illuminate these test data, and the most evident was different tires. Our current test car rolled on Goodyear NCTs, 225/50VR-16s; the previous numbers were recorded with Pirelli P7s of the same size. Curiously enough, Porsche specifies either make as standard equipment for the 928S (and optional with the previous Competition Package), and it's essentially luck of the draw as to which tires happen to be fitted on a given batch of cars. Could this be the difference? Are P7s better than NCTs?

In a word, no. But it took considerable time and help from a goodly number of people before this conclusion was reached. Our test car had the NCTs and it was straightforward enough to search out a set of appropriate P7s. However, we wanted to do direct back-to-back testing, and 928 wheels tend to be already attached to other 928s. Center Line Racing Wheels was prepared to offer us a set of its handsome aftermarket variety, but our leanings here were for retention of the stock wheel. Our rescue came from Bob Smith Porsche/Audi in Hollywood, where they were kind enough to pull a car from stock, put it on jack stands for a few days and let us swipe its wheels. In the meantime, we put some mileage on the fresh P7s to give them a fair run with the NCTs that had already traveled some 5000 miles. And 4-Day Tire Corp helped when it came to mounting all these various combinations.

We repeated three phases of our testing, 60–0 braking, 80–0 braking and the slalom, alternating between NCTs and P7s. After averaging two sets of data for each tire, we confirmed what we might have guessed, considering Porsche's usual thoroughness in engineering. In braking from 60 mph, the NCTs gave an average distance of 156 ft; the P7s averaged 153 ft, an insignificant difference considering run-to-run variations of as much as 5 ft. From 80 mph, the P7s were a bit more amenable to control-

ling the rear lock sensitivity and their 266-ft average compared favorably with the NCT's 280 ft, a difference outside the range of experimental error.

The slalom results were closer, however, with the NCTs getting the slight edge. Their best run was 58.4 mph; the P7s, only insignificantly behind at 58.1. Our tester noted that both tires turned in well and, as the car's limiting speed was approached, both got twitchy at the rear. However, he felt the NCTs were marginally better in transmitting torque while enduring the heavy side loads of the slalom's transitions.

In summary, we're convinced a 928S buyer needn't fret about luck of the tire draw; they're both excellent rubber.

The car is equally happy around town, racing down a canyon road or cruising across the desert at 120 mph, and the harder it's pushed, the more its breeding shows. The 928S is simply a marvelously competent car; more than that, it comes as close as anything to being the complete automobile, as understood in the year 1983. A time capsule car to show the future our best effort.

The cost is high; at $43,000 it is well up from last year's list price of $39,500. It's a judgment call to say a car this expensive is worth it, but at least the 928S gives you a great deal of substance to go with its costly image.

PRICE

List price, all POE	$43,000
Price as tested	$43,795

Price as tested includes std equip. (air cond, leather seats, elect. adj driver's seat, metallic paint, central locking, elect. window lifts, elect. adj and heated mirrors, rear-window wiper, cruise control), AM/FM stereo/cassette ($795)

GENERAL

Curb weight, lb/kg	3365	1528
Test weight	3520	1598
Weight dist (with driver), f/r, %	51/49	
Wheelbase, in./mm	98.4	2499
Track, front/rear	61.1/60.2	1552/1529
Length	175.7	4463
Width	72.3	1836
Height	50.5	1283
Trunk space, cu ft/liters	6.3+14.2	178+402
Fuel capacity, U.S. gal./liters	22.7	86

ENGINE

Type	sohc V-8
Bore x stroke, in./mm	3.82 x 3.11....97.0 x 78.9
Displacement, cu in./cc	285 4644
Compression ratio	9.3:1
Bhp @ rpm, SAE net/kW	234/175 @ 5500
Torque @ rpm, lb-ft/Nm	263/357 @ 4000
Fuel injection	Bosch L-Jetronic
Fuel requirement	unleaded, 91-oct

DRIVETRAIN

Transmission	5-sp manual
Gear ratios: 5th (1.00)	2.27:1
4th (1.54)	3.50:1
3rd (2.03)	4.61:1
2nd (2.85)	6.47:1
1st (4.27)	9.69:1
Final drive ratio	2.27:1

CHASSIS & BODY

Layout	front engine/rear drive
Body/frame	unit steel
Brake system	11.1-in. (282-mm) vented discs front, 11.4-in. (289-mm) vented discs rear; vacuum assisted
Wheels	forged alloy, 16 x 7J
Tires	Goodyear NCT, 225/50VR-16
Steering type	rack & pinion, power assisted
Turns, lock-to-lock	3.1

Suspension, front/rear: upper A-arms, lower trailing arms, coil springs, tube shocks, anti-roll bar/upper transverse links, lower trailing arms, coil springs, tube shocks, anti-roll bar

CALCULATED DATA

Lb/bhp (test weight)	15.0
Mph/1000 rpm (5th gear)	32.4
Engine revs/mi (60 mph)	1850
R&T steering index	0.98
Brake swept area, sq in./ton	250

ROAD TEST RESULTS

ACCELERATION

Time to distance, sec:

0–100 ft	3.3
0–500 ft	8.5
0–1320 ft (¼ mi)	15.4
Speed at end of ¼ mi, mph	92.0

Time to speed, sec:

0–30 mph	2.6
0–50 mph	5.5
0–60 mph	7.0
0–70 mph	9.4
0–80 mph	11.7
0–100 mph	19.3

SPEEDS IN GEARS

5th gear (4200 rpm)	136
4th (6100)	127
3rd (6100)	97
2nd (6100)	69
1st (6100)	46

FUEL ECONOMY

Normal driving, mpg	16.0

BRAKES

Minimum stopping distances, ft:

From 60 mph	156
From 80 mph	280
Control in panic stop	good
Pedal effort for 0.5g stop, lb	22

Fade: percent increase in pedal effort to maintain 0.5g deceleration in 6 stops

from 60 mph	nil
Overall brake rating	good

HANDLING

Lateral accel, 100-ft radius, g	0.818
Speed thru 700-ft slalom, mph	58.4

INTERIOR NOISE

Constant 30 mph, dBA	66
50 mph	72
70 mph	75

SPEEDOMETER ERROR

30 mph indicated is actually	30.0
60 mph	58.5

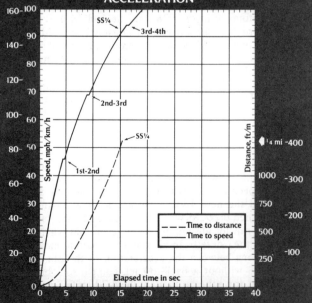

ACCELERATION

SUPERPOWER PORSCHE

For most of us, the Porsche 928 is fast enough. But a modified version now sold in Germany has two big superchargers that boost power to a claimed 340 kW and speed to an indicated 272 km/h. Hans-Jürgen Tücherer reports for CAR...

TRUE-blue Porsche owners and enthusiasts have taken some time to accept the 928 as one of the family — in some quarters, 928 owners have been regarded as people who lack the courage to buy a "real" Porsche. The aftermarket has so far followed this trend by virtually ignoring the 928 as a vehicle fit for tuning. In Germany even ten-year-old 911s are still being converted into 935s by a host of private tuning firms, but the 928 has remained the stepchild of the "tweakers".

Now all that has changed — a Bavarian tuning outfit, Auto-Vittorio, is offering the first all-round tuning package for 928s. Vittorio Strosek has sharpened his skills on various conversions performed on Jaguars, Ferraris and Lamborghinis and has turned his hand to producing the Auto-Vittorio 928 SK.

K for Kompressor

The letters SK are an indication of Strosek's thinking, for just as "K" indicated "Kompressor" (Supercharger) for those immortal pre-war racing and touring Mercedes Benz cars, so it indicates "supercharger" for the Strosek Porsche 928.

During a recent visit to Auto-Vittorio, I was able to sample one of these 928 monsters. Opening the bonnet reveals an engine compartment full of no-compromise machinery and the most obvious change is the addition of two huge Roots-type superchargers, nestling in the space where the fuel-injection manifolds used to be. The standard Bosch K-Jetronic system is retained but completely modified so that the fuel is injected upstream of the superchargers, which serves to cool the air entering the engine.

The main internal modification involves substituting a set of forged Mahle

---

Three-piece BBS rims wear 225 P7 Pirellis. A huge wing at the rear end is claimed to increase downforce by 150 per cent and improve handling considerably. GRP front spoiler, sills and fins add to the purposeful look of this 911 Turbo eater.

---

pistons to drop the compression ratio to 8,0:1 from the original 10:1.

75 kW per litre

Engine modifications are handled by Peter Baumann, a Swiss tuning expert who promises to give 928 owners at least 75 reliable kW from every litre of engine capacity, which indicates an awesome 340 kW at 6 200 r/min. And please remember that these aren't turbo horses that wake up only at higher revs, but real old-fashioned supercharger steeds that start working from idling speed onwards. The two toothed-belt driven superchargers start pumping effectively from below 2 000 r/min, at 3 000 the pressure is 0,4 bar and the full pressure of 0,75 bar comes up at 4 000!

Technical Specifications

Engine:
V8 Porsche, 4 664 cm³, 8:1 compression ratio, nominal power 300 kW (DIN) at 6 200 r/min. Bosch K-Jetronic injection, additional oil cooler.

Running gear:

Front	double wishbones
Rear	swinging arms with locating struts
Tyres	Pirelli P7 225/50 VR 16, BBS rims eight inch front, nine inch rear.

Claimed performance:

0-100 km/h	5,2 seconds
0-200 km/h	20,5 seconds
Top speed	272 km/h*

(* with taller gearing — 295 km/h).

Manufacturer:
Auto-Vittorio, Triebhof Rieden, D-8919 Utting am Ammersee, West Germany.

Driving this monster is like taking off in a jet fighter. To the accompaniment of barely-subdued thunder from its massive exhaust pipes, the 928 leaves long black strips of Pirelli P7 on the tar and sends a cloud of rubber smoke mushrooming into the air. A new tail section now being developed will enable Strosek to mount wide 345 Pirellis instead of the present 225s, which should cure the problem of getting all that power onto the road.

My most overwhelming impression of the car is that the accelerator is connected to the rear wheels in the most direct

fashion imaginable. With about 1 600 kg to move, the 928 SK takes only 5,2 seconds to reach 100 km/h.

Now 928 owners need fear the 911 Turbo no longer. The (indicated) top speed seems to be in the region of 272 km/h, although I backed off a little around top revs to spare the engine. With the new 345 tyres and taller gearing, top speed should be quite close to the 300 mark...

Risky at night

Exterior changes involve fitting a voluminous front spoiler which does away with the standard pop-up headlights. Four square headlights are provided but even with all four in use, night driving would be a risky experience. For those who love going fast at night, Strosek will retain the pop-up headlights as well (which could be illegal in some countries) although he is working on a new configuration which would allow the headlights to be fully integrated into the bodywork when folded away.

Two GRP sills are moulded to the body between the wheel arches to accentuate the car's low, wide look. The two fat original rear-view mirrors are discarded and replaced by two tiny but effective streamlined units.

Two small fins are mounted behind the rear wheels and a huge wing is fitted on the rear deck — claimed to increase rear downforce by 150 per cent. Changes to the running gear involve fitting three-part BBS rims to provide a slightly wider track, while the springs are shortened by 30 mm.

The rear wing provides so much downforce that even at the highest speeds the rear end shows no signs of misbehaving, as it sometimes seems to want to do with the production 928. To enable the driver to keep a firm hand on things, Strosek fits an Indianapolis steering wheel with thick leather rim.

Excellence costs money and in Germany this exercise will cost the 928 owner the equivalent of about R57 000 for the complete car. Individual prices are as follows, but any South Africans interested in importing equipment should allow for import duty and shipping charges etc: Front spoiler — R557; Sills — R275; Rear wing — R780; Wing mirrors — R215; BBS rims — R357. At the Auto-Vittorio workshops, the conversion to square headlamps costs about R1 295, lowering the suspension costs R526, the Indianapolis steering wheel costs R156 and the supercharger installation, about R11 600. ●

Two huge Roots-type superchargers (top) dominate the engine compartment. An ingenious drive arrangement provides correct rotation from a single cogged belt. An Indianapolis padded steering wheel (left) allows the driver firm control.

Porsche 928S

Series 2

PORSCHE'S success in the world markets, and particularly in Britain, throughout the recession remains a phenomenon. A brief cutback in production in 1982 was the result of lower demand in the States as the 928 model temporarily lost ground in the performance market and the 924 model yielded to the 944, but in the UK it was business as usual with higher registration figures being recorded year after year. Rival manufacturers looked for a downturn as the £22,000 4.5-litre 928 was phased out in favour of the 4.7-litre, 300 bhp 928S, which has now climbed over the £30,000 mark, yet UK sales remain solid at 300 units a year and in Stuttgart just over 5,000 8-cylinder models are made each year at the Zuffenhausen plant.

The 928 started life as "Car of the Year 1978" and was considered by Prof Dr Ernst Fuhrmann, then chairman of the company, as the eventual replacement of the 911. A less expensive version was introduced in Germany while the 928S was launched in 1979 to capture a higher performance image, but all the while Dr Ferry Porsche clung to the belief that the 911 captured the spirit of the company, appointing Peter W. Schutz as chairman in 1981. From then on the 911's future was safe, and the 928S was developed as a model with an entirely separate identity.

With hindsight, maybe the 928S should have been designed as a full four-seater right from the beginning. It has always been Porsche's philosophy to make sports cars which don't compete with Mercedes and BMW products and, of course, had the 928 been the 911's replacement it should not have had four seats. But the overall width of 72.28 inches (without exterior mirrors) was dictated by the width of the V8 engine, leaving chief stylist Anatole Lapine with the difficult task of designing a well proportioned car with a relatively short wheelbase of 98.4 inches, and an overall length of 176 inches.

Aesthetically, then, the 928S does not look quite right, too wide for its length (or too short for its width), and the limited amount of seating and luggage space must limit its appeal to some extent. We wonder if Porsche's management will grasp the nettle one day, extend the length of the flagship model and turn it into a reasonable four-seater with adequate luggage capacity?

That's a hurdle the prospective buyer has to cross. But having made that decision, the customer has a Grand Touring car *par excellence* with vivid performance, even in automatic form, outstanding roadholding and handling, superb brakes (now with the ABS system, at last), and a comfortable ride marred only by a higher-than-expected level of tyre noise. The high degree of comfort is taken for granted, and retained value, so important for the business-person, is high.

A package of improvements for the 1984 model year 928S has increased the appeal of the V8. With the introduction of the latest Bosch LH Jetronic fuel injection system, with an overrun cut-off, the power has increased from 300 to 310 bhp, the torque

ONE OF THE FAMILY: MOTOR SPORT'S 928 pauses in the pit-lane at Silverstone together with some of its Porsche cousins.

figure from 280 to 295 lb ft at 4,100 rpm, fuel consumption has been improved — especially at higher speeds, the figure at a steady 75 mph now being 27 mpg, rather than 22 mpg — and the model feels that much more responsive. Second generation ABS braking has been introduced, though not the latest system which the driver can switch off at will, and the appeal of the automatic version, which accounts for the majority of sales, has been greatly increased by the introduction of the Daimler-Benz four-speed box, with a better spread of ratios and enhanced acceleration.

We spent a day with the 5-speed manual version of the 928S, and the rest of the week with the automatic version to savour the best of both worlds. The manual's box had just been rebuilt after some abuse from another road-tester and felt unusually stiff, but if this proved anything it was that the 30 cwt car can accelerate almost as well from rest in third gear as it can in first!

The clutch is unusual, for a road car, in having a twin plate mechanism which is reasonably light in operation, while the Porsche 5-speed box is also unusual nowadays in having first dog-legged to the left, the four working ratios being in a normal H-pattern. First and third are close together and, with the heavy shift, it proved possible to select third by mistake a couple of times during the day. It took this without any protest at all, with none of the acrid smells that the early models used to exude after maltreatment.

The 928S is probabaly just too big, and too refined to be a true sports car, but the Grand Touring description fits it perfectly. In a straight-line thrash the manual will reach 60 mph from rest in six seconds flat, 100 mph in 15 seconds (little slower than the latest 911 Carrera), and a top speed of 160 mph. Before the 310 bhp version was announced it was put through a 24-hour high speed trial at the Nardo track in Italy. and with no more modification than taping over the brake cooling ducts, and removing the windscreen wipers, it averaged 156 mph for 24 hours running at close to 170 mph on the straights.

The car accelerates with a hard, but muted growl which is just about purposeful enough to satisfy the sporting customers. Oddly enough, since the rival BMW company specialises in saloon and GT cars, the new M635 CSi feels more of a *sports* car as we reported recently, though it's not likely to threaten the Porsche on the British market since it will have left-hand drive only, will be more expensive and more difficult to obtain.

The 928's handling is unbelievably good for such a big and heavy car. The steering has speed variable power assistance and is never feather-light, in fact at times the driver may not be sure if he has assistance or not, which is ideal by our reckoning. On Goodyear's 225/50 NCT tyres the handling is entirely neutral (the transaxle layout gives a near 50:50 weight distribution), the amount of grip is amazing, and the V8 whips round corners far quicker than most drivers would wish to attempt. Its ability to effect sudden changes of direction without a suspicion of instability, in a motorway hazard for instance, puts the car into a class of its own.

Road noise on any but the smoothest of surfaces is a distinct penalty, however. On the nice asphalt German roads the occupants

UNDERSTATED COMFORT characterises the cabin, with only detail changes in series 2 form.

would rarely be bothered by noise, but on less good British byways the intrusion is very noticeable and rather tiring for much of the time; inevitable, the designers say, in a model which is tuned for handling before compliance, and in which the rear suspension turrets are within the cabin, not isolated by a boot bulkhead.

The automatic version is now very nearly as quick as the manual, and since it makes even less demands on the driver we can see its popularity increasing still more, particularly in Britain where it's offered at the same price. In Drive, the 928S will shift up at 40, 63 and 110 mph, but by holding second and third gears and taking the engine speed to its 6,500 rpm maximum the shift into third can be delayed to 77 mph and into fourth to 121 mph, with 60 mph coming up in 6.5 sec and 100 mph in an impressive 16.3 sec, the top speed being a claimed 155 mph.

It seems that the smoothness of the shift can vary slightly from one car to another, the car we tested being one of the better ones, maybe, since we had no complaint at all about the quality of the transmission.

Both the manual and automatic versions should be able to return an honest 20 mpg most of the time — very hard driving, or heavy traffic conditions bringing this figure down, of course — so the 18.9 gallon fuel tank should permit a reasonable 350-mile touring range.

In fine conditions there is little to say about the ABS braking system. Sometimes the first application of the brake pedal brings a slight thump, just to remind the driver that the system is still working, but that's about it. The brakes are exceedingly powerful, as they always have been on the 'S' model, and completely fade-free.

In Series 2 form (though the description is used only in Britain, the figure 2 having been added to the rear inscription just for our benefit) there are a number of detailed improvements. The tailgate, for instance, now has an electrically operated release with *two* interior controls, one for the driver and one for the passenger, so you don't have to switch the engine off and go back with the key these days. The electrically operated windows can be opened and shut even when the ignition key is out, but only if the doors are open at the time.

As standard equipment the 928S has part-leather upholstery (on the sides of the seats, which are cloth trimmed), air conditioning, electrically operated seats, and an instrument panel that goes up and down with the steering wheel. The central locking system now has an override control on the centre console, so if anyone wishes to discuss your bourgeois taste in motor cars you can deal with the situation promptly, and such niceties as the illuminated vanity mirrors on both sides are retained.

At £30,678 such performance and luxury does not come on the cheap, but people who buy such cars (usually with a company transaction) are looking not so much for value-for-money as an expression of their life-style. So long as they don't need a full four-seater (or can afford another car) the 928S is a natural first choice for many.

M.L.C.

Shark's the word!

PORSCHE 928S

"When Porsche launches a car the enthusiasts can't get enough. The series two 928S is the first Porsche to offer ABS braking."

SUPERTEST

Shark's the word!

IN 1978 THE Porsche 928 won the title Car of the Year — the same title that is currently held by the slightly more humble Vauxhall Astra.

The difference, we suspect, is that by 1998 the Astra will be long forgotten, while the Porsche 928 will still be setting the standards for the rest of the Supercars. It won't be the same 928 as the one we test here but you can bet it won't be unrecognisable. It simply isn't Porsche's style to build a car that won't go the distance.

The first car with the name Porsche, the famous 356, was around in different versions for 17 years. The 911 is still the Porsche that this writer covets (and will order the minute the Littlewoods man comes knocking) and has been the cream of the cream for at least 20 years.

The problem (if you can call it a problem) is that when Porsche launches a car the enthusiasts simply can't get enough. The rumour was that the 928 was brought in to see off the 911 — a design that even the factory regarded as long in the tooth — but demand became healthy for both models. You can't, it seems, replace chalk with cheese no matter how desirable the newcomer might be.

The 928 may have pleased the motoring press but there was criticism from those who actually bought the things. It seems it wasn't fast enough, and Porsche — knowing that the customer was always right — did something about it.

The 928S, identified by its extra spoilers, appeared in 1980 boasting 20% more power and mind boggling performance. Two years later the S version became the norm and the 'slow' car was dropped from the price lists. So what's new?

How it goes

In series 2 form the 928S becomes the first Porsche to offer ABS anti-lock braking as optional equipment. And we'd say that the brakes are now at least as good as the best brakes in the world. That's the big news.

But there are other refinements. The 4.7 litre light alloy V8 engine is now equipped with the latest Bosch LH Jetronic fuel injection system with overrun cut-off. It is very high-tech indeed, using the change in electrical resistance of a platinum wire as the heart of the system — which means there are no moving parts to go wrong. This electronic wizardry has the added bonus of endowing the car with an extra 10bhp to lift the power output to a most impressive 310bhp. And Porsche claims the top speed has been raised in the process from 155 to 158mph with 0-62mph — more of that anon.

Naturally when quoting ultimate figures, Porsche is talking about the manual version. However, we have to say that for the first time in our experience it would seem that Porsche is exaggerating just a wee bit.

Surprisingly perhaps (after all this is very much a sports car) 77% of buyers opt for the automatic version now equipped with the latest four-speed gearbox from the Mercedes Benz stable said to offer a 12% saving in petrol bills over the previous auto. The figure you should bear in mind is 27mpg at 75mph. Our own figure is given to you without comment — 16mpg. And up at the test track we dropped to 13mpg. It doesn't mean this time that Porsche is stretching the truth, rather that here is a car that is made to be driven!

Completing the new features are electrically heated windscreen washer nozzles — what a clever idea!

As with most fuel injected cars, the 928S starts first time every time and runs without a trace of temperament from the word go.

Initial thoughts are that for a sports car the 928 takes up a lot of room on the road, but after a few miles the love affair begins. There are niggles of course: on the road the car seemed noisy and the ride is harsh, but then that was in direct comparison to the XJS we had just vacated. The Porsche has other qualities.

It goes round corners for instance at speeds which would make lesser cars simply fly off the road and take to the fields. Porsche says the lateral acceleration limits in cornering lie between .86G and .87G compared with the average .76 (their figure) of rival makes. In language you can hopefully understand this means that on a 100 metre radius circle the Porsche can go round 3mph quicker. It doesn't sound much, but it certainly feels impressive.

How's it done? Well, there's no one thing you can put your finger on but those Goodyear NCT tyres help a lot. Weight distribution is important too. The engine is set well back under the bonnet and the gearbox is behind the driver to match the poise of a mid-engined car. Then there are the patented complexities of the Weissach back axle geometry which enables the driver to avoid premature oversteer — it is confidence-inspiring in the extreme.

Our first port of call at Millbrook was the high speed bowl, where we discovered the speedometer over-read and the car couldn't deliver the promised goods. But it is hard to be critical of anything which can lap at 150mph with the ease of a Sunday afternoon cruise in the sunshine.

AA colleagues have been known to comment on the bravery they imagine one needs to drive at very high speeds but with this car no special skills were needed. With so many reassuring messages coming through your fingers and your seat . . . well, your granny could 'max' this one.

Don't get us wrong. Covering mile in 24 seconds-and-a-bit is always exciting, but it doesn't have to be frightening. Porsche, however, claims that the car is capable of 156mph in automatic form and 159mph as a manual. Our car couldn't make it and we can't help thinking that yours wouldn't either. While you may say it is fast enough, it isn't as fast as it is said to be.

Up there on the high speed 'wall' we did have one moment. 150mph gives you little time to start examining red flashing exclamation marks! But the cover on the brake fluid reservoir had parted company with the rest of it and enough fluid had been lost to set off the warnings. At least it shows that the fail-safe systems do just that!

A word in praise of the steering system. At 150mph many power-assisted steering systems would feel rather vague, but Porshe's isn't one of them, Servo assistance is related to engine speed or, to put it technically, the torque applied to the front wheels at low speed (such as when parking) is compensated for irrespective of the amount of force required to steer the wheels. As engine speed rises the pump reduces the servo assistance, minimising the risk of kick-back at ho-hum motorway speeds.

A subtle benefit too is the front wheel castor configuration which would require far too great a steering effort in a non-assisted system but which offers this Porsche improved straight ahead feel. It's brilliant.

An engineer from GM enjoyed spin around Millbrook's handling courses in exchange for can of brake fluid. He was more an happy with the deal, though comments were limited phrases like 'Magic damping' om one very impressed expert. ow right he was. We'd add that e way the car turns into corners also rather unreal at first, with e added weird feeling of the ack end steering the car.

To call this a sports car is a bit ke calling a Stradivarius a fiddle!

Despite the 928S's dislike of anging onto first gear (only up 5000rpm) acceleration is a little reath-taking. That, by the way, is situation which can't be hanged by using manual ver-ride as the move to second ear can't be held back by the nthusiastic driver. The acid test or a Supercar is its ability to each 120mph in less than 30sec, nd the 928S was there with lenty to spare. Millbrook's nile-long straight was an easy place to sprint to 120mph and eturn to zero with the ease of a vink.

The open mouths that seem to ine the streets as the 928S assed by are evidence that the stylists succeeded in one respect, but just how clean is the shape in aerodynamic terms? As with BMW and Mercedes we suspect that in the end eye-appeal is as mportant as a low Cd factor. That said, Porsche is quick to explain that a car's frontal area is just as important as its drag coefficient. The chief reasons for that banana-like profile were sure-handling and exemplary

road holding rather than the economy of the shape. Clearly, Porsche owners won't be financially embarrassed by a visit to the pumps. And anyone who wants the car to go faster must be standing on the wrong pedal.

As with all front engined Porsches, the trans-axle lay-out provides near perfect weight distribution, achieving the benefits of a mid-engined car without the space penalties. The big V8 engine rests on the front axle, while the gear box, differential, fuel tank and battery are located across the rear axle. The engine and gearbox are joined by a steel tube containing a drive shaft only 25mm in diameter running at engine speed, supported by maintenance free bearings.

How comfortable

The quick answer is that for much of the time the Porsche simply isn't as comfortable as the Jaguar XJS V12, which still sets the standards in quietness and refinement.

However on twisting roads the Weissach axle and that 'magic' damping make the Porsche much more reassuring and poised. And when it comes to attention to detail and quality control, well the German horse wins by a neck. Maybe one's thoughts are influenced by the Porsche's superior ergonomics — the science of placing controls at your fingertips and making instruments that are easily read.

On this Porsche it isn't just the steering wheel you adjust, for the whole instrument binnacle and the stalks shift too, retaining their relationship with your finger tips.

Some drivers have criticised the Porsche's seating for its lack of lumbar support but perhaps they didn't notice that it is possible to insert extra padding into the backrest. In any case our tester's back did not protest at the standard article. Both front seats are electrically adjustable for height, leg room, squab angle and backrest rake.

Adults will object to a ride in the rear of the 928S, where there is a distinct lack of legroom. It is fine for children of course but we must remain unhappy about the lap-belt-only seating safety for our youngsters. It's unusual to see visors for rear passengers too, but the 928S is a bit like that — when people say 'Has it got ..?' the answer is always Yes.

We remained unimpressed, however, by the test car's air conditioning system which, while looking good on paper, failed to keep us cool through an English heatwave. The controls couldn't be simpler — you merely set a slider to the desired temperature between 18 and 30 degrees Centigrade while moving the bottom slide control to 'automatic'. Our system was set to 18 degrees at most times and rarely got there. Maybe the system needed charging up?

On the in-car entertainment front the 928S series 2 sees a complete change with the introduction of the new Blaupunkt Atlanta stereo radio/cassette player. This 18-station memory unit has PLL synthesiser tuning (whatever that might be), and a tape track search. There's a four channel stereo amplifier hidden somewhere crashing out 20 watts per channel through eight speakers. Not surprisingly it sounds almost as good as your singing in the bath.

The ride can seem harsh at times as the Porsche encounters road ridges or cats eyes, and we'd have to say that the NCT tyres transmit too much noise. Porsche tells you why:

'Comfortable' must be understood properly. Too softly sprung vehicles with excessively yielding upholstery can lull the driver into a false sense of security. They insulate him from vital information about the state of the road and behaviour of his car. In its turn this can lead to a dangerous loss of concentration and quicker onset of fatigue ...'

A word or two about the cockpit. In front of the driver are reflection-free dials. There's water temperature and fuel (you can watch the fuel needle move

Shark's the word!

at 150mph) with a tank that holds about £30 worth. The speedometer is graduated up to 170mph. The matching rev counter is red-lined at a modest 6000rpm and the oil pressure goes up to five something-or-other. There's a *battery* condition indicator too.

There are more warning lights than you can count but that description is perhaps over simplifying what happens when anything goes wrong. When the top came off the brake fluid reservoir we actually got a written warning in red lights telling us exactly what was wrong. Either side of the driver you find meaty looking switches. There's a light switch on top — the pop-up design means you can flash the lights without having to pop them up — and fog lamps front and back. On the right side sits the heated rear screen and hazards. The screen heater, by the way, switches itself down in power without being asked, when its job is done — a small energy saving refinement.

There are just three stalks. Lights and indicators on the left and on the right sits the headlamp washer and sophisticated cruise control. The washer is a two-tank device which will actually remove the corpses of insects encountered at 150mph!

The electric window switches sit on the centre console — we've got to criticise something — and occasionally get fouled by the driver's elbow on the way in.

VERDICT

Can the Porsche 928S series 2 be the best sports car in the world? Well, until Porsche sees fit to lend us a 911 Turbo we'll say nothing.

But we'll have to say that the £32,212 Supercar didn't excite us as much as the far cheaper 911 Carrera. It's a problem, but the more competent that Porsche makes its cars, the more likely some tester is to interpret it all as a bit dull!

Seriously though, the 928S is an absolutely glorious Supercar, with few faults other than noise levels and ride. Let's just say there are some who would regard the car more suited to the racetrack than the road.

One's first thought is that no car could be worth such a pricetag. The second thought is that, with the wherewithal, we'd join the long waiting list without a moment's hesitation. The final thought is that we are still young enough to prefer a manual gearchange and a 911 Carrera.

The heart of the beast — 4.7 litres of burbling V8

Always a perfect view — the steering wheel is adjustable

An electrically-powered seat is standard equipment

PERFORMANCE
Maximum speed 149mph mean, 153mph best, 128mph in 3rd, 76mph in 2nd, 41mph in 1st (at 5000rpm)

Acceleration from rest

mph	time (sec)	indicated mph
30	2.7	34
40	3.9	44
50	5.0	55
60	6.6	65
70	8.4	75
80	10.2	85
90	13.6	95
100	17.0	107
110	21.5	118
120	26.0	128

Standing ¼ mile 15.0sec
Terminal speed 94mph
Maximum G 0.9

ENGINE
Type and size front-mounted V8, water cooled, 97mm bore x 78.9mm stroke = 4664cc; aluminium alloy head and block
Compression ratio 10.4:1
Valve gear Single overhead cam per bank driven by toothed belt
Fuel system Bosch LH-Jetronic injection
Ignition Electronic
Max power (DIN) 310bhp at 5900rpm
Max torque (DIN) 295 lb ft at 4100rpm

TRANSMISSION
Gearbox Four speed automatic. Ratios 1st 3.676:1, 2nd 2.412:1; 3rd 1.436:1, top speed 1.000:1, reverse 5.139:1, final drive 2.357:1. Mph/1000rpm 30.5mph in top, 21.3mph in 3rd.

CHASSIS
Suspension Front: Independent by double wishbones, strut dampers with co-axial coil springs, anti-roll bar. Rear: Independent by lower wishbones, upper transverse links and Porsche-Weissach back axle geometry, coil springs, anti-roll bar.
Steering: Rack and pinion with power assistance
Wheels 7J x 16 aluminium alloy wheels, Goodyear NCT radial-ply (225/50 VR 16) on test car
Brakes: Front ventilated discs 11.1in diameter. Rear ventilated discs 11.4in diam, circuit split front to rear. ABS anti-lock system. Park brake operates on separate rear drums.

Porsche 928S4

Porsche raises the price and the rewards of automotive hedonism one more time.

• Ten years ago, the Porsche 928 appeared like a bolt of lightning in an automotive industry whose future looked forever drab and gray. Most carmakers had been shell-shocked by the combined effects of the first fuel crisis, a worldwide recession, and the heavy hands of the U.S. government's safety and emissions regulators. In reaction to these debilitating influences, automotive design had shifted in a sensible, practical, and largely unimaginative direction. The new 928 defied the prevailing trends by emphasizing speed, comfort, and driving pleasure rather than utility,

fuel efficiency, and low cost.

Today, with performance back in vogue, OPEC's choke hold broken (at least temporarily), and horsepower and low emissions peacefully coexisting, it's hard to remember just how gutsy a move the Porsche managers made when they introduced the 928 during the economic nadir of the last decade. Led by Prof. Ernst "Four Cam" Fuhrmann, they not only ignored the conventional wisdom of the time but also forsook their own rear-engined, air-cooled traditions.

Prescient and daring they may have

been, but they weren't interested in foolish risks; they equipped the 928 with the most advanced technology they could muster. Porsche's new flagship had an all-aluminum engine, sixteen-inch 50-series tires, a rear suspension that steered the rear wheels slightly to promote stability, fully integrated soft bumpers, and unusually low maintenance needs. The package was wrapped in a highly distinctive cocoon.

Despite few changes, this remarkable design has held up well through the years. Until recently, in fact, the 928 was the standard by which all high-performance GTs

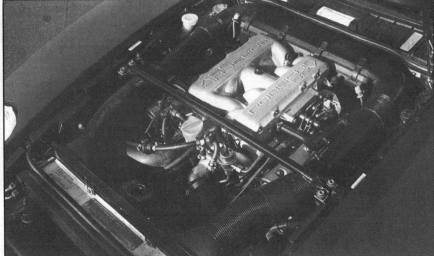

were judged. However, the competition—including some of Porsche's own models—has begun to crowd in. Recognizing the threat, Porsche is breathing new life into its second-oldest design for the 1987 model year. And because the 928's fourth series of modifications is its most extensive yet, the revised edition also gets a new name: 928S4.

The most obvious changes are to the bodywork. The 928's aerodynamic drag has always been an Achilles' heel of sorts. The original car had a drag coefficient of 0.42, a mediocre value even in 1978. This was later improved to 0.39 with the addition of front and rear spoilers, but in an era of 0.30 sedans, that's still a lackluster number. The changes for 1987 drop the figure to a much more respectable 0.34.

As significant as it is, the improvement has been accomplished without any alterations to the 928's original sheetmetal. A

soft new urethane nose cap has rounder contours, light clusters that are more nearly flush, and a completely different lower section. Instead of the previous air-dam lip, which shunted low-lying air to the sides, the new bottom section appears to direct more air underneath the car. This flow is smoothed by a new belly pan, which extends from the nosepiece to the front of the doors. A soft new tail complements the new nose; it's smoother and rounder, and the taillights are no longer deeply recessed, though they're still not quite flush. The bottom of the stern section is contoured to clean up the undercar airflow. Along the lower sides of the car are a pair of new sill panels, which help guide the air-

stream around the rear tires.

A casual observer might overlook these styling revisions, but one would have to be blind to miss the 1987 car's new rear aerodynamic aid. Instead of the previous small rubber spoiler, the 928S4 has a full-fledged wing trailing from its rear window. It's every bit as startling as the first 911 ducktail you ever saw, and according to Porsche it both reduces drag and increases downforce. To keep it from hanging up in a carwash, it can be folded forward to lie flat against the rear window—though only a philistine would take a 928 through an automatic carwash.

A redesigned cooling system also contributes to the aerodynamic improvement.

A set of adjustable horizontal louvers between the grille and the radiator, similar to the systems used on heavy trucks, regulates the cooling airflow, and two variable-speed electric fans have replaced the previous engine-driven cooling fan. A computer varies the angle of the louvers in three stages and the speed of the fans, according to the coolant temperature, the Freon pressure in the air-conditioning system, and, if an automatic gearbox is fitted, the transmission-oil temperature. Naturally, the system tries to keep the louvers closed as much as possible; the drag coefficient increases to 0.36 when they are fully open.

The thirteen-percent drag reduction of the new body would have a salutary effect on the 928's performance all by itself, but the new car also benefits from a power increase. The engine is still basically the same four-valve, four-cam, 5.0-liter V-8 that was introduced to the American market in 1985, but it's been substantially redesigned for S4 duty. Its power is up from 288 hp at 5750 rpm to 316 at 6000, and its torque has increased from 302 pound-feet at 2700 rpm to 317 at 3000.

Behind the increases in output are numerous mechanical changes. The cylinder heads have slightly shallower combustion chambers, larger intake and exhaust valves, a narrower angle between the valves, and revised valve timing. The 1987 engine also has two knock sensors and individual control of each cylinder's ignition timing. A new, more compact intake manifold has two plenum chambers and variable breathing characteristics. The two chambers are fed air by a Y-shaped passage from the throttle body. A second, shorter passage with its own butterfly valve also ties the two plenums together. Between 3500 and 5350 rpm, depending on throttle position, the butterfly automatically opens to improve the intake system's resonant effects. This variable tuning helps the breathing over a much wider rpm range than is normally possible. In fact, Porsche engineers claim that the new V-8 develops 300 or more pound-feet of torque all the way from 2700 to 4750 rpm.

We have the German market to thank for these improvements, because 1987 is the first year in which the home market gets the four-valve design. Although the 288 hp of our original four-valve V-8 was a big increase over the power output of the previous U.S. two-valve engines, the two-valve, 4.7-liter engine formerly sold in Europe produced 306 hp. In switching to a

Compared with last year's 928, the 928S4 (on right in both photos) has sleeker extremities, new side sills, and a most serious-looking rear wing.

four-valve design worldwide, therefore, Porsche had little choice but to pump in more power: it would hardly have been seemly to present the home market with a power reduction. We benefit from the improvements as well, in accordance with Porsche's new policy of offering identical engine outputs, with and without catalysts, in all markets.

Porsche power may be the same worldwide, but that doesn't mean we get the same gearing. To enhance fuel economy, the American 928S4 has the same tall (2.20:1) final-drive ratio and transmission ratios as last year's models. The European car has a closer ratio five-speed and a 2.64:1 final-drive to maximize top speed and the ease with which it is reached. The European automatic gets a 2.54:1 final-drive ratio.

Still, the American 928S4 should be significantly faster than its predecessor. Porsche claims a top speed of 165 mph for

the manual version and 162 mph for the automatic, both 10-mph improvements over the 1986 car's performance. Acceleration has also been energized. According to the factory, the new five-speed car reaches 60 mph in 5.7 seconds, the automatic in 6.3 seconds. Those times represent improvements of, respectively, 0.4 and 0.3 second.

To support this elevated performance, the 928S4, like Porsche's other top models, has wider wheels and tires in the rear than in front. The rear end is anchored by 245/45VR-16 tires on eight-inch wheels, while the front stays with 225/50VR-16s on seven-inch rims.

Except for the larger rear wheels and tires, little is altered in the 928's chassis. Anti-lock brakes became standard in the U.S. with the 1986 model. Slightly larger pistons in the front calipers of the 928's massive brakes were the only change deemed necessary to deal with the S4's

higher speed capability.

Inside, only the seat adjustments are different. In addition to the familiar power controls for fore-and-aft position, front and rear height, and seatback angle, lumbar support can now be adjusted as well. A bladder can be inflated electrically to provide the desired amount of lower-back support, and its vertical position is also power-adjustable. Three four-way switches on the door side of each seat control all of these variables. A memory panel on each door stores up to three combinations of seat positions and side-mirror settings.

All of these changes should add up to a radically improved car. To find out for sure, we arranged to borrow an early 928S4 prototype; unfortunately, it wasn't completely up to snuff. Not only did its engine feel sluggish, but its curb weight was a porky 3620 pounds. That wasn't too surprising, because every available option (including an automatic transmission) was

present and accounted for.

Although we did test the one and only S4 prototype available in the U.S., the resulting performance figures were so far out of line in every category but braking that we've decided not to soil the record with misleading information. We'll follow up with a test of a production 928S4 as soon as the factory can deliver us a car with representative performance.

We were able to draw some conclusions from our time with the prototype, however. On the road, the S4's larger rear tires are a definite improvement. Contrary to the claims Porsche makes for the self-steering Weissach rear axle, a typical 928 will kick its tail out smartly if its throttle is released in midcorner. The 928S4, however, is noticeably tamed in this respect. There is still enough oversteer to help rotate the car in tight turns, but not so much that you have to hold your breath when you use it.

Another addition to security is the anti-lock brakes. Despite our test car's prodigious weight, it stopped from 70 mph in 183 feet without requiring any fancy footwork from the driver. And we observed absolutely no brake fade.

Interestingly enough, the restyled 928 didn't generate any rubbernecking on the street. Perhaps that's not surprising: except for the eye-popping rear wing, the changes are rather subtle. Indeed, the rounder contours and the almost flush lights give the car less of a sculptured appearance than it had before. If the 928 looks better and sleeker now, it's also a bit less distinctive.

All of the improvements have a price, of

Vehicle type: front-engine, rear-wheel-drive, 2+2-passenger, 3-door coupe

Base price: $58,900

Available options: high-output air conditioning, limited-slip differential, heated seats, variable lumbar support, memory seats, sport shocks, raised steering-wheel hub, burglar alarm

Standard accessories: power steering, windows, seats, locks, and sunroof, A/C, cruise control, tilt steering, rear defroster and wiper

Sound system: Blaupunkt Monterey, AM/FM-stereo radio/cassette, 8 speakers

ENGINE

Type	V-8, aluminum block and heads
Bore x stroke	3.94 x 3.11 in, 100.0 x 78.9mm
Displacement	303 cu in, 4957cc
Compression ratio	10.0:1
Engine-control system	Bosch Motronic with port fuel injection
Emissions controls	3-way catalytic converter, feedback fuel-air-ratio control, auxiliary air pump
Valve gear	belt- and chain-driven double overhead cams, 4 valves per cylinder, hydraulic lifters
Power (SAE net)	316 bhp @ 6000 rpm
Torque (SAE net)	317 lb-ft @ 3000 rpm
Redline	6100 rpm

DRIVETRAIN (Manual)

Transmission 5-speed
Final-drive ratio 2.20:1

Gear	Ratio	Mph/1000 rpm	Speed in gears
I	4.07	8.0	49 mph (6100 rpm)
II	2.71	12.0	73 mph (6100 rpm)
III	1.93	16.8	102 mph (6100 rpm)
IV	1.46	22.2	135 mph (6100 rpm)
V	1.00	32.5	165 mph (5100 rpm)

DRIVETRAIN (Automatic)

Transmission .... 4-speed automatic
Final-drive ratio 2.20:1

Gear	Ratio	Mph/1000 rpm	Max. test speed
I	3.68	8.8	54 mph (6100 rpm)
II	2.41	13.5	82 mph (6100 rpm)
III	1.44	22.5	137 mph (6100 rpm)
IV	1.00	32.5	162 mph (5000 rpm)

DIMENSIONS AND CAPACITIES

Wheelbase	98.4 in
Track, F/R	61.1/60.9 in
Length	178.1 in
Width	72.3 in
Height	50.5 in
Frontal area	21.0 sq ft
Ground clearance	4.7 in
Curb weight	3500–3620 lb
Weight distribution, F/R	50/50%
Fuel capacity	22.7 gal
Oil capacity	7.9 qt
Water capacity	16.9 qt

CHASSIS/BODY

Type	unit construction
Body material	welded steel and aluminum stampings

INTERIOR

SAE volume, front seat	53 cu ft
rear seat	21 cu ft
trunk space	8 cu ft
Front seats	bucket
Seat adjustments	fore and aft, seatback angle, front height, rear height, lumbar support
General comfort	poor fair good **excellent**
Fore-and-aft support	poor fair good **excellent**
Lateral support	poor fair good **excellent**

SUSPENSION

F: .... ind, unequal-length control arms, coil springs, anti-roll bar
R: .... ind, unequal-length control arms, coil springs, anti-roll bar

STEERING

Type	rack-and-pinion, power-assisted
Turns lock-to-lock	3.0
Turning circle curb-to-curb	37.7 ft

BRAKES

F: .... 12.0 x 1.3-in vented disc
R: .... 11.8 x 0.9-in vented disc
Power assist .... vacuum with anti-lock control

WHEELS AND TIRES

Wheel size	F: 7.0 x 16 in; R: 8.0 x 16 in
Wheel type	forged aluminum
Tires	Dunlop SP Sport D40 F: 225/50VR-16; R: 245/45VR-16
Test inflation pressures, F/R	36/44 psi

MFR.'S PERFORMANCE RATINGS	manual	auto
Zero to 60 mph	5.7 sec	6.3 sec
Standing ¼-mile	14.1 sec	14.7 sec
Top speed	165 mph	162 mph
Fuel economy, EPA city	15 mpg	16 mpg
EPA highway	23 mpg	21 mpg

course—and the fact that the dollar has fallen so dramatically with respect to the deutsche mark in the past year doesn't help matters any. The 928S4's base tariff is $58,900, and a car equipped like our prototype with every conceivable option will cost about five grand more. If that seems like a lot, keep in mind that the 928S4 will

run with the Ferrari Daytona and Lamborghini Miura of legend and lore, and with a lot more practicality.

In the 928's league, normal concerns of price and value simply don't apply. The only question is this: How much automotive hedonism can you afford?

—Csaba Csere

PORSCHE APPEAL

The Porsche 928 was originally designed to replace the evergreen 911, but became popular in its own right. There are excellent second-hand cars for sale as Graham Robson reports

The amazingly successful Porsche 911 was always going to be a difficult act to follow, and even the resourceful Stuttgart concern did not find it easy. After agonising for some years on the right way to replace the 911, it produced a car diametrically different in every way — front-engined where the 911's engine had been at the rear, water-cooled instead of air-cooled, anonymously styled rather than broadhipped and aggressive.

The howls of dismay could be heard all the way across the Atlantic. To its astonishment, Porsche found that the 911 steadfastly refused to die, the 928 did not sell as fast as it had hoped — and the result was that both types have been built, side-by-side in the range, ever since.

Nevertheless, the 928 is a supercar in every way — and, at the price asked, so it should be. Even the original versions had astonishing straight line performance (a top speed of 142 mph, for instance), the roadholding has always been impeccable, and the cars have improved significantly over the years.

Nearly 2000 examples have been imported to the UK, and a significant number are now on the secondhand market. Against obvious rivals like the Jaguar XJ-S and the BMW 635CSi, how does it stand up, today?

WHAT IS A 928?

Compared with the 911 range, the 928 family is easy to describe, because it has only appeared, so far, in one guise though in a variety of mechanical tunes. The 928 is a front-engined, rear-drive coupé, with smooth, somewhat characterless styling, and headlamps which peer upwards to the sky, but flush with the bonnet, when not in use. There is two plus two seating (that in the rear is strictly 'occasional') and, because of the rear-end style, the boot is rather small, though you can enlarge the space by folding forward the rear seats.

Mechanically, the 928 is everything you might expect from Porsche — big, torquey light-alloy V8 engine, choice of manual or automatic transmissions, all independent suspension, all-disc braking installation and, although the shape is not all that aerodynamically efficient by 1985 standards, it still looks good, allowing 17-20 mpg economy from what is a ferociously powerful car.

The big advance, Porsche claimed, was in the rear suspension, where the new 'Weissach' linkage tamed the on-limit handling completely. In all respects, in fact, the 928 is a very efficient car which, paradoxically enough, means that it seems to lack character in certain ways.

ENGINE

For the 928, Porsche designed an all-new V8 unit, with principal castings in light-alloy, one single overhead camshaft per bank, hydraulic tappets, driven by toothed belts, and with Bosch fuel-injection.

The original 928 had 4474cc, and 240bhp, plus 257lb/ft peak torque at 3600rpm. Although that gave high performance by any standards, it was not enough to satisfy some customers so, in only two years, the 928S version was announced.

For 928S, apart from its new aerodynamic aids, had a larger 4664cc engine, in which power had leapt to 300bhp at 5900rpm, and 283lb/ft torque at 4500rpm. As the comparison makes clear, this was an altogether more sporty (but no less flexible) unit, with much of the extra urge coming in above about 3500rpm. This engine was never made available on the 'basic' 928, which was withdrawn from the UK market in mid-1982.

The latest change, phased in from September 1983, was when the 928S became 'Series 2'. In this guise, the 4.7-litre engine was given Bosch Type LH electronic fuel injection, and electronic ignition, boosting peak power to 310bhp at 5900rpm, and peak torque to 295lb/ft at 4500rpm. Porsche claims better fuel economy by about 10 per cent in day-to-day driving, though our 1984 test didn't confirm this.

TRANSMISSIONS

Ten or 20 years ago, would we ever have considered a car like this with automatic transmission? Nowadays, there is no doubt — a good proportion of 928s and 928Ss have this fitting.

The manual transmission is a solidly-built five-speed, all-synchromesh unit. For the 928S2 the ratios were altered very slightly but, all-in-all, the box helps provide towering performance. The overall gearing is such that the 928s can all beat 60 mph in second gear, and achieve nearly 120 mph in fourth.

Until the autumn of 1983, the automatic transmission (a conventional torque-converter type, from Daimler-Benz) had three forward ratios, and a direct top gear but, for the S2 model only, the latest four-speed/direct-top Daimler-Benz transmission has been used instead. The ratio-change lever is between the seats and, as you might expect, the top speed is a few mph down on the manual version, but well over 100 mph is available (at more than 6000rpm) in second or third as appropriate.

MODEL CHOICE

For the secondhand buyer, there is very little confusion. At first only the 928 model was available, for which there was no choice of

The Porsche 928 has so far only appeared in one body shape, although in differing levels of mechanical tune. It is a front-engined, rear-wheel drive coupé powered by a torquey light-alloy V8 engine with a choice of one manual or two automatic transmissions

shapes, and only the major option of manual or automatic transmission.

Then, from the beginning of 1980, the new 928S was marketed alongside the 928 — 300bhp and spoilers, versus 240bhp and original smooth style. In the case of the 928S, however, there was no

only a transmission choice, but the possibility of specifying a limited-slip differential, for £335 at 1980 prices). In 1980 and 1981, 928 and 928S sales in the UK were almost equal (289 to 292) but the 928 faded out in 1982, with 62 cars delivered.

The 928S S2 took over direct from the 928S, and is still with us. The limited-slip differential price had risen to £460, and it is worth noting that there was an £846 electric sunroof option too!

AVAILABILITY

Figures supplied by Porsche show that 1865 928s of all types were sold in the UK by the end of 1984 — and we think that more than 1000 of these will already have changed hands at least once. The choice, therefore, is somewhat limited — statistically most will be original-type 928s, of which 739 were imported.

There is, of course, another major consideration. Remember that there are only 28 Porsche dealers, nationwide and, to get service, you might need to travel a considerable distance from your home.

Once you find your Porsche dealer (the importer's HQ is in Reading, by the way), there should be no problem in finding parts. Even the oldest 928s are only seven years old in this market, the basic design of body, running gear and suspension has not changed, so mechanics should be thoroughly familiar with all derivatives.

WHAT TO LOOK FOR

Before even sallying forth to buy a 928, ask yourself several questions: Can you afford one? Can you find enough choice? Is it the right size? What about insurance and parts prices?

Although we are sure that you could eventually find an early-model 928 for around £10,000 (that's the price for a new Ford Capri 2.8i Special, by the way), you should come to terms with the enormous cost of insurance — it is Group 8 — and the price of parts. Take a look at the standard *Autocar* table for confirmation. How about £448 for just a silencer box, or £233 for an exchange starter motor?

Still with us, and still breathing freely? Then here are some opinions about the worth, and the little ways, of the 928 range, which we assembled with the help of London's principal dealership, AFN of Isleworth, and the ▶

BUYING SECONDHAND
PORSCHE 928

APPROXIMATE PRICES

Price Range	928	928S
£10,300–£10,700	1979	
£12,300–£12,700	1980	
£14,700–£15,200	1981	
£15,500–£16,000		1980
£17,700–£18,200	1982	
£18,700–£19,300		1981
£21,700–£22,300		1982
£25,300–£26,000		1983

There was no new-car price difference between manual and automatic transmissions, and no significant difference in secondhand values.

PARTS PRICES

	928	928S	928S Series 2
Engine assembly — (new)	£6,051.30*	£12,092.25	£12,990.40
Short engine (exchange)	£2,389.70	£2,542.65	£2,542.65
Gearbox/transmission (exchange)	£2,234.45	£2,234.45	£2,234.45
Clutch driven plate (exchange)	£57.21	£51.75	£62.32
Clutch, complete (exchange)	£218.52	£215.04	£225.61
Automatic transmission, with converter (exchange)	£2,150.50	£2,150.50	£2,620.85
Brake pads — front set — (new)	£51.75	£51.75	£51.75
Brake pads — rear set — (new)	£40.48	£40.48	£40.48
Suspension dampers — front (each)	£63.99	£63.99	£63.99
Suspension dampers — rear (each)	£63.99	£63.99	£63.99
Water radiator assembly (new)	£434.75	£434.75	£434.75
Tyre price, typical	£173.65	£267.95	£267.95
Alternator (exchange)	£180.19	£180.19	£161.84
Starter motor (exchange)	£232.85	£232.85	£232.85
Headlamp unit — (each)	£102.71	£102.71	£102.71
Taillamp unit — (each)	£70.51	£70.51	£70.51
Front wing panel	£384.92	£384.92	£384.92
Front door — assembly	£626.75	£626.75	£626.75
Bumper, front, complete (new)	£125.12	£125.12	£125.12
Bumper, rear, complete (new)	£146.08	£146.08	£146.08
Windscreen, laminated	£253.00	£253.00	£253.00
Exhaust system — main silencer box	£382.37	£448.38	£448.38
Exhaust system complete	£941.45	£1,132.39	£1,132.39

Exchange   All the above prices include VAT at 15 per cent

RECOMMENDED REGULAR SERVICES

	Service Interval		
Change	300–1,200 miles	12,000 miles	24,000 miles
Engine oil	Yes	Yes	Yes
Oil filter	Yes	Yes	Yes
Gearbox oil	Check	Check	Yes
Sparking plugs	No	Yes	Yes
Engine air cleaner	No	Yes	Yes
Labour at £27.60/hour		£83.70	£83.70

SPECIFICATION AND PERFORMANCE

Specification:	928 5-speed	928 Auto	928 Auto	928S	928S Series 2
Engine size (cc)	4,474	4,474	4,474	4,664	4,664
Engine layout	ohc V8	ohc V8	ohc V8	ohc V8	ohc V8
Engine power (DIN bhp)	240	240	240	300	310
Car length	— 14ft. 7.1in. —				
width	— 6ft. 0.3in. —				
height	— 4ft. 3.9in. —				
Boot capacity (cu.ft.)	7 or 14.1 cu.ft.				
Turning circle (kerbs)	36ft. 6in. approx.				
Unladen weight (lb)	3,350	3,347	3,342	3,390	3,390
Max. payload (lb)	926	926	926	713	713
Performance summary:					
	23 Dec. 1978	28 Oct. 1978	18 Apr. 1981	5 Apr. 1980	5 May 1984
Tested in *Autocar*:					
Top speed (mph)	142	138	140	152	158
0-60mph	7.5	8.0	7.2	6.2	6.2
Overall fuel (mpg)	17.1	14.6	15.9	17.5	16.6
Mpg at steady 70mph	n.r.	20.2	n.r.	n.r.	n.r.

General manager, Campbell Finlay.

Look for a car which has been properly serviced by a Porsche dealer (some have not), and particularly be sure you are being offered a 'genuine' UK-market example. Quite a few, apparently, have been personal imports, in a West German specification which is not nearly as complete as that of UK models.

Cheap and cheerful rebuilds have already been detected, of cars once written off officially by insurance companies after an accident, but then reconstructed. Beware — and it is this sort of cautionary note which makes a study of the service record doubly important. If you find a suspiciously cheap 928 for sale privately, try to arrange to have it inspected by a Porsche dealer—if the seller won't allow it, there will be a good reason.

Most 928s are kept for between two and three years by their first owners, and it is only with subsequent owners that upkeep starts to be neglected. The majority of all 928s, when new, go to high-flying professional men, entrepreneurs, and the like — most being driven well, and sympathetically, at that stage.

MECHANICAL

As you might expect from Porsche, well-kept 928s stand up very well to their high-speed jobs. The new-car warranty, after all, was for two years/unlimited mileage (the second year being borne by the concessionaires). They should be looked at every 6000 miles by a dealer, with a thorough service every 12,000 miles. At that point, brake pads will almost always need to be changed, for the 928 is a fast and heavy car which needs its brakes.

On the earlier cars, hard driving resulted in grooved discs which, if not changed, then continued to chew up pads fast, and not stop the car so well. With the latest braking system, things have improved, but it's worth a look, on the ramp, before clinching the deal.

Exhaust systems, incidentally tend to be another mechanical item needing early replacement, and these are costly, like most 928 parts. Clutches, too, tend to have a hard time on fast driven cars. You should be able to get a feel of the condition during the test drive.

The engine lasts well — even after seven years, very few need major rebuilds. The hydraulic tappets, if kept clean with regular oil changes, help give the valve gear an easy time. Check that the cogged camshaft drive belts are OK — any lack of performance, or a smoky exhaust might mean that the belt has jumped a cog, the timing might be deranged, and a valve might even have touched a piston.

A good way to be sure that the suspension geometry, and all the bushes, are in good condition on a secondhand car, is to get a feel for the steering on a test drive, particularly under braking, and also to look for uneven wear characteristics (or too-rapid wear in terms of tread consumed per 1000 miles) on the very expensive Pirelli P7 tyres. There is a good alternative now — the latest 928s are being delivered on Dunlop D4s.

Incidentally, no-one really seems to know why, but long-stored cars seem to 'sulk' — and not work well for a time when re-activated — so perhaps you should think twice about a 'summer-use' only example. As a guide, something like 19-20 mpg is an average day-to-day fuel consumption figure, very creditable for a car with such high performance.

It is worth noting that almost every 928 sold secondhand by a Porsche dealer will automatically carry the 'Official Porsche Centre Car Plan', which is a discreet way of saying 'Extended Warranty'. This covers the cars for 12 months against mechanical breakdown and is a good deal, which you should not miss.

BODY AND TRIM

The news regarding corrosion is very good—but, then, this is only to be expected of a car which carried a seven-year warranty against corrosion 'from the inside, out'. Many body panels are in galvanised steel, while all the opening panels — bonnet, doors, and hatch, together with front wings (which bolt on to the main monocoque) are in light alloy. The polyurethane 'bumpers' are deformable, and recover from light bangs.

Nevertheless, it is possible to inflict stone damage on some areas of the car, occurrences not covered by the warranty and, on earlier cars, there was evidence of this on the sills and the bottom of the doors (plus rear wings behind the wheel arches); later cars feature extra protection in this area.

Another minor defect, not entirely cured by all accounts, is that the headlamp setting adjus-

Above: 928 boasts true supercar performance and impeccable roadholding. It has also been steadily improved during its eight year history. Left: Every 928 sold here had air conditioning. Below left: Dealer servicing is essential

YEARLY IMPORTS

1978	928 4.5-litre	23
1979	928 4.5-litre	365
1980	928 4.5-litre	238
	928S 4.7-litre	164
1981	928 4.5-litre	51
	928S 4.7-litre	128
1982	928 4.5-litre	62
	928S 4.7-litre	221
1983	928S 4.7-litre	302
1984	928S 4.7-litre	311
Total Number		1,865

MODELS AVAILABLE

September 1977: Porsche 928 announced in West Germany. All-new 2+2-seater fastback Coupé, with 4.5-litre V8 engine, choice of five-speed manual or three-speed automatic transmission, all independent suspension.
Spring 1978: First UK imports in 240bhp/4.5-litre form.
January 1980: First imports of 928S model, like 928, but with 4.7-litre, 300bhp, and extra spoilers front and rear.
July 1982: Final imports of original 928 model. All UK imports now of 928S.
September 1983: 928S became Series 2, with Bosch L-Jetronic instead of K-Jetronic injection, ABS braking, four-speed automatic transmission and full air-conditioning all standard.
1985: Still in full-scale production, only one basic model.

ter cables — from lamps back to the driving compartment by the drivers' seat — may break. This will not be obvious until a new owner comes to use it, perhaps weeks or months after purchase, so check it out.

At the same time, it is worth carrying out a complete systems check of all the electrics in the car. It is a complex machine, and — Murphy's Law being what it is — there is always likely to be some minor defect, somewhere. Every 928 sold here, by the way, had full air conditioning, many had electric opening sunroofs, and quite a proportion, more recently, had leather trim.

If you intend to carry rear seat passengers on a regular basis, we think you should get them to join you on the test drive, to see that they have enough space (leg room in particular is limited), and that they don't feel claustrophobic behind those high-back front seats.

Finally, be sure that the character (or, even, the lack of idiosyncracies) of the 928 is right for you. Porsche dealers readily admit that these cars are completely different from the evergreen 911s, and attract a completely different class of owner. Which type are you? ∎

Facelifted 928S gains new 32 valve head, 320bhp and clever aerodynamic aids in latest guise. Storming performance takes in higher 168 mph maximum and handling is even better than before, making the Porsche a really fabulous car to drive

HEAVY METAL PLUS

The cold, hard facts say that the new Porsche 928S4 amounts to an extra £8015 for an extra ten brake horse-power. A lot more money for not much more power you might think. But the 928S4 is a lot of motor car, expensive or not. And continuing along the stat-istical theme, it costs £46,534, has 5.0-litres of V8 engine, 32 valves, 320 hor-sepower, and hits 168mph. That's the most impressive statistic of all.

Its new found handful of miles per hour has swept the 928S4 up into a very small supercar elite. It's not those extra 10 bhp that have wrung another 9 mph from the big Porsche. The reason for its improved performance lies in subtle aerodynamic improvements.

The plastic at the front and rear ends has been reshaped; there's an under-tray, a front spoiler, and a larger black plastic rear wing designed to kill lift. But, most clever of all, is a new system of electronically controlled slats in the nose that open or close – venetian blind style – to admit air into the engine bay.

It's a complex system with sensors picking up readings from coolant, air conditioning, the engine bay, the auto-matic transmission and so on, so that the electronic brains can determine how to position the slats – movement effected by servo-motors.

Greatest aerodynamic gain, with the slats fully closed, is just 0.01 reduction on the new 0.34 Cd value – Porsche can't (or won't) translate that into real life gains of speed or fuel usage. From anyone else it would look like overkill – but not from Porsche; it just lets you start to grasp the sheer depth of tech-nological detail that has gone into the development of the 928S4

For the new S4 is a demonstration of Porsche's current engineering prin-ciple that all versions of their cars should have identical performance, whether they run on leaded or unleaded fuel, with or without catalytic converters. The design parameters for the S4 were even more rigid: not only did all versions need identical per-formance, but they should also all be capable of running on lead-free fuel,

have the minimum possible servicing requirements, and – here's the tough one – have more performance and more torque than the previous version.

Now that's good news if you live in the USA or Sweden, or other such environmentally sensitive markets where tough emission rules have usually dictated lower powered ver-sions of most new models. Here in the UK where we still pollute the air fairly liberally, the S4 buyer gains more engine capacity and more valves but only that small improvement in power. The gain in torque is similarly small – from 295 to 317lb ft, but the torque peak is down a thousand revs to 3000rpm and the low-down torque considerably improved. The new S4 engine is, in fact, a development of the American specification 32-valve unit sold there since last year. Each exhaust camshaft of the twin-overhead cam heads is directly driven by belt, with the intake cam driven from it via a short chain. The head layout and cam drive is the same as that of the new 944S model.

The new model is quicker all round: 168mph and 0-60mph in 6 secs com-pared with 159mph and 6.2secs for its predecessor. The figures are all Porsche's own and they are usually conservative. Not that we managed to improve them. Even a 25 kilometre stretch of Black Forest autobahn wasn't sufficient to give the car free reign. At 160mph plus speeds the road unravels very quickly. With a Mer-cedes Benz 500SEL disappearing backwards in our dust, we saw the 928's speedometer needle glide smoothly – and quite effortlessly – past 260kmh (160mph). Our manually geared (and catalyst equipped, remember) Porsche was still willing but the autobahn exit was looming – and our nerves were fraying. The 928S4 is a car that can devour even the biggest of roads. If the speed wasn't

impressive enough – and it was, for few even of the supercars are as smooth, stable and unflurried at such speeds – then the sheer strength of the engine most certainly was. It's a sportscar V8, responsive to the throt-tle, keen to rev and with a hard-edged rasp to its exhaust note. Sample its torque by flooring the throttle at almost walking pace in fifth and it will pull away with unconcern.

Such torque and power make gear changing almost superfluous. For almost all practical purposes, even when travelling fast, one simply slips the shift occasionally between fifth and fourth. Little wonder, in fact, that 70 per cent of 928 buyers opt for the automatic transmission version with its four-speed Mercedes-Benz 'box. Indeed, the manual shift rules itself further out of favour by having that unfamiliar and slightly awkward dog-leg first change.

Unsporting though it might seem, the autobox does provide a near ideal combination of docility and response. The car can be cruised at relaxed revs in a high gear but the quick shifting 'box gives instant down-changes to the lowest available gear when the throttle is floored.

And, better still, the remarkable 928, with its rear-mounted gearbox puts that power straight down onto the road. Traction is superb and so too is the handling. Wider rear wheels and tyres are a detail change on the S4 model and have made a superb car that little bit better still.

It has the neutral handling balance of a racer, turning into corners with negligible body roll and no sign of understeer however determinedly the driver tries. Assisted steering, almost heavy such is its handling-biased set-ting, and which is quick and accurate, helps bring the car to life, too.

Powering hard through a bend will eventually edge the rear wheels out of

line, as will easing back the throttle in mid-corner. And if this remarkable chassis has a vice, it is that when over-steer is induced the tail pops out rather messily because of the weight concen-trated around the rear end.

Brakes are solidly reassuring – from the light pressure of a check stop to the standard ABS system for dire emerg-encies. Nevertheless, though it is a remarkable machine to drive hard, it is a daunting one as well. First im-pressions are of its size and width – of the sloping sides and bonnet disap-pearing from sight. Its width is not easy to judge on a narrow road and revers-ing can be a nightmare, such is the lack of visibility.

Rather like the Jaguar XJS, the 928S4 is a very self-indulgent machine; a lot of car surrounding a very small interior. It's a close-fitting 2+2: with the front seats comfortably adjusted, there is precious little rear room.

The seats already adjusted electri-cally – new on the S4 is a lumbar adjustment (electrically operated, nat-urally) and memory system to record and recall three different seat and door mirror positions.

Overall, though, the 928 remains something of an enigma. Despite the ferocious performance and superb handling it isn't an out and out sports car. being just that bit too big and brutal, yet it doesn't have the refine-ment of a grand tourer like the XJS.

But even if it can't easily be categor-ised, it is still a masterpiece.

MODEL:	PORSCHE 928S4
DATE IN UK:	October 1986
ENGINE:	4957 cc V8, 320 bhp
PERFORMANCE:	168 mph, 0-60 mph 6.0 secs
MPG:	14.4-30.0
PRICE:	£46,534

When it appeared out of the blue ten years ago, Porsche's exotic 928 shocked many people. Firstly, it dared to proclaim itself the successor to the revered 911 — but it had a front engine, and water-cooled at that. And then it sported that bulbous bumperless one-piece styling with window openings seemingly punched out of it. In the intervening decade, we have learned that the flat-six will continue alongside the V8, and we have seen the influence of this design watershed spread in diluted form to a wider range of cars. At the same time, the range of cars from Stuttgart has advanced on many fronts, with each of the types having its moment of glory. Lately it has been the four-cylinder cars in the limelight; now, with a completely revised four-valve per cylinder design, it is the turn of the V8.

Most important to the Porsche marketing effort is the fact that the proper order of things has been restored. With one of the most enviable development programmes of any sportscar maker, the Stuttgart cars constantly edge forwards like over-eager drivers sitting on the grid waiting for the green light. Pole position is meant to stay with the 928S, which Porsche calls its flagship, but it has been eclipsed on price not only by the almost mythical 959, but also by the rather ugly 911 Turbo SE.

But if there is one thing more confusing than a flagship which is not the dearest in the range, it must be a flagship which is not the fastest in the range. Being out-sprinted by the 911 Turbo was acceptable; losing out to a four-cylinder of half the size was not. This is exactly what happened when the 944 Turbo roared into the picture with performance in the upper reaches which equalled or surpassed the V8; however, the fifth-generation 928 has been given back the edge over its precocious junior.

This is not the first four-valve-per-cylinder version of the alloy V8 to be offered to the wealthy businessman: American customers have been driving a 5-litre 32-valve 928 known as the S3 since 1985, although this "smog special" was rated at 288 bhp, some 30 horsepower less than the current S4, whose vast but wholly controllable 320 bhp output applies to all markets, with or without catalytic exhaust converter.

Feeding fuel to the eight hefty cylinders of the 928 is a Bosch LH-Jetronic system with over-run fuel cut-off, linked to the EZK solid-state digital ignition computer; supremely accurate fuel-flow and individual timing adjustments for each cylinder, controlled by separate knock sensors, allow a high compression ratio of 10:1 in the TOP (Thermodynamically Optimised Porsche) head. In fact this ratio is slightly less than before, but accompanies all-round improvements: not only does the revised design produce considerably more torque, now totalling a mountainous 317 lb ft, it also burns lower octane fuel, and suffers no loss of

Grandest Tourer

power whatever when fitted with the catalytic convertor required by Germany and the USA.

A central spark-plug makes for even ignition within the silicon-coated cylinder, while there is no evidence of the low-rev flaccidity which afflicts small-capacity four-valve engines: peak torque is churned out at a textbook 3000 rpm, with the crest of the power curve at 6000. This means significant gains in mid-range overtaking performance over the S2 whose lesser torque peaked at 4100 rpm.

Hydraulic dampers locate the broad and massive power-plant within the narrow-lidded engine-bay. Induction is accomplished in the classic V8 manner, through the centre of the vee, with softly-polished inlet tracts adding only a couple of inches to the unit's height. Belt tension for the two camshafts per bank is monitored electronically, and the distributor is mounted on the end of one camshaft.

A variety of ducts is carefully blended within the curves of the revised nose, which also incorporates a discreet spoiler: the huge ventilated brake discs are rammed full of cool air by one set, while the flow to the combined oil and water radiator is automatically controlled according to thermal load, thus minimising drag whenever possible. Undeni-

ably a bulky car, the 928 has never been particularly sleek, a fact which one family car manufacturer's advertising exploited in boasting that its own product had "a lower Cd than a Porsche". But now that embarrassing 0.39 figure has dropped to 0.34, a real achievement which is due to the softer and longer nose and tail (making the S4 3in longer than the S2), subtly widened sills, a narrow but free-standing tail spoiler, and a large undertray.

Like all current cars from the company, the gearbox is at the back, though in the front-engined models it is attached to the engine by a substantial torque-tube through which the prop-shaft runs. This solid connection reduces any drive-line movement, and provides a firm mounting for the gear shift, should you specify the no-cost option of a five-speed manual 'box. Standard issue, though, is the four-speed auto, and with the pulling power of an ocean-going tug surging through it, I found myself for the first time quite content to let the machine choose its own ratios.

In many cases the torque-converter of an auto dulls the response of the engine it is attached to; not so the 928. Push the smooth throttle pedal and acceleration is immediate, building up forcibly as the revs rise and accompanied by a brief five-litre snarl. Press harder and the Mercedes-Benz four-speeder snaps down one ratio, shoving the occupants deep into the seats while the tach needle lingers at maximum torque and the speedometer spins in moments towards licence-threatening levels. The response is instant and predictable: the driver can feather the throttle to surge ahead in the same ratio, or instantly twitch the box into a lower gear at any point he likes. Determined foot pressure will call up a second downshift with even more dramatic results, but even here the nose lifts only a whisker during take-off.

No need to anticipate overtaking moves by using the selector lever to change down, as I usually do in lesser autos — the Porsche can do the job as quickly and with no effort, at the expense of a thump as it changes from second to third at full stretch. On dry roads, the new larger 245/45 VR 16 Dunlops at the back (the front retains the previous 225/50s) are easily capable of coping with the car's power, not a chirp being heard during gearshifts, and they remain impressive over wet roads, more so probably than the benchmark Pirelli P7. But maximum throttle needs respect in the rain.

It seems a pity that much of the engineering splendour of this vehicle is concealed beneath the flawless paint, for every component has been shaped from the best material for the job,

Well-fitted boot with luggage net and removeable soft cover.

and hang the expense — or at least pass it on to the customer, because there are seemingly plenty who will not bat an eyelid as the bill passes the £50,000 mark. The writer of that cheque will probably never see the elegant light alloy castings which comprise the suspension, or the compact four-piston brake calipers which bring race-track stopping power to the motorway, but he will feel the evidence of such care every time he puts the key in the ignition. There is a satisfaction which derives not from bhp figures or acceleration times but from putting a crafts-man's best work to its intended use.

Those alloy front wishbones are mounted in a conventional double set-up, with a combined spring/damper, to hold the front wheels in place, but the plump rump of this Grand Tourer is the home of the trend-setting "Weissach axle" which has inspired a new branch of chassis technology — positive rear wheel movement. Many manufacturers have now followed Porsche's engineers in putting the inevitable angle changes to good use, and indeed the 928 design seems rather simple in comparison with that of the Mazda RX-7 tested last month. It responds only to fore-and-aft inputs, but the effect is similar — it tends to introduce toe-in on the loaded outer wheel, minimising the likelihood of oversteer if the throttle is snapped shut half way through a roundabout.

However, like any car the 928 responds best to smooth driving, and it clings through the tightest bends in a supremely predictable way. A modicum of understeer tells the driver how hard he is pressing on, and if it starts to increase, a gentle lift of the throttle edges the fat coupé back into line. Its width is not difficult to cope with in itself, given the direct steering, but be prepared to give way in country lanes.

Steering action is good, though perhaps falling short of the super-sharp feel of the same company's 944 Turbo; assistance varies with both speed and load, giving roughly the same pleasant weight to the leather-bound wheel whether parking or travelling at 120mph. At such speeds directional stability is very good, with little reaction to side-winds, although vertical deflections do set up a squirming sensation which feels more to do with the suspension than the tyres. This is most pronounced when cresting a brow, when the car seems to wiggle its hips before resuming its course. And I was surprised to find that it bottomed out at the end of some (admittedly severe) dips.

Overall it deals well with bumpy roads, particularly at higher speeds when the rather sharp ride smooths out, but like other Porsches the wheels crash and thump over holes and even cats-eyes, sounding uncomfortable rather than feeling uncomfortable. Tyre rumble is about the loudest single noise; the engine, sadly perhaps, is completely insulated from the driver's ear except on full throttle. Another exception to this vow of

Recessed controls in seat-edge are fiddly; but overall cabin layout is excellent.

silence is when the letter-box of a sunroof is open, which introduces a roar like an express train.

ABS is part of the package, but I did not manage to invoke it, being sufficiently impressed by the normal action of the large ventilated discs and the four pads which grip each one. Dunlop, too, deserves credit for such rapid and consistent stopping.

Opening the heavy door and tipping the seat forward exposes the two rather dainty perches in the back, separated by the massive hump of the transaxle. These are small even for older children, and adults are unlikely to be squeezed in at all. Folding the backs down extends the luggage space quite usefully, though, giving a flat surface almost to the front seats. Surprisingly, cargo is better catered for in this supreme sports coupé than in most estate cars — not in terms of volume, of course, but in appointments: a tough luggage net covers the boot floor, there are strap anchorage points, and a quickly detachable cloth cover screens the boot alone or extends individually over the folded rear seats.

Supporting the crew is a pair of rather curvaceous seats which grip the hips much better than they look as if they should, with electric adjustment by some rather muddling switches down the side, and three memory positions. Yet despite all these variations, including lumbar adjustment, which I fiddled with constantly, I could not sit comfortably

for more than half an hour at a time.

Other aspects of the driving position are good: the bulky instrument housing moves up and down with the wheel, retaining a good view of the clear orange-needled dials and keeping the switches in fingertip reach. The ignition switch is also in this housing, instead of concealed at some awkward angle down on the column, while the climate is influenced by small sliders on a central panel. There are stalks for flashers (left) and wipers (right), plus another for the Tempostat cruise control for the lazy. The handbrake lever is of the fall-away type and well sited to the driver's right, together with a headlamp adjuster and the rear hatch release.

Extra vents are let into the door panels, and the driver also has the seat memories and the mirror controls by his right arm. Window and roof controls, though, are easily confused with the rear wash/wipe rocker, all of these being behind the T-bar gear selector.

Wide-angle driving lamps in the bumper allow for instant flashing, and augment the already superb headlamps, while further safety features include heated washer nozzles, and a secondary windscreen wash system which blasts the glass with concentrated cleaner strong enough to remove the usual messy peppering of massacred insects.

Well-equipped, but still inviting you to spend money on options, the 928S4 is far from being the stereotypical luxury car: a Jaguar

XJ-S for half the price would be that. Instead it argues forcibly to be a real sportscar, despite its great bulk and its mostly automatic sales. Even at high cornering speeds the 928S4 feels absolutely settled, asking for more acceleration to squirt from the exit of the bend, which can be fed in with complete confidence in the traction available. Pinpoint accuracy is there to be exploited through the wheel, and the massive-looking vehicle flicks one way or the other with almost ludicruous ease.

Combine these qualities with the beautiful finish of components and trim, the busy quiet it exudes on the motorway, and the uncomplaining way it will trickle through M1 roadworks jams, and it is difficult to draw a distinction between the Grand Tourer and sportscar labels. It is a fine compromise in function with no compromise in execution — a hatchback with luggage space which will quarter Europe in a day and provide immense satisfaction while running rings around many another sports aspirant.

And if you are likely to be one of the 300 or so who will buy one in a year, who cares what sort of car it calls itself?   **GC**

Model: 928S4
Maker: Porsche AG, Stuttgart
Importer: Porsche Cars GB Ltd, Reading
Engine: Front-mounted all-alloy V8, four valves per cylinder, four belt-driven cams. 4957cc (100 x 78.9mm), 10:1 cr, Bosch LH-Jetronic fuel injection, EZK electronic ignition. Power: 320 bhp. Torque: 317 lb ft.
Transmission: Rear-mounted transaxle: four-speed automatic
Suspension: (Front): alloy double wishbones, coil springs, telescopic dampers. (Rear): upper transverse link, lower semi-trailing arm, coil springs, telescopic dampers
Steering: Power-assisted rack and pinion
Brakes: 4-piston calipers and ventilated discs all round, servo, anti-lock system standard
Wheels: Alloy rims, 7J x 16 front, 8J x 16 rear
Tyres: 225/50 VR 16 front, 245/45 VR 16 rear
Performance: 0-60 mph: 6.5 sec; Max speed: 161 mph
Economy: 18.4 mpg overall
Price: £48,935. Test car extras: electric sunroof, £1221; heated seats, £148 per seat; total, £50,452
Summary: Striking shape, first seen ten years ago, brought right up to date. Practical, as all Porsches are; displays muted brio — breathtakingly fast but placid and smooth, without the hard edge of, say, the BMW M635. A glorious piece of engineering for the price of a house.

Narrow bonnet reveals V8 set well back in crammed engine bay.

If these cars were clothes this review would be Turnbull & Asser tussling with Hugo Boss. Or, if you prefer, bespoke old-money English meets cosmopolitan, slick-cut German. There are technical comparisons to be drawn certainly: both the Aston Martin V8 Vantage and the Porsche 928S4 are bulky, assertive V8 coupés, with heritages verging on the legendary. What separates them are the design attitudes they pig-headedly stick to.

In pure design terms, both are particularly self-indulgent. There is comfortable space for only two adults in each and, if the back-seat passengers are youngsters rampaging through a bout of pre-school hyperactivity, they won't be comfortable for long either — these are cars for couples. The Porsche weighs in at a beefy 3526lb with the Aston lumbering behind at 3985lb; the 928S4 is a cigarette under 15ft long and the Aston a cigar over.

For European roads these fat-bellied cars are never less than hefty. As two-seaters they make as much sense as running a Boeing 737 as an executive jet.

Turn the ignition key in the Aston and the starter clanks while the engine teases, chuckles and catches with a grunt. Suddenly it's alive

It takes 16 weeks to build a Vantage, its hand-applied paintwork is glossier than the production-line metallic of the Porsche, but chips more easily

Turn the ignition key in the Porsche and it will start instantly — the engine note dry and sexless. At this point you may notice that the typography on the instrument faces is not the only feature to resemble the Volkswagen Golf GTI 16V; the soft, early-morning whirr of the V8 is also a distant cousin of the Golf's suburban rasp.

Twist the Aston into life and the starter clanks while the engine teases, chuckles, catches with a grunt — suddenly, the car is alive. Once awoken this engine has a deep V8 backbeat. It snuffles and bellows, reminding you of its eagerness to have fun.

The Porsche turned heads in its first incarnation 10 years ago with the soft-edged convex curves of its exterior. Its cockpit mouldings flow and mimic the exterior in gentle contours — while the upholstery leather and pinstripe cloth carpeting are cleverly toned, muted, subdued and restful. Porsche is not afraid to specify exactly the right materials for the job: the dashboard is plastic, a lot of switches are rubbery turn-knobs, the treads on the doorsills are black plastic with a transparent 928 logo let into them so that the body colour gleams through.

In contrast, Aston Martin designers have had it drilled into them that plastic is bad. Their PVC phobia has resulted in a cloying aroma of Connolly hide wafting among fingerprint whorls of walnut veneer while the door treads on the Vantage are burnished, easy-scratch stainless steel.

Even the steering wheel has a rim of mirror-lacquered wood. A bank of identical switches are a stretch away down on the console, the pedals are hung from oddball stalks which sprout from the floor and the handbrake is a heavy, chromed, fly-off lever nuzzling your left leg.

The Aston's interior is a peculiar form of design shorthand. It has the formality of a stateroom and the visual codes of old England: that sickly, playing-cricket-on-the-village-green symbolism to be found in fashion magnate Ralph Lauren's American advertising campaigns.

It is every bit as considered as the Porsche's '80s functionalism, but after a while you start to wish the Aston interior had a solitary feature approaching the ergonomic delight of the 928S4's instrument binnacle.

This ovoid pod has seven important displays within the circumference of the leather-wrapped steering wheel, which move with the column as you adjust it up or down so that the instruments are always visible. Tall Aston users, on the other hand, find the outer reaches of column adjustment on the Vantage comprehensively mask all the minor dials, leaving only the speedometer and tachometer in view.

Drive the 928S4 first. Surprise number one is that it seems noisy, although not from the engine — which remains dry and slightly metallic-sounding throughout. The 225/50 fronts and 245/45 rear Goodyears swoosh and the suspension has a slightly intrusive throb. But the noise is — and this is absolutely clear after the first 400 yards — a by-product of the continual feed of useful, unclutted information coming to the driver through the steering and the seat of his pants.

Initially, and at low speed, there is a stickiness to the steering and the throttle feels weighty and long-travel: you would have to jab it to make the Porsche sprint. The combination

of these characteristics has a two-fold effect. First, the car is a sweetheart around town and in traffic. You can place it accurately on traffic-cramped urban roads and creep along on the throttle. You also get the feeling that driving this car fast is going to be an extremely rewarding experience.

Start off in the Aston and, compared with the Porsche, it is like going back 10 years. In the 928S4, with its Bosch electronic fuel injection and engine management, everything is microchip-monitored. The Aston, with four rally-car Weber carburettors clambering out of the vee of this huge 5.3-litre engine, has a much more shambling character.

It takes four or five miles for both the engine and the solidly clonky ZF manual gearbox to warm up. Until then, double-declutching up and down the box smooths out the long-throw, notchy shifts. The throttle is incredibly ▶

After four or five miles the Aston's 5.3-litre engine and ZF manual gearbox warm up. Until then you have to double declutch up and down the box to smooth out the long-throw notchy shifts. The throttle is incredibly sensitive; blip it when the car is stationary and the whole front end shimmies and trembles

The Porsche is astonishingly capable; there is grip aplenty, but also a surety of control and poise that has been refined through lap after lap at the old Nurburgring

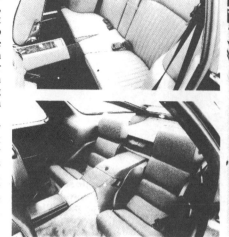

The Aston's interior is all Connolly hide and walnut veneer. Even the steering wheel has a rim of mirror-lacquered wood. The Porsche's cockpit mouldings flow and mimic the gentle curves of the exterior. The dash is a plastic pod with seven displays within the circumference of the leather-wrapped wheel

sensitive; blip it when the car is stationary and the whole front end of the Aston shimmies. There is an enormous feeling of power from the moment the temperature gauge needle swings into the middle of its arc. The clutch is heavy, while the brake pedal is not only hard work but also feels dead unless the brakes are warmed up gently. The steering is lighter than the Porsche and the low-speed ride more supple, although the Porsche dives more dramatically under braking. But generally, the major controls on the Aston seem intended to be handled by big blokes who believe real driving demands a touch of gymnastics.

On the motorway, the Porsche holds few surprises. The noise level increases, but not beyond the volume that can be drowned by listening to a radio news bulletin. Wind rush is muted and the air conditioning is quiet. You could drive this car from Calais to Nice in a day or run from Munich to Hamburg at twice Britain's legal limit without suffering any kind of sensory deprivation at the end of the trip.

The Aston is noisy at 80mph or more on the motorway: not merely sports car-cliché noisy but Polonez noisy, irritatingly noisy. There's wind roar, induction-roar and tyre roar plus a few bodyshell creaks over transverse ridges. Yes, the Vantage will top 165mph but you suspect you might suffer marked hearing loss during the run-up to two and a half miles a minute. Away from the motorway, the characteristics of the Porsche are the easiest to explain. Its detractors would imply that it is efficient to the point of *ennui*: a more upbeat description is that it is astonishingly capable.

There is grip aplenty, but also a surety of control and poise which hints that the car has been refined through lap after lap at the old Nurburgring. Make a mistake, misjudge a corner and take it too fast or turn too late, and the Porsche is with you all the way — neutral, able and waiting to react.

Initially it understeers and then sets into a stable neutrality. The stickiness disappears from the steering and the throttle seems to become lighter and more sensitive. Yes, it oversteers in moments of abject stress, but you always feel that you can control it and master the car. That level of supreme controllability is, presumably, due to two factors. First, the front engine, rear transaxle layout pushes the car towards an optimum 50:50 weight distribution. Second, the patented Weissach axle stops the outside rear wheel destabilising the car into the nearest hedge, should you find it necessary to lift off in mid bend.

It is not perfect, though. The four-speed automatic gearbox shifts smoothly and slides unobstructed from drive to three when you require lightening acceleration. But, on winding roads when time is pressing, you may want to drop from three to two for some head-down overtaking or fast exits out of tight corners.

There is a chasm lurking between ratios three and two: and not being able to use the vast engine braking effectively within the 5-litre V8 — as you could in the five-speed manual option by, say, dropping from fifth to third gear — takes the edge off the car. Yet the autobox is so good in every other driving condition that it is the only sensible transmission to specify for the Porsche 928S4.

The Aston, as befits the menace inherent in the blanked-off grille with its bull mastiff's sneer, is much more of a traditional driver's car, which makes it a harder proposition. It has a manual five-speed box with a racing shift

pattern that has first down and left on the basic H-gate, and it requires a far greater physical effort to hustle on winding roads.

On A-roads it feels really good. Compared with the Porsche it takes a greater swing of the steering wheel to get the Vantage to turn in, even though the cars share a three-turn lock-to-lock steering response. It feels clumsy, but it's not: the ride is better than the Porsche's on A-roads with its long-travel springing and prodigious grip. It takes longer to become confident in the Aston because the suspension and steering feel slightly less direct than the satin-wired reactions of the 928S4. The steering is also more upset by bumps.

The Aston is far quicker than the Porsche. Aston Martin has now come out of the closet and revealed that the Vantage specification V8, with hotter cams, quad-Webers instead of Bosch injection and a boosted compression rate, produces 403bhp at 6200rpm with a torque peak of 390lb ft at 5000rpm. The Porsche figures are much lower: 320bhp at 6000rpm and 317lb ft at 3000rpm.

The Vantage is astonishingly fast, especially given the bulk of the machine. Torque and acceleration are both thunderous: floor the throttle in gears three, four or five and the Vantage snorts and flies off. The 928S4, by contrast, is quick in Drive, but has to be snatched into three to really move. Even then it will be humbled by the Vantage on any kind of

The Aston is far quicker than the Porsche. It has hotter cams, quad-Webers instead of Bosch injection and a boosted compression ratio. The hand-built 5.3-litre V8 produces 403bhp compared with 320bhp from Porsche's 5-litre unit. The Aston's torque and acceleration are awesome: floor the throttle in three, four or five, and the Vantage snorts and powers away

The Aston's menacing blanked-off grill with its bull mastiff sneer tells it like it is: this is a real drivers' car. The curvaceous skin of the 928S4 hides a more-refined engine and transmission

rewarding. In many ways, especially if you gloss over the silliness of the heavyweight two-seater concept, it is a design paragon.

Aston Martin claims it takes 16 weeks to build a Vantage. Every engine is constructed by one man who signs the motor off by placing a brass plaque with the craftman's name engraved on it on a rocker cover. So what? Any automotive engineer will tell you that computer-aided design and robotic assembly makes the family box of today a finer car than the handbuilts of yesteryear. The hand-applied paint of the Vantage is glossier than the production line metallic of the Porsche, granted, but it chips more easily.

There is one other factor to consider. Even though the Porsche costs £54,827 you probably don't need to talk to your accountant before buying. Porsches might not hold their value quite as well as they did in the early '80s but a glance at the car ads in *The Sunday Times* or *Autocar* will confirm that you can turn your 928S4 back into a stack of readies quite easily. The Aston, at £79,500, is more of an acquired taste and less easy to sell.

In the end, Aston versus Porsche comes down to craftmanship versus design. The Porsche is slower outright, but quicker A-to-B than the Aston. With its V8-bellow and trad appearance, the Aston is much raunchier than

straightline drag contest.

The Porsche also lacks the panache of the Aston's V8: the all-British motor bellows, roars and feels constantly alive and direct. In contrast, the Porsche V8 is cool, austere and trustworthy; the Aston Martin has a big hearted, prop-forward of an engine.

The Porsche has a fine anti-lock, all-ventilated disc brake system. Porsche claims it will slow the car from 62mph to a standstill in 3.3 secs on dry tarmac and our experience of its everyday performance hints that such a claim is no idle boast.

In the Vantage, the brake pedal demands much higher pressure and the discs are often cold and grabby on first application, which is disconcerting. What is more worrying, even morally questionable, is the fact that you cannot purchase this two-ton, 168mph car with any form of anti-lock braking system. This also

raises the question of whether the Aston Martin, for all its gut-busting performance, should be regarded as a serious performance car while it displays such an omission.

Should you take the Aston upcountry onto tight, bumpy, patchwork surface roads you will find that it loses its composure long before the Porsche. It bucks and writhes while the Porsche exudes an unruffled calm as it buckles down to coping with any shenanigans. Although slower in absolute terms, it is probably faster than the Aston in A-to-B driving because it is so much more restful and, thanks to that neat instrument binnacle, fools you into thinking that it is a narrow car, narrower even than its baby sister 944. The Aston never feels less than massive, nor shrinks around the driver like the Porsche does.

You adapt faster to the 928S4. It is more 'user-friendly' than the Aston but always

the comparative austerity of the 928S4. The Vantage is Arnold Schwarzenegger flexing his muscles in a silk suit; a hand-stitched two-piece cut by tailors who ask which way 'sir' dresses. It is definitely not a ready-to-wear shoulder-padded number aimed at light beer drinkers. That is the difference.

The Porsche is the better car. The Aston transmits a more subtle series of codes about the driver. It is an old school tie sporting four Weber carburettors. The Porsche has a crushing arrogance, plumbed through its awesome capabilities: the people who buy the 928S4 expect it to be as reliable and as useful a lifestyle accessory as a cellular telephone. The fact that it will happily cruise at 140mph may be less important.

For all its foibles, you would love the Vantage. For all its competence, you would grow to respect the Porsche. ∎

The Business

There's a belter of a Press release that accompanies Porsche's new £56,000 928S4 SE into the hands of its appraisers. Its message is plain and unequivocal. Yuppies, contrary to the media-induced hype, don't buy Porsches. It's not that they wouldn't like to. Simply that they can't afford to. What a relief.

As Porsche GB MD Peter Bulbeck has intimated many times in recent months, the spotty City brats can't hack the repayments. What with the phone number mortgage, the platinum plastic and all those career-smart subscriptions, the fabled six-figure salaries are all but devoured by the priority trappings of a Docklands lifestyle. According to Porsche's research, these do not include garage space for an expensive German sports car with a nickable badge.

Although Porsche GB don't dwell on this revelation, it seems chillingly compatible with the company's increasingly lofty pricing policy and shrinking share of the UK market. To quote from the release, "34 per cent of owners are aged between 40 and 49 (average age 39) . . . 62 per cent admit that they earn over £40,000 a year . . . Managing Directors, Director/Partners and Chairmen collectively account for the bulk of Porsche owners". Not an over-committed yuppie in sight. The word is, *they* all drive 3-Series BMWs and Golf GTis, cars which offer entry-level one-upmanship but conspicuously good value for money at the same time.

The most obvious conclusion to draw from all of this is a depressingly cynical one: Porsches are overpriced and driven by super-successful ageing businessmen who, having 'made it', can afford to 'spend it' in an indulgent and

Yuppies, contrary to the media-induced hype, don't buy Porsches

thing to an American musclecar of the Sixties

totally gratuitous manner.

If this is indeed the case, then the 928S4 Special Equipment is a very curious creation indeed. In essence, it's the 928 Club Sport – a stripped, lightened and tweaked version of the S4 developed for a spot of production sportscar racing among other things – with all the standard S4's luxury kit re-applied. The point is that it's a UK 'special': no one over here would buy the plain CS off the peg. They wanted all the goodies; as, indeed, the in-house customer profile research predicted they would. So Porsche GB made it easy for them by tarting up the CS, hiking the price and calling it the SE.

On paper, it adds up to the ultimate 928: all the svelte sophistication and habitability of the mainline S4 with the grunt, grip and handling of the quasi-racer CS. In reality, however, it adds up to serious schizophrenia.

Without wishing to give too much away at this stage, the SE is probably the nearest thing to an American musclecar of the early Sixties a great deal of money can buy. I don't say this lightly. The original 928S which charmed the world's motoring Press at the beginning of the decade with its peerless combination of grand touring abilities is but a distant relation of the red-raw SE. You wouldn't want to tackle 500 miles of autobahn in this car. It would be too tiring. Think of a Shelby Mustang with handling, brakes and superb build quality, however, and you're getting closer to the mark. I hardly like to say it, but the SE could seriously damage your health.

The weight paring that shaved a substantial 210lb from the S4 for its CS incarnation is largely irrelevant here. The SE carries all the standard equipment of its S4 running mate plus wider wheels and tyres. The good-looking 8J/9J 16in forged alloys wear 225/50 VR 16 and

245/45 VR 16 uni-directional Bridgestones. The 'fat foot' aesthetics are enhanced by a brace of spacers at the tips of the rear driveshafts which widen the rear track by 0.6in. The car also sits lower on shorter springs which are 10 per cent stiffer and work with the recalibrated gas-filled dampers to provide a much tauter chassis. It almost goes without saying that a limited slip differential is standard.

As for the engine modifications, Porsche are surprisingly reticent to divulge their exact nature. The 34-valve quad-cam 5-litre V8 develops, in standard form, a claimed 320bhp and 317lb ft of torque. These outputs are unchanged for the SE, despite the use of recalibrated camshafts with greater valve lift, modified engine management and a freer-breathing exhaust system. The intention, say the Weissach engineers, was to change the engine's response characteristics, not to build more muscle. If that was the case, I'd say they failed magnificently. As the figures in the performance table show, with due allowance for the previously tested S4's auto transmission, the SE is more flexible, more accelerative and faster flat out than the standard article.

It must be said that the transmission mods have a part to play here. The big V8 drives to the rear wheels via an uprated five-speed manual transmission with a 2.73:1 final drive, some 3.4 per cent shorter than the standard S4's. But let's not mince statistics: any car that will blast round Millbrook at 163.5mph (a true 175mph on the flat), thump its occupant from 0 to 60mph in 5.3 seconds and dispose of all the fourth-gear 20mph increments between 30 and 100mph in around four and a half seconds apiece is monstrously quick.

There's nothing about the hollow, slightly gutteral, timbre of the burbling engine note at tickover to warn the unsuspecting of what lies in wait. At rest, or trickling round town, this Porsche is docility personified. Progress is smooth, well damped, almost anti-climactic. Feed the power in gently and the SE responds in kind, wafting forwards with almost benign indifference.

The clutch is remarkably light and the gearchange, while no paragon of slickness and distinctly vague in the 3/4 plane, is far from being a trial of strength. So far, so suave.

That said, the cabin – which, as ever, looks as if it's been sculpted from a solid chunk of leather – remains a masterpiece of Teutonic design. Both ergonomically and aesthetically, it's close to flawless with big, chunky controls, man-sized seats with decent thigh, lumbar and lateral support and a huge range of adjustability. The only major drawback here is that the gap between brake and accelerator pedals makes heel and toe downchanges too awkward to ever seem natural. Instrumentation hasn't changed at all over the years, nor has it needed to. The large oval binnacle, which moves up and down as a unit with the adjustable steering, contains some of the clearest dials in the business. In these respects, at least, the SE plays the luxury long-distance GT with real conviction.

The thing that strikes you about the cabin is the subtle infiltration of contemporary hot-hatch decoration. Porsche call it a full black leather interior with special black/red velour pinstripe seat inlays. I call it 928 à la Peugeot 205 GTI. It's nothing like as tasteless as the black and white tablecloth check seat facings that afflicted the original (pre-S) 928, but neither is it a patch on the genuine full leather number in the regular S4.

Take to the open road after a heavy expense-account lunch, though, and it's a dramatically different story. All the ease and effortlessness experienced drifting through the suburbs suddenly vanishes like a pleasant daydream. To move fast in the SE requires a mental as well as a physical change of gear. If it's your intention to feel the carpet with your right foot you'd better tense your neck muscles in preparation. If you don't, giving the SE its head means losing yours to the will of gravity. Heavy acceleration equals g-force, it's as simple as that. The big car growls, grabs the horizon by the collar and hauls it in. In real terms, it's quicker than a 911 Turbo and, this side of a 959 or F40, you don't get

Magnificent 5-litre quad-cam V8 uses LH injection/ management and undoubtedly develops more than the factory's claimed 320bhp. The proof is in the driving

much quicker than that. The ordinary S4 feels tame by comparison.

What you do with a charging SE if the road to the golf club is twisty and bumpy, however, is a matter of some concern. Whatever subtlety or finesse the 928's chassis may once have had it has lost. Its grip remains little short of phenomenal and you won't find a car of similarly generous proportions or weight with better body control. But the fatter tyres and stiffer suspension have turned what was once a minor irritation – a propensity to tramline over road markings and follow transient road camber changes – into a major issue. A car as wide as the 928 doesn't have the luxury of choosing its own course down the road – if it did, it would end up on the wrong side. What's worrying is that it isn't always possible to

persuade the SE of this, especially under braking. It weaves and squirms like a line-half. Without committing yourself to the laws of chance and probability, conducting the SE down a challenging country road with even a moderate degree of brio simply isn't on. Here's a supercar that really must fear to tread where hot hatchbacks regularly go.

More bad news for boardroom jockeys comes in the form of a board-hard ride and a level of road roar that, on a coarse surface, could easily send you crazy. A limited slip diff that makes the transition from a neutral cornering balance to very sideways indeed excitingly abrupt is another trait that the successful businessman with money to burn is bound to find fascinating.

Me? I loved it. Now, where did I put the 'fax . . .   M

PERFORMANCE

	928S4 SE	928S4 auto
Max speed, mph	163.5	158.7
Best 1/4 mile	166.3	161.5

Acceleration		
from rest, mph	sec	sec
0-30	2.1	2.7
0-40	3.0	3.7
0-50	4.1	4.9
0-60	5.3	6.4
0-70	6.8	8.1
0-80	8.5	10.6
0-90	10.3	13.2
0-100	12.7	16.1
0-110	15.4	19.5
0-120	18.6	25.5
0-130	23.2	—

Acceleration in 4th/5th*		
30-50	4.6/6.2	2.2
40-60	4.4/6.2	2.7
50-70	4.2/6.4	3.2
60-80	4.2/6.3	4.2
70-90	4.4/6.2	5.1
80-100	4.6/6.7	5.5
90-110	5.2/7.3	6.3
110-120	6.1/7.7	9.4

Overall mpg	16.2	17.4

*in kickdown for S4 auto

PORSCHE 928S4 CLUB SPORT

Little cause but great effect: We drive the quickest 928 ever made, one that will, sadly, remain in Europe.

BY GEORG KACHER

PHOTOGRAPHY BY MERVYN FRANKLYN

Stuttgart—

Autobahn Leonberg to Heilbronn. The speedometer needle accelerates toward the 135-mph mark, suggesting we pull the gear lever down into fifth. Eagerly picking up speed, the red 928 darts into a dip and up the following crest, briefly heading right for the sky. It's five in the morning, and traffic is still light on this three-lane autobahn, so it seems safe to press on. At the end of the long straight, the instruments indicate 180 mph and 6500 rpm, but even at this pace the 928 feels as solid as the *QE2*.

Time to back off. The nose dips only a fraction as the car slows down for the Bad Rappenau exit. Under braking, the fat Bridgestones tramline emphatically, but there is very little body roll, and the car instantly regains its poise as the horses are unleashed again to tackle this delicate third-gear right-hander. Although the power comes in forcefully

enough for the Japanese rubber to paint black stripes on the asphalt, keeping the balance is easy for this special 928. It simply surges ahead with vigor. As a change in road surface eventually kicks out the tail, the dialogue between driver and machine is so direct that even a moderately gifted driver can steer the Porsche back into line with no trouble at all.

As we pull into a filling station, the attendant notices the white-on-red Club

Sport graphics on the front fender. "A trick version again, eh?" is his rather casual remark. "The boss has a lightweight 911, but he isn't happy with it. Too stiff, no equipment, and not exactly a bargain, either. I'd be interested to see if they did a better job with the V-8."

We were interested, too, since Porsche's previous sport specials have indeed been quite controversial. The 911 Club Sport is a lot of fun but extremely uncompromising. In the case of the 944

Turbo S, some of the benefits of the serious engine and chassis are diluted by too many goodies that push up price and weight. The 928 Club Sport, however, turns out to be a well-balanced compromise that combines the best of both worlds: a sensibly tuned engine and suspension and a level of equipment that can satisfy the basic needs of both driver and passenger.

Although the marketing experts would have preferred the 928 Club

Sport to have been a big-money *boulevardier*, the engineers eventually had it their way. "This car is strictly for the performance-oriented customer," points out former Weissach chief Helmuth Bott. "It provides a lot more driving pleasure at the expense of a little luxury." Designed as a true lightweight model, the 928 Club Sport spent its first weeks in the body shop to shed as much surplus fat as possible, so the list of missing items is rather long. It includes

PORSCHE 928S4 CLUB SPORT

piles of sound-deadening material, rear wiper, central locking, power seats, rub strips, cruise control, rear sun visors, remote-control tailgate release, cassette boxes, oddments trays, and the original wiring harness, which was replaced with a less complex design.

Encouraged by the success of the first round of weight-saving measures, the engineers returned for an encore. This time, they tore out the windshield washer unit, reduced the contents of the tool kit, fitted lightweight aluminum wheels, and replaced the standard air conditioning unit with a lighter, more efficient one. And last, they removed the vibration damper from the transaxle tube and installed an uprated free-flow exhaust system with twin tailpipes. Thus modified, the car was rolled onto a platform scale and weighed in at 3263 pounds, down 201 pounds from the standard European production model.

After the slimming cure, the car went back to the shop for fine-tuning of the driveline and the suspension. The front springs, for instance, were lowered and stiffened by ten percent, the rear track was extended by one inch with a set of spacers, the shock absorber damping rate was increased by a couple of notches, and the wheel widths went up one inch, to sixteen by eight inches in the front and sixteen by nine in the back. The catalyst-equipped engine received hotter camshafts and a recalibrated injection and ignition system to push the redline up from 6000 to 6775 rpm. The five-speed manual transaxle (sorry, no automatic) is still rather balky and vague, but it now incorporates a limited-slip differential and a final-drive ratio shortened by three percent.

Despite this comprehensive catalog of changes, the performance data for the 928 Club Sport have—at least on paper—improved only marginally. The

figures Porsche quotes for power and torque are still the same (320 bhp at 6000 rpm and 318 pounds-feet of torque at 3000 rpm), but the V-8–engined weight watcher is three-tenths of a second quicker from zero to sixty (5.6 versus 5.9 seconds) and 4 mph faster overall (173 versus 169 mph). Did I hear you say, "It's hardly worth the trouble"? That was our initial reaction, too, but looking back at a memorable day in a very early 928 Club Sport, I can assure you that these figures don't tell the whole story. Driving is believing.

At a glance, it is difficult to tell the Club Sport V-8 from any off-the-peg 928S4, and yet this *déjà vu* impression changes the instant you turn the ignition key. The carefully revised 5.0-liter powerhouse not only sounds different, it also reacts differently to accelerator input. Low-end torque is unchanged, but there seems to be quite a bit more oomph on tap above 4000 rpm. Throttle response is lightning fast, the sheer unrestrained urge above 125 mph is second only to the 959's, and the unit's willingness to rev certainly equals that of the best Italian thoroughbreds.

Although the performance benefits of the low-calorie Club Sport may not be particularly impressive against the stopwatch, they become obvious out on the open road, where the engine's abilities team up with those of the modestly modified suspension. Yes, the chassis is rather harsh, traction can be a problem, and there is still too much bump-thump, but we gladly pay this price in exchange for fine handling, a most communicative steering system, superb brakes, and a degree of roadholding that cannot be matched by any other front-engine, rear-wheel-drive sports car. Especially at the limit, where too many high-performance machines feel twitchy and vague, the 928 Club Sport is incredibly sure-footed and unambiguous. As the saying goes, "When you do this, I'll do that." It never leaves the driver in doubt about its reactions, it always gives plenty of warning, and it requires no more than a quick flick at the leather-rimmed wheel to step back in line.

For drivers of the right bent—a profile Porsche considers too rare in the United States to justify sending over the lightweight 928—this biggest Club Sport model is the best 928 ever conceived. It is also arguably the most desirable Porsche this side of the mega-money 959. ∎

Although its appearance, trim, and specs are little changed, the lightweight 928 is faster, tougher, and more serious.

PORSCHE 928S4 CLUB SPORT
(European model)
Base price (approximate) $69,400

GENERAL:
Front-engine, rear-wheel-drive coupe
2-passenger, 2-door steel body

POWERTRAIN:
32-valve DOHC V-8, 302 cu in (4957cc)
Power DIN 320 bhp @ 6000 rpm
5-speed manual transmission

CHASSIS:
Independent front and rear suspension
Rack-and-pinion steering
12.0-in front disc, 11.8-in rear disc brakes
225/50ZR-16 front, 245/45ZR-16 rear
Bridgestone tires

MEASUREMENTS:
Wheelbase 98.4 in
Curb weight 3263 lb
Fuel capacity 22.7 gal

WESTERN WHEELING

California to Colorado in Porsche's V-8
▲
BY JOHN LAMM
PHOTOS BY THE AUTHOR

IT'S THE CONTRASTS that make life so interesting. That's why, when crossing the dry, brown, featureless landscape in that area where corners of Wyoming, Utah and Colorado meet, I couldn't help thinking of Vence, France. We were headed east on Interstate 40 toward Dinosaur, Colorado, site of the Dina Freeze, home of the Bronto Burger—in a bright red Porsche 928S 4, about to turn onto state route 64 for Rangely and Meeker, before cutting south on 13 to Rio Blanco and then the freeway at Rifle. Oddly enough, the drive brought back memories of the Alpes-Maritimes, and an earlier 928 route that I believe went inland from Vence to Courségoules, and then turned back to St Vallier de Thiey and Grasse before catching the *autoroute* near Mougins for Nice. No Bronto Burgers there, but great croissants.

These are not just the scattered thoughts of someone who has been standing in unleaded premium fumes. A journey from Los Angeles to Colorado Springs not long ago was my most recent trip in a 928, while the drive in France was the first for any journalist, because it was at the introduction of the car in early 1977.

Think of it, the 928 is that old. Just by chance, I'm writing this story on my 44th birthday, and when I first drove a 928, I was 33. I hope to have aged as gracefully.

There was tremendous anticipation by the automotive press leading up to the 928's launch. We loved the timing, because the introduction story fit perfectly in *Road & Track's* 30th Anniversary issue in June 1977. Interestingly, the new Porsche shared the spotlight with another German automobile that was brand-new, is still in production, and also looks as good today as it did then: BMW's 6-series coupe. Our cover car the following month was the also-new DeLorean, which goes to prove something, though we're not certain what.

There were two controversies over the 928 at

We'd be hard pressed to find a driving environment more conducive to touring than the 928S 4's interior. But back-seat accommodations leave much to be desired for all but the most diminutive adults.

the time it was launched, one being whether or not enthusiasts were ready to accept a very expensive ($26,000 at the time, about 20 percent less than a 944 today) front-engine, water-cooled super Porsche. Journalists agonized over this question (and over their gin and tonics) at the introduction, but shouldn't have wasted their time. Even if the traditional Porsche fans weren't about to love the 928, there was a whole new group of Porsche buyers who would . . . and have.

The second matter was the car's styling, and all the press musings were again unnecessary. Yes, the 928 did look different, but that was because instead of following an old design trend, it was beginning a new one. The problem was that Porsche's engineers gave Tony Lapine's design department a rather large chassis for which the designers then had to create a body that looked as "unlarge" as possible. For example, the rear taillights are set in angled corner cuts to keep the car from having square corners that would make it look larger.

Then there were the headlights looking skyward. In fact, they do an excellent job of keeping the hood from being too large an expanse of sheet metal. Besides, the technique had already been used on the Lamborghini Miura, and who

are we to fault that design? That sort of logic never got in the way of many writers, and the 928's exterior design was a difficult one for them to understand at first. It's one thing to make a styling judgment about the next in a long line of sedans, but another when you're looking at a design leader.

This matter of the ageless design of the 928 came back several times as we put more high desert miles behind us. Although we're well used to the car's shape in Southern California, where a significant portion of worldwide 928 production has been sold, I was struck once again by how much attention it still draws when you get away from the west coast. That our car was bright red obviously made a difference, but it was interesting to see the car elicit stares, smiles or a thumbs-up, followed by an "all-l-l right." Just the sort of reaction we got 11 years earlier in France.

When people look at you when you're driving a 928, there seems to be an assumption in their eyes that you're having a wonderful time. And they're correct, because when you're in this Porsche you aren't so much in a car as a system. Like an aerospace project, with every part carefully designed and fitted, not picked out of a parts bin. You feel almost self-contained and sufficient, the way Bruce Dern finally did in the great movie *Silent Running*. I have no idea how many times I've done the LA to Vegas to St George and Cedar City, Utah freeway run, but I've never noticed the miles go by quite so quickly before.

This spaceship aspect to the 928 is, of course, in stunning contrast to philosophy of the first Dr Porsche, when he created the original Volkswagen Beetle. Never mind, because the rules are all different now.

The new rules, for instance, call for a cocoon cockpit. Like the 928's instrument panel with its deep-set dials for engine and vehicle speeds, coolant temperature, oil pressure, amps and fuel level. Necessary buttons, such as those for lights, are at both ends of the instrument pod. Nice meaty knobs you can grip. And the entire business can be adjusted up and down.

Supplementing those buttons are the usual steering-column stalk controls and a large center console that contains the heating/ventilation controls and the typically mediocre Blaupunkt radio. This console also does a nice job of separating the cockpit into a definite right and left side, somehow adding to the aircraft systems feeling.

Perhaps the best thing about the 928's interior is the seats. Upholstered in leather, they are electrically adjustable in the usual directions, with lumbar supports that can harden or soften and move up and down.

Behind these seats is another pair, deeply molded and sufficient only for small children. More practically, the deep seat bottoms make a neat hiding place for things like cameras when you fold the seatbacks forward to increase the rear luggage area.

Even in the dry, almost forbidding open spaces, you feel secure in the 928. You sense you could drive through hell in a 928 and not be subject to the usual restrictions . . . except the one disappointing aspect of the car, its un-

impressive air conditioning. Porsche has realized the problem it has keeping the cockpit cool, what with that huge rear window letting in so much sun and heat. There are sun visors for the back window to minimize all this, and a separate air-conditioning system with outlets between the back seats. They do valiant work, but are just barely adequate, or so it seemed in the 85- to 90-degree (Fahrenheit) heat.

And you have a great deal of time to think about these things as you head north to Salt Lake City. The desert turns to green at this point, though in fact it's the result of the irrigation systems that so efficiently use the water that drains from the nearby mountains. We were aimed at the small town of Minden, not far from Logan, to visit with Bert and Cookie Tanner, and arrived late in the day. With the warm sun slanting across the valley, you can appreciate why the Mormons were so happy to settle in when they got this far. Clean air. Quiet. Why does anyone live in a city?

Minden, Utah to Aspen, Colorado is a long haul, particularly if you take the scenic route, but then that's the point of all this. First to gigantic Bear Lake, then lop off a corner of Wyoming getting to the Flaming Gorge National Recreation Area and its impressive red rock formations. Knock off a corner of Utah and you finally get to Colorado, with miles to go before you get to the state's famous mountains.

It's during these long stretches that you also

Neither precarious 10-mph hairpin turn, nor glee of hot-air balloon event nor enjoyment of Bronto Burger shall stay our man Lamm from his appointed touring rounds.

Porsche 928 S 4

List price ....(late 1988) **$69,380**
Price as tested ....(late 1988) **$72,855**
Price as tested includes std equip. (air cond, AM/FM stereo/cassette sound pkg w/15-watt amplifiers, leather interior, elect. window lifts, elect. sunroof, metallic paint, adj driver's seat with memory, adj steering wheel & instrument cluster, central locking, cruise control, rear-window wiper), lumbar adj for front seats ($1030), passenger-seat memory ($864), alarm sys ($507), heated front seats ($370), gas-guzzler tax ($650)

0-60 mph	**5.5 sec**
0-¼ mi	**13.9 sec**
Top speed	**163 mph**

IMPORTER
Porsche Cars North America, Inc, 200 S. Virginia St, Reno, Nev. 89520

HANDLING
Lateral accel, 100-ft radius, g...**0.86**
Speed thru 700-ft
  slalom, mph **62.6**

ENGINE
Type .... **dohc 4-valve V-8**
Bore x stroke,
  in./mm .... **3.94 x 3.11/**
      100.0 x 78.9
Displacement,
  cu in./cc **302/4957**
Compression ratio **10.0:1**
Bhp @ rpm, SAE net ...**316 @ 6000**
Torque @ rpm, lb-ft....**317 @ 3000**
Fuel injection ...... Bosch LH-Jetronic
Fuel requirement .... premium
  unleaded, 91-octane
Exhaust-emission control equipment:
  twin 3-way catalytic converter, oxygen sensor, air injection

GENERAL
Curb weight, lb **3525**
Test weight....................**3660**
Weight dist (w/driver), f/r, % ..**52/48**
Wheelbase, in. **98.4**
Track, front/rear.........**61.0/60.9**
Length **178.1**
Width **72.3**
Height **50.5**
Ground clearance **4.7**
Trunk space, cu ft.......**6.3 + 14.2**
Fuel capacity, U.S. gal. **22.7**

FUEL ECONOMY
Normal driving, mpg **16.5**
Cruising range, mi (1-gal. res) ...**358**

CHASSIS & BODY
Layout ....front engine/rear drive
Body/frame ....unit steel
Brake system, f/r .... 12.0-in. vented discs/11.8-in. vented discs, vacuum assist , ABS
Wheels ...... cast alloy; 16 x 7J front, 16 x 8J rear
Tires .....Dunlop SP Sport Super D4; 225/50ZR-16 front, 245/45ZR-16 rear
Steering type...........rack & pinion, power assist
  Overall ratio 17.8:1
  Turns, lock-to-lock 3.1
  Turning circle, ft 37.7
Front suspension: upper & lower A-arms, coil springs, tube shocks, anti-roll bar
Rear suspension: upper lateral links, lower trailing arms, Weissach axle, coil springs, tube shocks, anti-roll bar

DRIVETRAIN
Transmission ....**5-sp manual**
Gear ratios: 5th (1.00) **2.20:1**
  4th (1.46) **3.21:1**
  3rd (1.93) **4.25:1**
  2nd (2.71) **5.96:1**
  1st (4.07) **8.95:1**
Final-drive ratio **2.20:1**

ACCELERATION
Time to distance, sec:
  0-100 ft **3.0**
  0-500 ft **7.7**
  0-1320 ft (¼ mi) **13.9**
Speed at end of ¼ mi, mph...**101.0**
Time to speed, sec:
  0-30 mph **2.1**
  0-50 mph **4.4**
  0-60 mph **5.5**
  0-70 mph **6.9**
  0-80 mph **8.9**
  0-100 mph **12.9**

BRAKES
Minimum stopping distances, ft:
  From 60 mph **137**
  From 80 mph **234**
Control in panic stop ....**excellent**
Pedal effort for 0.5g stop, lb **20**
Fade: percent increase in pedal effort to maintain 0.5g deceleration in 6 stops from 60 mph ....**nil**
Overall brake rating ....**excellent**

MAINTENANCE
Service intervals, mi:
  Oil/filter change..**15,000/15,000**
  Chassis lube ....**none**
  Tuneup **30,000**
Warranty, mo/mi **24/unlimited**

SPEEDS IN GEARS
Maximum engine speed, rpm ..**6100**
5th gear (rpm) mph .....**(5050) 163**
4th (6100) **134**
3rd (6100) **100**
2nd (6100) **72**
1st (6100) **48**

INSTRUMENTATION
Instruments: 180-mph speedometer, 7000-rpm tach, oil press., coolant temp, voltmeter, fuel level, clock
Warning lights: central warning system, handbrake, ignition, hazard, seatbelts, high beam, directionals

INTERIOR NOISE
Idle in neutral, dBA................**51**
Maximum, 1st gear **74**
Constant 30 mph **63**
  50 mph **67**
  70 mph **71**

CALCULATED DATA
Lb/bhp (test weight) **11.6**
Bhp/liter **63.2**
Mph/1000 rpm (5th gear) **33.0**
Engine revs/mi (60 mph) **1850**
R&T steering index.............**1.17**

appreciate the 928's engine. The thought of a big Porsche V-8 may have been offensive to some Porsche purists of 1977, but now it's an accepted part of the program. What enthusiast can't appreciate the aluminum head and block, the twin camshafts per head and four valves per cylinder? It's a shame we don't get to see more of that engine, as we do with the Lotus-designed LT5 V-8 in the Corvette, but at least Porsche has given us the lovely intake manifold with fat runners to look at.

ACCOMMODATION

Seating capacity, persons	**2 + 2**
Head room, f/r, in.	**36.5/32.0**
Seat width, f/r	**2 x 20.0/2 x 15.0**
Seatback adjustment, deg	**70**

▲ **Test Notes...**

■ Quick, without a lot of mechanical protestation from its all-aluminum V-8.

■ Ride is firm, but controlled.

■ On bumpy roads, you're aware that there's a lot of mass to those wheels and tires.

■ Although redline is 6100 rpm, the engine will easily rev to 6800 at which point the limiter cuts in.

■ One staffer said the shifter felt clumsy, but others disagreed.

■ From 80 mph the S 4 stops in just 234 ft.

THE LOVELY THING about a V-8 is its loaf-when-you-want-to, roar-when-you-need-to nature. You can just putter along with the Porsche V-8. I had the opportunity to put it in the hands of someone who had never driven an automobile this powerful. No problem. Or you can dump all 316 bhp on those 245/45ZR-16s if you like and find it to be much more manageable than turbo power.

Backing all this is a 5-speed manual transaxle that is smooth, authoritative and really unnecessary, considering that with the V-8's torque you don't have to spend a great deal of time shifting. Considering the car's image, the Daimler-Benz 4-speed automatic offered in the 928 might be a better choice.

At 0–60 mph in 5.5 seconds, the 5-speed 928 is only about a sneeze slower than a 911 Turbo, with the automatic 928 another half-second behind the manual version. Our mileage on the 1500-mile trip ranged from a low of 19.6 mpg to a high of 26.8, with two adults, moderate luggage and the air conditioning on the entire way. In our latest World's Fastest Cars test at Ohio's Transportation Research Center, a stock 928S 4 topped at 163 mph . . . and looked very nice roaring, but not too loudly, around the banking.

Because the 928 is as much a system as an automobile, you can expect every piece in the mechanism to be as good as the drivetrain, which isn't always the case in fast cars. The chassis has independent front and rear suspension, the latter with the highly touted Weissach axle. The Los Angeles-Colorado Springs route was a perfect chance to try this design, with everything from smooth freeways to the sort of rutted, uneven mountain roads that take quite a weather beating each winter. It's an excellent example of what makes independent rear suspension worth the cost, soaking up the bumps and making certain that 316 bhp is being put down here and now, not on the next bump or in the air in between.

The steering is a power-assisted rack and pinion that seems to provide just the right effort with sufficient feedback. In a car of the 928S 4's class, the brakes are large vented discs at each wheel with anti-lock; the latter is particularly nice when you're making tracks down a mountain road that has rivulets of water running across the corners.

I've never skied at Aspen, but it must be wonderful, the slopes butting right up to the town. But even during summer the chamber of commerce has done an excellent job of bringing in interesting substitutes. We arrived too late to enjoy one of the evening concerts, so we had to settle for a nice dinner, and made up for the lack of Vivaldi with a bottle of Far Niente Chardonnay. The hot-air balloon festival had just ended, but on Monday owners of several of the huge, colorful monsters were up enjoying the crisp morning air.

Lovely place, Aspen, but the best part of the trip came next. All the miles of freeway from Los Angeles to Salt Lake City, and then the lonely stretches of back-country 2-lane blacktop, were worth it as soon as we began to climb east on Colorado 82 out of Aspen toward Independence Pass. Forget it in winter, because then the pass is closed, but in summer it's a wonderful drive, twisting along a narrow road that at times is only a lane-and-a-half wide. The route does widen, of course, but the speed limit is kept low. Not that many non-turbo vehicles are up to their best performance as you wind up to the 12,095-ft pass. Even the 5.0-liter German V-8 was a bit anemic at that altitude.

You're crossing the Continental Divide at this point, and you need to stop to admire it all. Although we went through in July, a cold storm had been through the night before—we'd taken along a stash of chocolate chip cookies just in case the storm returned and isolated us—so even at 10:00 a.m. there was a layer of frost all around. Ice coated many of the bushes along the roadside, but there wasn't a cloud around, and you sort of expected Julie Andrews to come prancing over the hilltop singing, "The hills are alive . . . "

Somewhat ironically, that image brings us right back to Vence, France, and that original Porsche 928 trip. From Aspen on to Colorado Springs you're in countryside that is not all that different from what you could find back in the Alpes-Maritimes. The 928 that Joe Rusz and I shared then was red. There's a different front spoiler on it now, new wheels and a rear-deck spoiler that offers high-speed advantages on the *Autobahn*, but is worth more in the U.S. for the way it makes it easier to open and close the rear hatch. Horsepower is up from the original 240 in the 4.5-liter version of the V-8 to 316 in the 5.0-liter. Torque has taken a similar jump, from 250 to 317 lb-ft, and is now generated at 3000 rpm instead of 3600. Acceleration from 0–60 mph has dropped 1.5 sec from 7.0, while top speed has jumped from 138 mph to 163.

A dozen model years later the 928—survivor of critics, a fuel crisis that put many V-8s into the history books, and now a weak dollar—has aged with all the grace of a nobleman. Have we done as well?

There is another aspect to consider: A new 928S 4 will put you back about $75,000. This is not the fault of Porsche, which is just trying to keep up with the weak dollar. But would you rather have the Porsche or, for about the same price (author's choices here), a Toyota Celica All-Trac, a 1969 Mustang Boss 302 or Camaro Z-28, a nice Austin-Healey 100/4 *and* a Honda Civic for around-town use?

Tough choice, but then it's choices, like contrasts, that make life so interesting.

Luggage space isn't cavernous, but there's enough space for two people's bags, a cargo net to prevent them from sliding around and a hinged panel to keep them out of sight.

A MORE POWERFUL PORSCHE . . .

Porsche has added a more powerful version of the 928 to its range. The new model has a lower final drive ratio, lightweight wider-rim alloy wheels and sports suspension.

The £55,441 Porsche 928 GT's 5.0-litre V8 engine develops 10bhp more than the standard car's 320bhp. Modified exhaust and electronic management systems, as well as special camshafts, give the engine better mid-range response.

With the lower gearing and fat,

ultra-low profile Bridgestone tyres, the 928 GT has a claimed top speed of 170mph and acceleration from zero to 60mph in 5.6secs.

Suspension has been altered, with gas-filled dampers and slightly wider rear track. Anti-lock braking and a tyre pressure monitoring system is fitted as standard. Out of sight are modified inner wing panels to accommodate the wider wheels and tyres. Inside, the standard seats are replaced by the lighter sports version.

Sporting 928: the GT's 5.0-litre V8 develops 330bhp

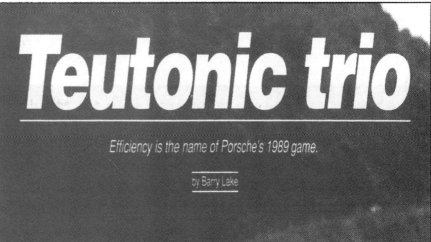

Teutonic trio

Efficiency is the name of Porsche's 1989 game.

by Barry Lake

About every second year — give or take a bit — Alan Hamilton of Porsche Cars Australia treats a collection of Oz motoring writers to the latest selection of Porsches available on the Australian market. This year he has broken his release into two events, first a trio of front-engine/rear drive models and — still to come (before the end of 1989 we are promised) and anxiously awaited — the latest developments of the 911 range, which will this year include the Carrera 4 all-wheel drive model.

The three new front-engine cars are, as is normal Porsche practice, difficult to detect from the outside; the improvements are mainly hidden within the mechanical specifications. Bystanders might find them hard to pick as they flash by, but Porsche drivers will readily recognise the difference: all three cars are markedly improved in performance. They are the Porsche 944 S2 with greatly upgraded engine, the 944 Turbo with detail mechanical refinements, and the 928 S4 — the latest upgrade of the company's flagship model.

Alan Hamilton, son of Norm Hamilton who began importing Porsches to Australia in the early 1950s and thereby founded the world's longest-standing Porsche importing business, is a top racing driver and an astute businessman but above all a motoring enthusiast. Alan has had a lifelong love affair with Porsches. His employees share his feelings and it would be hard to find a company so laden with enthusiasm for the product.

Alan and one of his key men at Porsche Cars Australia, Roger Watts, had planned a route from Melbourne's Tullamarine Airport that took in the Otway Ranges and the famed Great Ocean Road to Apollo Bay. Like previous Porsche test routes it was one which could show the cars to their best advantage without the necessity to exceed speed limits — although there was the opportunity on the day to experience high speeds safely if so desired.

Improvements to the 944 S2 are the greatest. The car has what is virtually an all-new engine, despite the fact it is the same basic design as the 2.5-litre unit it replaces. Already Porsche's 2.5 four-cylinder, along with Mitsubishi's 2.6, was one of the giants of the world's four-pot powerplants, a feat made possible by Mitsubishi's patented contra-rotating balance shaft system which Porsche uses under licence. Four-cylinder engines — with two pistons going up and two down — have inherent balance problems that are otherwise all but impossible to balance out. And the bigger the parts, the more pronounced the problem becomes.

Porsche has now relocated these balance shafts higher in the block of this new power plant and the system is further refined to cope with the previously unthought of 3.0-litre capacity. Forged pistons provide added strength and reliability, the digital engine electronics are modified to suit, engine compartment ventilation is via a computer-controlled three-speed fan, the intake system has been improved, and there is electronic control of the oil cooling via a light alloy cooler.

Contributing to performance is a new 16-valve head (the Turbo version retains the two-valves per cylinder layout).

But the improvements are not only with the engine. Gearbox, driveshafts, shock absorbers, suspension and anti-roll bars have been upgraded using technology developed on the high-performance Turbo version, while four-piston, fixed-caliper disc brakes with forced air cooling look after the stopping.

Wheels are seven inches wide by 16 inches front and eight inches by 16 inches at the rear, with 205/55 and 225/50 ZR rated tyres front and rear respectively.

Detail changes to the aerodynamics, including the nose section which also has a higher grade plastic to resist stone chipping and damage from low-speed bumps, have improved the aerodynamic drag coefficient from a claimed 0.35 to 0.33.

Power output of the engine is 161 kW (211 PS hp) which gives the car a top speed of 240 km/h. More dramatic is the torque figure of 280 Nm at a mere 4000 rpm — and 196 Nm already in operation at just 1500 rpm — which aids the impressive zero to 100 km/h time of 7.1 seconds.

Driving the 944 S2 is sheer pleasure, mainly because it is so easy to drive point to point. Where the 944 Turbo requires concentration and a certain amount of brio to get the best from it, the S2 has torque aplenty at all rpm speeds. We tried idling it along at 1500 rpm in fifth gear, then pressed the accelerator pedal down and the car just surged steadily onwards up to its maximum speed with no sign of cam or turbo-like bursts of power, just a turbine-like surge. Winding the 944 S2 through the tight turns the driver had a choice of gears — second or third — it would still pull strongly.

The 944 Turbo, by comparison, had the potential to be quicker, but the driver had to work at it. Try a corner in third gear when second was required and the engine would lug along without boost and lose time. Use the right gear and punch it, the car would leap forward with a burst of power that could have the rear tyres scrabbling for grip.

A good driver, concentrating and working at it, would be quicker point to point on a tight road in the 944 Turbo. But a lesser driver or even a good driver on a lazy day, would more likely be quicker in the 944 S2. It's certainly less tiring, physically and mentally, to drive.

The 944 turbo has a number of factors working for it, however. Firstly, in this latest guise, a larger turbo with higher boost and with the digital electronics for ignition and injection upgraded accordingly, it has a 30 horsepower increase of engine power from its four-cylinder, 2.5-litre, eight-valve, turbocharged unit, to 191 kW (250 PS hp) and torque is a healthy 350 Nm at 4000 rpm. The Turbo does the zero-100 km/h dash in 5.9 seconds — more than a second quicker than the S2 — and has a top speed of 260 km/h (20 km/h higher than the S2).

To harness this extra performance, the latest Turbo has a limited-slip differential (the S2 doesn't — although didn't appear to need it even on damp twisty roads) and

Brake dust tells the story. The mouth watering 1989 Porsche line-up cooling off after a run or two down one of Australia's best driving roads, the Great Ocean Road in Victoria.

928 S4's 32-valve, 5.0-litre V8 has 235 kW.

944 Turbo's 2.5-litre in-line four has 184 kW.

The 928 S4 — one of the most deceptively efficient, fast and safe cars of all time.

944 S2's 16-valve, 3.0-litre four has 157 kW.

anti-lock braking system (which the S2 also does not have, though we had no problems with locking brakes on that car, even when driving hard into tight corners on a wet surface).

Additionally, the Turbo has wider rear wheels — still seven inches wide by 16 inches at the front, but nine inches by 16 inches at the rear. The tyres are wider — 225/50 ZR at the front, 245/45 ZR at the rear.

Also standard on the Turbo model are cruise control, and sunroof. Both S2 and Turbo have central locking, power steering, power windows, power external rear-view mirrors, electrically adjustable driver's seat, automatic climate control, Porsche alarm system, driving lights and fog lights, rear window wiper, leather covered steering wheel, rear spoiler, head-light washers, and 10-speaker hi-fi radio/cassette system. The 944 S2 and 944 Turbo are virtually indistinguishable in appearance on the road; only the detailed badgework gives the clue to which is which — and to a keen observer, the engine note.

For the incredible torque and smoothness — both to degrees we have never before experienced in a four cylinder car — of the 944 S2 you are asked to pay $99,969. There is also a Cabriolet (soft-top convertible) model available without a rear spoiler but with a power-operated soft-top for $122,506.

The 944 Turbo comes in hard-top coupe form only, at $129,023. All are beyond the reach of we mere mortals, but those who can afford to indulge don't need to ask the price of quality . . . and they know Porsches have good long-term investment potential.

After the nimbleness of the 944 S2 and the bursting performance of the 944 Turbo, switching to the 928 S4 was like climbing into a too-large, ungainly, and heavy-to-drive behemoth . . . but only for the first couple of kilometres.

The 928 has always been one of the most deceptively efficient, fast, and safe cars of all time. The fourth major update, the S4, is all of that and more.

In situations where the 944 Turbo might step its rear end out of line as the turbo power rushes into play on the exit from a tight, damp and bumpy corner, the 928 just sits flat and unfussed.

Most, other than Porsche devotees, might have forgotten the 928, with its "Weissach axle", had actually started the current all-wheel steering era. This Porsche design put formerly unwanted changes to suspension geometry as the suspension bushes flexed in cornering to work for it rather than against it. By turn-

ing this flexing into rear-wheel steering that aided, rather than detracted from, the cornering power, Porsche gained a degree of four-wheel steer that gives the car uncanny road manners.

I remember some years back a photographer asking me to attack a corner faster and faster in a 928 to try to get some attitude on it to make for a spectacular photograph.

Even after adding, little by little, 50 per cent to the original perceived maximum speed for the corner, I could not get the car to do anything other than corner flat and on-line at ever-increasing speed. Its cornering limits were well beyond my threshold of fear.

The latest version is all that and more. This could well be the most efficient car — in handling terms — ever created, barring race cars and super cars like the almost unbelievable all-wheel drive 959.

Power comes from the now-veteran 5.0-litre V8, one side of which is the basis for the 944 four-cylinder engine. The output is now 235 kW (320 PS hp) and this gives the car acceleration figures of 5.9 seconds 0-100 km/h for the manual version and 6.3 seconds for the automatic, with top speeds of 270 km/h and 265 km/h respectively.

Wheels are six-inch and eight-inch (by 16-inches diameter) front and rear, with tyres 225/50 ZR 16 and 245/45 ZR 16 front and rear.

The auto transmission version has been upgraded to give sportier performance from the box and items like anti-lock braking and power steering are standard.

The 928 S4 has leather seats and all of the usual luxury items one would expect in a $200,629 car, but there is more to come in this 1989 model year with the soon-to-arrive 928 GT, a sports version, which will have the same level of interior fitments and instrumentation as the 928 S4. The price

Three ingredients for a great driving experience — 928 S4, sunshine and a challenging road.

will be the same as the S4 but both cars can be loaded up to an even greater price with a long list of optional equipment.

Moving further into the technological age, the 928 S4 has a tyre pressure monitoring system which has sensors in each wheel.

If the pressure of any tyre drops below the recommended levels, it shows up as a red warning light on a diagram of the car on the dash which indicates which tyre is at fault.

The other electronic gizmo is the Porsche Information and Diagnostic System (PIDS) which reports to the driver in words and symbols on 21 different functions including fuel consumption, outside temperature, average speed (all of which most modern trip computers will do) but also has a "dobber" function which records any occasions of exceeding the rpm limit

by the driver, any high temperature running, driving with low oil level, and other factors which will affect engine life. This information can be accessed by the Porsche technician, who will then know how hard the car has been used and will be able to service or repair it accordingly.

Although visually barely different from their predecessors, the new 1989 Porsches are significant steps forward in efficiency — and they have arrived earlier then expected. Alan Hamilton puts this down to the slump in sales of Porsches in the US after peaking in the mid-1980s, a scare which prodded the factory into an accelerated rate of development. Hamilton and other Porsche distributors hadn't expected these cars until 1992 or 1993. Now, in those years, we will be driving even better Porsches. A testimony to the power of competition. ❑

TEST EXTRA Porsche 928GT

The GT is the enthusiast's 928 — faster than ever and
with sharper handling but far from silent or smooth-riding

Price £55,441 **Top speed** 165mph **0-60** 5.6secs **MPG** 14.2
For *Tremendous grip, progressive power delivery, cabin*
Against *Road noise, economy, rear cabin space*

WITH PORSCHE 911 TURBO PRICES moving smartly upwards and big-league Ferraris already skimming the stratosphere, the Porsche 928GT — yours for £55,441 — is beginning to look like the only cost-effective way to join the 165mph-plus club. Its fundamental appeal has never been in doubt: it is very much the *practical* supercar, the one with four seats, a hatchback and decent boot.

And in GT form, as tested here, it's faster than ever. We've tested just three current supercars that have the legs of the 928: the Ferrari Testarossa, the Lamborghini Countach and the Aston Martin Vantage. The Italian pair owe as much to racing ideology as they do to road car design. Fine instruments of speed as they are, few would enjoy driving them in London traffic. Even tempered, the 928 doesn't mind going slow. It's a car for all reasons.

At a glance, only the forged light alloy road wheels distinguish the 928GT from its less powerful stablemate, the 928S Series 4, but where the S4 gets an auto box and the 320bhp 5-litre engine, the GT comes with a manual five-speeder and the big V8 tweaked to release a further 10bhp. The extra power comes courtesy of special camshafts and exhaust system, and a modified engine management system which allows the revs to climb higher — to 6775rpm as opposed to the 6600rpm of the S4. Peak torque of 317lb ft remains the same as the S4's but is pushed higher up the rev range from 3000 to 4100rpm.

To benefit fully from the extra power, the GT is equipped with an electronically controlled limited slip differential. It also has lower gearing, 'Sport' gas-filled dampers and a marginally wider rear track. The 16ins diameter forged wheels are an inch wider than the S4's at 8ins front and 9ins rear to accommodate Bridgestone ultra low-profile rubber, 225/50 fronts, 245/45 at the rear, Z-speed rated.

The GT's sharper performance profile is obvious as soon as you get behind the wheel. In place of the cosseting upholstery of the S4's seats, a shapely Recaro-style 'Sport' item clamps the driver firmly in place. Electric adjustment is restricted to height only and the memory facility is lost. The extra support is fair exchange. The only other visible deviation from S4 spec is the gear-lever, which is shortened by about an inch.

The second reminder that this is no regular 928 comes when you crank the key. The engine has a deep, even beat that seems to be an octave lower than the S4's. The 800rpm idle is rock steady, irrespective of engine temperature.

Easing through traffic gives no clue to the engine's full potential. The Porsche trickles along at walking pace, clutch fully out, with no trace of transmission snatch or backlash. But flatten the accelerator from low revs and the 928's considerable bulk surges rapidly towards the horizon.

PETER BURN

PORSCHE 928GT

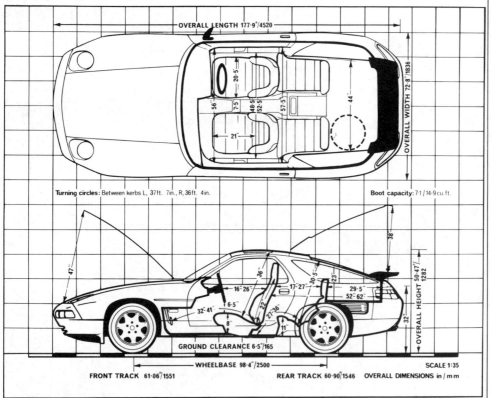

Turning circles: Between kerbs L, 37ft. 7in., R, 36ft. 4in.
Boot capacity: 7·1 / 14·9 cu. ft.

OVERALL LENGTH 177·9"/4520
OVERALL WIDTH 72·8"/1836
OVERALL HEIGHT 50·47"/1282

GROUND CLEARANCE 6·5"/165
WHEELBASE 98·4"/2500
FRONT TRACK 61·06"/1551
REAR TRACK 60·90"/1546
OVERALL DIMENSIONS in / mm
SCALE 1:35

PERFORMANCE

MAXIMUM SPEEDS

Gear	mph	km/h	rpm
Top (Mean)	165	266	6300
(Best)	169	272	6500
4th	127	204	6600
3rd	96	155	6600
2nd	69	111	6600
1st	46	74	6600

ACCELERATION FROM REST

True mph	Time (secs)	Speedo mph
30	2.3	33
40	3.2	45
50	4.4	56
60	5.6	66
70	7.2	77
80	8.9	87
90	10.8	97
100	13.4	107
110	16.3	117
120	19.5	127
130	24.1	137
140	30.2	148

30-70mph 4.9secs
Standing mile: 13.8secs, 102mph
Standing km: 25.0secs, 131mph

ACCELERATION IN EACH GEAR

mph	Top	4th	3rd	2nd
10-30	7.6	5.3	3.8	2.6
20-40	6.6	4.7	3.5	2.5
30-50	6.4	4.5	3.3	2.3
40-60	6.5	4.4	3.2	2.4
50-70	6.5	4.2	3.1	—
60-80	6.5	4.2	3.3	—
70-90	6.2	4.3	3.6	—
80-100	6.6	4.6	—	—
90-110	7.3	5.2	—	—
100-120	7.9	5.9	—	—
110-130	8.9	—	—	—
120-140	10.9	—	—	—

FUEL CONSUMPTION

Overall mpg: 14.2 (19.9 litres/100km)
Touring mpg*: 18.6mpg (15.2 litres/100km)
Govt tests mpg: 30.1mpg (urban)
22.8mpg (steady 56mph)
14.4mpg (steady 75mph)
Grade of fuel: 4-star (97RM) or Eurosuper unleaded (95RM)
Tank capacity: 19 galls (86 litres)
Max range*: 353 miles
* Based on Government fuel economy figures: 50 per cent of urban cycle, 25 per cent each of 56/75mpg consumptions.

BRAKING

Fade (from 102mph in neutral)
Pedal load (lb) for 0.5g stops

start/end		start/end	
1	25-20	6	30-25
2	25-20	7	30-28
3	25-25	8	30-25
4	25-30	9	30-30
5	25-25	10	30-30

Response (from 30mph in neutral)

Load	g	Distance
10lb	0.38	79ft
20lb	0.62	49ft
30lb	0.95	32ft
40lb	1.05	29ft
50lb	1.10	27ft
Parking brake	0.35	86ft

WEIGHT

Kerb 3449lb/1566kg
Distribution % F/R 53/47
Test 3819lb/1734kg
Max payload 969lb/440kg

TEST CONDITIONS

Wind	9mph
Temperature	30deg C (87deg F)
Barometer	998mbar
Surface	dry asphalt/concrete
Test distance	977 miles

SPECIFICATION

ENGINE
Longitudinal, front, rear-wheel drive. Capacity 4957cc, 8 cylinders in 90deg V. **Bore** 100.0mm, **stroke** 78.9mm. **Compression ratio** 10.0 to 1. **Head/block** al alloy/al alloy. **Valve gear** dohc, 4 valves per cylinder. **Ignition and fuel** breaker-less electronic ignition. Bosch LH-Jetronic multi-point fuel injection. **Max power** 330bhp (PS-DIN) (242kW ISO) at 6200rpm. **Max torque** 317lb ft (430 Nm) at 4100rpm.

TRANSMISSION
5-speed manual.

Gear	Ratio	mph/1000rpm
Top	1.000	26.13
4th	1.354	19.30
3rd	1.790	14.60
2nd	2.512	10.40
1st	3.764	6.94

Final drive 2.73 to 1. Limited slip diff.

SUSPENSION
Front, independent, double wishbones, coil springs, telescopic dampers, anti-roll bar.
Rear, independent, semi-trailing arms, upper transverse links, coil springs, telescopic dampers, anti-roll bar, self-levelling.

STEERING
Rack and pinion, power assisted, 3.0 turns lock to lock.

BRAKES
Front 12.0ins (304mm) dia ventilated discs.
Rear 11.8ins (246mm) dia ventilated discs. Four channel Bosch anti-lock.

SOLD IN THE UK BY
Porsche Cars GB Ltd, Bath Road, Calcot, Reading, Berks RG3 7SE.

COSTS

Prices
Total (in UK)	£55,440.83
Delivery, road tax, plates	£130.00
On the road price	£55,570.83
Options fitted to test car:	
Full feature alarm	£581.81
Cellular telephone preparation	£480.90
Sunroof	£1341.76
Total as tested	£57,975.30

SERVICE
Major service 12,000 miles — 5.4 hrs.

PARTS COST (inc VAT)
Oil filter	£11.87
Brake pads (2 wheels) front	£93.60
Exhaust complete	£352.71
Headlamp unit	£118.48
Front wing	£477.31

WARRANTY
24 months/unlimited mileage, 10 years anti-corrosion, 3 years against paint defects, 24 months breakdown recovery.

EQUIPMENT

Anti-lock brakes	●
Self levelling suspension	●
Alloy wheels	●
Auto gearbox	●
Power assisted steering	●
Limited slip differential	●
Leather trim	●
Air conditioning	●
Cruise control	●
Radio/cassette player	●
Front fog lamps	●
Driving lamps	●
Headlamp wash	●
Electric tilt/slide sunroof	£1342
Metallic paint	NCO

● Standard — Not available NCO No cost option

Figures taken at 7942 miles by our own staff at the Lotus Group proving ground, Millbrook.
All *Autocar & Motor* test results are subject to world copyright and may not be reproduced without the Editor's written permission.

1. Headlamps, front/rear fog lamps, 2. Water temperature, Fuel gauge, 3. Speedometer, 4. Revcounter, 5. Oil pressure, Battery voltage, 6. Rear screen demist, 7. Hazard warning lights, 8. Ignition switch, 9. Windscreen, headlamp wash-wipe, 10. Cruise control, 11. Indicators, main beam/dip, 12. Electric windows, 13. Rear hatch wipe, 14. Digital clock, 15. Air conditioning, heater/ventilation controls.

◀ Third gear punch is formidable. Overtaking opportunities are created out of thin air. From 2000rpm there's solid torque but, beyond 4000rpm, the 928 really picks up its heels and sprints all the way to the redline.

At the test track the difficulty was getting power down effectively. It either spun away as tyre smoke or the wheels tramped with alarming force. Failing to ease off the power once on the move simply spins the wheels all the way through first gear, resulting in a slower run. This makes the 5.6secs sprint to 60mph — the same as for a 911 Carrera or a Ferrari Testarossa — even more impressive than it sounds. Reaching a three-figure speed takes just 13.4secs from rest and the standing quarter takes a mere 13.8secs. Keep the pedal buried in the plush cream carpet and the big Porsche's acceleration keeps you moulded to the seat until the needle nudges 130mph.

Then you change into top. The process continues, only with less intensity, climbing to 165mph on the banked Millbrook track. On the flat, without power-sapping tyrescrub, the 928GT is certainly capable of 170mph. Our best half-mile sector topped 169mph.

Check through the in-gear figures and the engine's flexibility becomes clear. The 928GT will pull cleanly from as low as 10mph in top. In fourth, 10-30mph takes 5.3 secs; 90-110 in the same gear takes 5.2secs.

Make no mistake, this engine is a gem. It has ferocious acceleration on tap but power is spread over such a prodigious range that it is never unmanageable and always easily accessed. Throttle response is instant, and it is as happy in traffic as it is blasting down a mountain road or at 140mph on the autobahn.

Driven hard and fast, the penalty is an overall fuel consumption of around 15mpg. The best we got was 18.5mpg. The option to use unleaded makes it a little easier on the pocket and the environment. Even with a 19-gallon tank, fuel stops are fairly frequent.

Beneath the GT's seductive curves lies a chassis of immense competence, though it is by no means perfect. Once acclimatised to the low seating position and high scuttle line, the 928GT is as friendly as a hot hatchback. Its bulk and weight become little more than an illusion as confidence in the car's abilities grows. And those abilities are put to best use not on the motorway, but on quieter backroads where it is uncannily easy to maintain outstandingly high average speeds over long distances.

The gutsy engine takes care of getting past slower-moving traffic while the fat Bridgestones play a star role in keeping it all firmly on the tarmac. They are also partly responsible for an over-harsh and noisy ride, every bump transmitted through to the cabin as a thud. Nevertheless, the suspension is surprisingly supple on rough single track roads.

But while seat-of-the-pants feedback is exceptional for such a large car, steering feel isn't all it should be. Direct and accurate most of the time, the helm's responses are corrupted by the effects of cambers, ridges and even lane markings. The four-spoke wheel with its soft leather rim is good to grip but the steering weights up considerably with any side-loading on the tyres. The 928GT is not for the limp-wristed.

The steering is geared high enough to counteract quickly the results of over-enthusiasm with the throttle. Better still, the chassis is forgiving enough to allow the driver to ▶

All-alloy V8 develops 330bhp, 10bhp more than S4. Max torque comes higher up rev range. V8 is smooth and refined with fine flexibility and prodigious acceleration. Instrumentation and controls hard to fault. Leather trimmed cabin is strict two-plus-two; seats hug tight

928GT is sharper than S4 and has stronger grip. It won't bite back unless severely provoked

◄ take such liberties and get away with it.

Some of the credit can go to good weight distribution, but the 928's independent rear suspension arrangement also plays a significant role. This compensates for toe-change under weight transfer, thus having a self-stabilising effect on handling.. Unlike the rear-engined, rear-drive 911, the 928's handling is almost foolproof. Go in too hard and the front tends to run wide. Gently ease off and it runs back on line. On slower turns the power can be used to push the rear wheels out and point the nose towards the exit earlier.

Bumpy bends can cause the back end to leap across momentarily, but lateral movement is always arrested before it can precipitate a slide.

Engine braking is good and the massive ventilated discs have fine pedal weighting and haul the 928's bulk down from legal speeds most effectively. But from higher speeds — and remember the 928GT is capable of around 170mph — they lack that initial bite. Anti-lock is standard.

No manual gearbox that can handle well over 300lb ft of torque is going to be slick and light. Considering the great chunks of metal whirring around the inside, the 928's change is lightning quick but the quality of lever movement leaves a lot to be desired. The downchange from fourth to third is the worst offender. Spring assistance is minimal and it is all too easy for the lever to baulk in the no-man's-land between third and fifth.

On the motorway, the 928GT loses a great deal of its charm. Here, there is nothing to take your mind off the constant thrum from the tyres or the road vibrations that come unchecked through the steering and seats. It's

as bad at 50mph as at 150mph, though wind roar is never a concern and the powerful beat of the engine is always restrained. At least the hip-hugging seats are supremely comfortable over long periods behind the wheel and the Blaupunkt radio/cassette with 10 speakers has ample power to drown out the road noise.

Outside the UK, the GT is similar in concept to the 911 Club Sport, losing equipment in favour of reduced weight. For the UK, the GT buyer gets the same lavish trim levels as the S4, and that includes air conditioning, leather seats, central locking with alarm, electric windows and mirrors, cruise control, and the Porsche information and diagnostic system. The test car also had a sliding sunroof, which was tiny but allowed improved ventilation, and a cellular telephone set into the centre console in the armrest position. A further refinement was the full alarm system which operates automatically from the remote locking and automatically closes windows and sunroof.

The Porsche appears to be superbly made and the impression when driving is of almost unrivalled integrity. But that's not to say that the 928GT's reputation for durability remained intact in our week with the car. The electric seat height adjustment worked on one side only, the tyre pressure sensors gave out persistent warnings of low pressures when they were actually correct, and the air conditioning system spurted all its fluid over the road following our Millbrook test session.

Despite the inoperative air conditioning, the 928's cabin always proved to be a pleasant environment. It is roomy with all controls and instruments set out almost to perfection. All the dials can be viewed clearly through the

wheel and even the minor switches are easy to find. The contoured facia is as attractive as it is functional, and there is no lack of oddment space, unlike many cars of this calibre.

The two fairly sizeable rear seats can be reached rather uncomfortably by folding forward the front seat backs, but the lack of headroom and legroom makes them suitable only for children on anything but very short journeys. Rear seats can be folded flat to create more luggage space and a large hatch allows easy access to the load floor. Luggage space is sufficient for the weekend requirements of two people. Add the requirements of one or two small children and the 928's limitations are obvious, but that's only to be expected of a sports coupe.

A space-saver spare is carried beneath the luggage floor. Should a puncture occur, it must first be inflated using the compressor also carried in the rear of the car.

The latest interpretation of the 928 theme is a car of towering abilities. It's a devastatingly quick road car and one that is a pleasure to drive — it's almost as easy to drive and as forgiving as any good hot hatch. The tremendous punch and flexibility of the smooth V8 engine are matched by a chassis of outstanding competence. The combination won't bite back unless severely provoked.

But the 928GT is still a compromise. Those fat tyres and firm dampers produce the desired effects but a by-product is excessive road noise and a rough-edged ride that many would find unacceptable. For them, the S4 is a better bet. But there is still a place for the 928GT. Its rawness gives it a sporting appeal that has been lost in the clinical functionalism of the S4. ■

PORSCHE 928 GT   £55,441

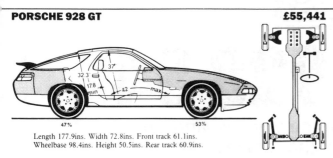

Length 177.9ins. Width 72.8ins. Front track 61.1ins.
Wheelbase 98.4ins. Height 50.5ins. Rear track 60.9ins.

GT version of 928 is quicker and more responsive than S4 and has manual gearbox as standard. Handling and grip are superb but big V8 is thirsty. Very spacious and comfortable cabin for two (but a cramped 2+2), excellent driving position and instrumentation, but ride and refinement needs to be better in view of its touring aspirations

Capacity	4957cc
Power	330bhp at 6200rpm
Torque	317lb ft at 4100rpm
Max speed	165mph
0-60mph	5.6secs
30-70 through gears	4.9secs
ss ¼ mile	13.8secs/102mph
30-50 in fourth	4.5secs
50-70 in fifth	6.5secs
MPG overall/touring	14.2/18.6
MPH/1000rpm in top	26.13
Kerb weight	3449lb
Date tested	23.8.89

ASTON MARTIN VIRAGE   £120,000

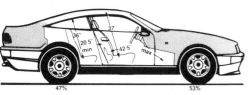

Length 186.5ins. Width 73.0ins. Front track N/A.
Wheelbase 102.7ins. Height 52.0ins. Rear track N/A.

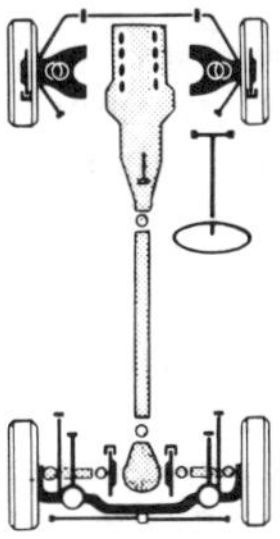

British Virage is a complete contrast to the Italian exotics. We've yet to try one but with the same all-alloy V8 engine as the Vantage, performance is sure to be immense. It's beautifully finished using traditional coachbuilding skills. Latest of an ancient breed of all-British supercars. There's a long waiting list already and it's likely to remain that way

Capacity	5340cc
Power	350bhp
Torque	N/A
Max speed	155mph*
0-60mph	6.0secs*
30-70 through gears	N/A
ss ¼ mile	N/A
30-50 in fourth	N/A
50-70 in fifth	N/A
MPG overall/touring	N/A
MPH/1000rpm in top	N/A
Kerb weight	3948lb
Date tested	not tested

*Manufacturer's figures

BMW M635 CSi   £45,780

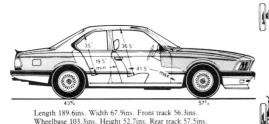

Length 189.6ins. Width 67.9ins. Front track 56.3ins.
Wheelbase 103.3ins. Height 52.7ins. Rear track 57.5ins.

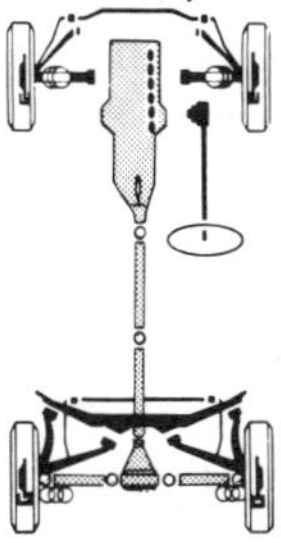

Seventies four seat near-supercar is just begining to show its age, but fabulous 24-valve six still delivers lusty performance with good refinement. Handling is enjoyable but tricky in the wet, ride firm but well controlled. Generally well equipped with first class build. About to be replaced by stylish new 8-series V12 coupe

Capacity	3453cc
Power	286bhp at 6500rpm
Torque	251lb ft at 4500rpm
Max speed	150mph
0-60mph	6.0secs
30-70 through gears	5.5secs
ss ¼ mile	14.6secs/99mph
30-50 in fourth	6.7secs
50-70 in fifth	9.3secs
MPG overall/touring	20.6/22.4
MPH/1000rpm in top	24.0
Kerb weight	3458lb
Date tested	18.1.89

FERRARI MONDIAL 3.2   £51,995

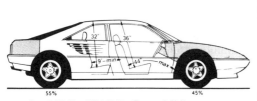

Length 178.5ins. Width 70.7ins. Front track 59.8ins.
Wheelbase 104.3ins. Height 48.6ins. Rear track 59.4ins.

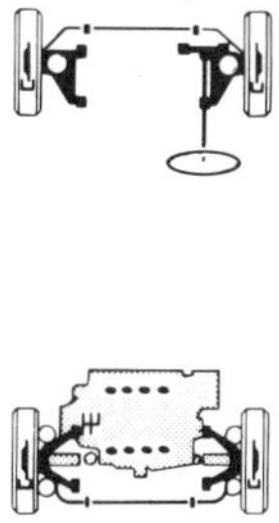

Ferrari's 2+2 shares the same wailing V8 that powers the 328GTB. Greater weight blunts performance but the Mondial is still very rapid. Handling is well balanced, brakes are excellent and the ride supple. It's beautifully made and the engine note is unforgettable. A Ferrari you can live with very comfortably from day to day

Capacity	3186cc
Power	270bhp at 7000rpm
Torque	224lb ft at 5500rpm
Max speed	143mph
0-60mph	6.8secs
30-70 through gears	6.3secs
ss ¼ mile	14.9secs/95mph
30-50 in fourth	5.6secs
50-70 in fifth	8.1secs
MPG overall/touring	16.8/20.1
MPH/1000rpm in top	20.9
Kerb weight	3265lb
Date tested	25.6.86

JAGUAR SPORT XJR-S   £45,000

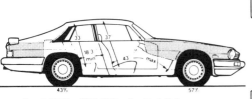
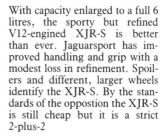

Length 186.7ins. Width 70.6ins. Front track 58.6ins.
Wheelbase 000.0ins. Height 58.0ins. Rear track 58.0ins.

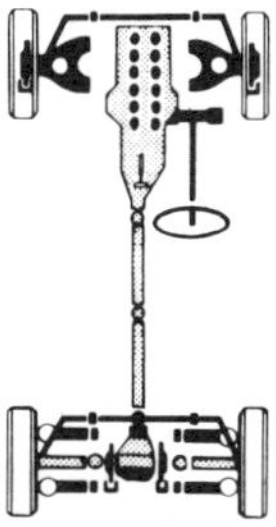

With capacity enlarged to a full 6 litres, the sporty but refined V12-engined XJR-S is better than ever. Jaguarsport has improved handling and grip with a modest loss in refinement. Spoilers and different, larger wheels identify the XJR-S. By the standards of the opposition the XJR-S is still cheap but it is a strict 2-plus-2

Capacity	5993cc
Power	318bhp at 5250rpm
Torque	362lb ft at 3750rpm
Max speed	150mph
0-60mph	7.1secs
30-70 through gears	6.6secs
ss ¼ mile	15.5secs/93mph
30-50 in kickdown	2.7secs
50-70 in kickdown	3.9secs
MPG overall/touring	—/15.4
MPH/1000rpm in top	N/A
Kerb weight	N/A
Date tested	23/8/89

MERCEDES-BENZ 560 SEC   £63,200

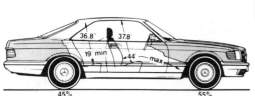

Length 203.1ins. Width 79.0ins. Front track 61.2ins.
Wheelbase 120.9ins. Height 56.9ins. Rear track 60.1ins.

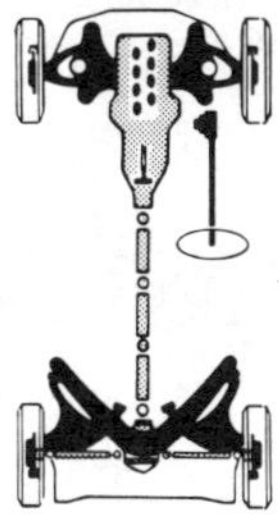

The 5.5-litre V8-engined S-class coupe delivers effortless performance. Torque is smoothly transmitted via Mercedes' excellent four-speed automatic gearbox and limited slip diff; manual is not available. Ride and handling standards are predictably high, as is the level of luxury and equipment. This is a full four seater opulent cruiser

Capacity	5547cc
Power	300bhp at 5000rpm
Torque	335lb ft at 3750rpm
Max speed	147mph
0-60mph	7.1secs
30-70 through gears	6.2secs
ss ¼ mile	15.8secs/93mph
30-50 in fourth	N/A
50-70 in fifth	N/A
MPG overall/touring	18.6/19.9
MPH/1000rpm in top	N/A
Kerb weight	3572lb
Date tested	30.7.86

PORSCHE 928 S4

Even more muscle, extraordinary verve and an image that still galvanises the dollies on the boulevard: all this and competence, too...

ELEVEN years after it was first launched, the Porsche 928 retains that menacing elegance. Standing in our car park, the metallic copper S4 was vaguely reminiscent of a jacketed parabellum projectile.

CAR's last test of one of these supercars was of an S2 version in January 1986. The S4 embodies mild but effective styling changes and its engine gains another two camshafts and 16 valves over the S2. For the record, the S4 is not the first 928 to have a 32-valve twin-cam engine, however, for that distinction goes to the S3, a United States market clean air special.

Bodywork changes for the S4 are confined to the front and the tail. Up front there is now an impact absorbing nose, fluently rounded with flush fitting lights and a considerable improvement on the S2's. Much the same applies to the new tail section which is complemented by a larger spoiler. Surprisingly for such a low, sleek car the S2's Cd (drag) figure was a relatively poor 0,39 but the nose, tail and spoiler changes of the S4 bring it to a more acceptable 0,34 when the automatically adjustable engine duct is in its optimum postion. Barring the changes to the tail and nose mouldings, the 928 body retains the same classic lines it had when it was launched.

Porsches are known for their build quality and the bodywork gives the general impression of toughness and durability. Not so the interior of the test car, where the almost white lamb's wool carpeting and leather seats, though durable enough, showed even very mild soiling. Certainly the effect was plush, even opulent but the constant attention that it demanded was a rather wearying and impractical aspect of the car.

Otherwise it's difficult to criticise the 928 interior - always assuming that it's accepted that this is a 2-plus-2 configuration and that adult rear seat passengers are rarely expected. Unlike other Porsches there has been no cost cutting on interior fittings. The 928 is designed and styled for a custom look and defined ergonomic results. Front seat occupants could hardly ask for extra space or a more comfortable seating position and they are faced with a functionally beautiful dashboard.

LUXURY SPEC

The test car contained a full spectrum of luxury accessories ranging from automatic air-conditioning to fully adjustable three-position memory and power seats. Ergonomics for the driver have been particularly well thought out within the configuration constraints of a low centre of gravity sports coupé. The driver even has the luxury of a steering wheel and instrument pod which tilt up and down as a unit.

Floor pedals are a minor exception in that the brake pedal is well forward of the accelerator, though they are large and the accelerator is of the comfortable, organ-pedal type. Since

The 928 comes into its own on the the open road (above). Its mighty 235 kW S4 V8 (below) has four overhead camshafts, four valves-per-cylinder and full electronic engine management. Both cylinder block and cylinder heads are made of aluminium.

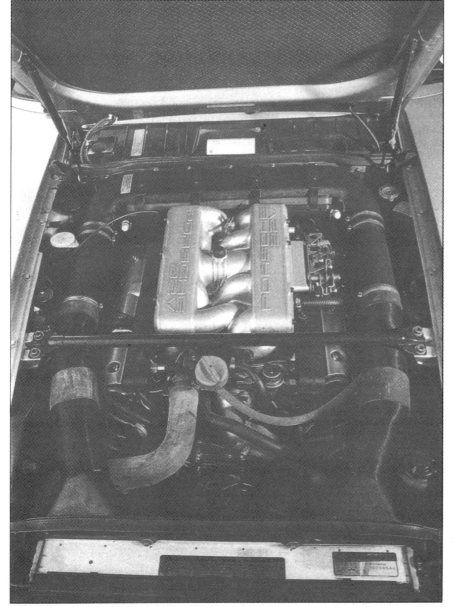

the seating position is close to the ground it was possible to give the driver the benefit of an elbow height gearshift, console mounted and followed by a sloping panel of easily reachable controls.

Electronics have been used to provide an LED dot matrix warning panel, so that the driver can be appraised of important malfunctions as they occur. Tyre pressure was one of the monitored functions and it presented a novel feature which 'malfunctioned' a number of times during our test. When the display warned us of pressure loss we would stop and check the pressures, only to find that things were normal.

Dot matrix displays are also used for time, distance and fuel consumption indications which can be called up

KEY FIGURES

Maximum speed	262 km/h
1 km sprint	26,29 seconds
Fuel tank capacity	86
Litres/100 km at 100	N/A
Optimum fuel range at 100	N/A
*Fuel index	N/A
Engine revs per km	1 320
Odometer error	3,39 per cent over
National list price	R449 800
(*Consumption at 100 plus 40%)	

when required. Two tripmeters as well as the odometer are also displayed in LED rather than with traditional revolving mechanical cylinders. Hopefully the odometer's electronic memory is fail-safe.

The long nose and slightly restricted visibility, especially through the spoiler-obscured rear screen, and the feel of the controls of the car at low speed make it rather cumbersome in urban traffic conditions. On the other hand the 928 is an autobahn-eating grand tourer, the luxury flagship of the Porsche line-up.

AUTOMATIC PREFERENCE

Though manual transmission is an option, most 928s are ordered as automatics and this is probably a sensible choice for a car of nearly 1700 kg with 430 N.m of torque on tap, since a suitable manual gearbox is likely to have a heavy shift action, making it awkward in traffic conditions.

The test car was fitted with a four-speed automatic transaxle which gave 45,46 km/h per 1000 r/min in top – well matched to the stump-pulling torque of the big V8. The all-aluminium power unit has a V-block which is essentially two 944 S2 blocks mated together.

Bores are silicon-coated and the pistons chrome-plated. S4 engines have had their bores enlarged by 3 mm to 100 mm, so that with the same 78,9 mm stroke, capacity is 4 957 cm³ compared to 4 664 cm³ for the superseded engine. The main changes, of course, are the double overhead cams and four valves per cylinder. The cylinder heads are also fitted with hydraulic tappets and are, incidentally, the same heads used on the new 944 16-valve engines.

Bosch LH-Jetronic with an air mass meter supplies the fuel mixture which is ignited by a Bosch mapped ignition system. Peak power of 235 kW at 6 000 r/min is only 7 kW up on that of the previous engine but the rationale behind going to 16 valves in this case was mainly to achieve cleaner burning and improved fuel consumption.

At a South African price of around R500 000 the buyer of one of these cars is unlikely to be concerned with fuel consumption - which was why we refrained from delving into the dense array of wiring and plumbing in order to fit our fuel metering equipment. Nevertheless an indication of its thirst can be gained from our overall figure achieved during driving and testing. This came to 19,34 ℓ/100 km – in line with the claimed ECE urban cycle figure of 17,1 ℓ/100 which, in this case, equates with our inclusion of the onerous full power demands made during road testing.

MUSCLE ON TAP

Sheer muscle must of course be high on the requirements list of many 928 buyers and they won't be disappointed. Flooring the throttle brings about a sensation similar to taking off in a Boeing. The driver is pressed back into those futuristic seats and the scenery begins to flick past ever more rapidly.

A glance in the mirror shows any following traffic shrinking to dinky toy dimensions. Not surprisingly, the power-to-weight ratio of 148,7 watts to the kilogram makes this one of the most powerful production cars around and the low frontal area and Cd efficiency make overall wind resistance less of a factor than usual.

During our acceleration tests 0 to 100 km/h came up in 6,61 seconds and the kilometre sprint in a blistering 26,29 seconds with a terminal speed of 204 km/h. At the maximum speed of 262 km/h the scenery was really moving rapidly, giving an impressive demonstration of the the 928's capabilities.

One member of the test team complained that the sharply raked windscreen's tendency to reflect off the dashboard made distance perception more difficult, while another commented on the heaviness of the steering around the centre point. Nevertheless, all agreed that the 928 comes into its own at speed.

Ideally suited to wide open roads and long sweeping bends, it's capable of covering a lot of ground very quickly if the driver so desires. And

most importantly, it inspires a great deal of confidence in the competence of its cornering and braking.

EYEBALL BRAKING

Braking is by Bosch ABS and with the massive 225/50 ZR 16 tyres in front and 245/45 ZR 16s at the rear, stopping was eyeball-straining and very consistent. Standing on the beefy brake pedal for ten stops from 100 km/h resulted in a best stop of 2,9 seconds and a worst of 3,0 seconds with the rapidly pulsating ABS system keeping the car in a straight line.

Hard cornering provides yet another convincing demonstration of the 928's superior capabilities. The S4's suspension is unchanged, using the same double wishbones and coil springs up front and at the rear, the coil-sprung Weissach axle. Anti-roll bars are fitted front and rear and the engine is joined to the transaxle by a rigid torque tube.

Built for leech-like road-holding, it has the low centre of gravity, even weight distribution and wide track required to complement the sticky tyres and superior suspension. Body roll is almost non-existent and the Porsche exhibits gentle understeer.

With so much power available it can be driven on the throttle in grand style but it's advisable to select third rather than top (drive) or the kickdown intervenes inopportunely to spoil the fun. Nevertheless, when the driver does bring the tail out, it's a snip to marshal it back into line.

From our point of view ride quality was the 928's worst feaure if it was to be regarded as a luxury tourer. Low profile tyres and firm suspension settings are largely the cause of the macho ride quality but there is also a significant amount of road noise which finds its way into the cabin. Over coarse grade tarred surfaces taken at speed the result is annoying and makes normal conversation difficult; but a Porsche enthusiast might regard it as a necessary characteristic.

Necessary, because the feel of the tyres on the road is communicated very clearly to the driver. It's a live, seat-of-the-pants feel which signals the car's state of motion to the driver to give him quicker awareness of the car's reactions, if he is sensitive to them.

Surprisingly, our test S4 proved quicker in acceleration and top speed than a 7 kW difference would suggest and perhaps the previous test car was not at its best, since it was 0,75 of a second slower to 100 km/h and top speed was down by 9 km/h.

TEST SUMMARY

Living with the mighty 928 S4 was an experience to be savoured and remembered. It was just so much faster and more capable than anything that we normally get to drive that coming

back to reality was one of life's little knocks.

It's a large car with enough room in the back for two children and a little luggage. If you have a flat tyre there's a space saver wheel that you have to inflate with a small electric pump. But so what, it goes like the clappers, corners like it's on rails and what's more, it's built to do it all day and all night. ●

SPECIFICATIONS

ENGINE:
Cylinders	V8
Fuel supply	Bosch LH Jetronic
Bore/stroke	100/78,9 mm
Cubic capacity	4 957 cm³
Compression ratio	10,0 to 1
Valve gear	d-o-h-c per bank
Ignition	electronic
Main bearings	five
Fuel requirement	97-octane Coast 93-octane Reef
Cooling	water

ENGINE OUTPUT:
Max power I.S.O. (kW)	235
Power peak (r/min)	6 000
Max usable r/min	6 400
Max torque (N.m)	430
Torque peak (r/min)	3 000

TRANSMISSION:
Forward speeds	four plus torque converter
Gearshift	console
Low gear	3,870 to 1
2nd gear	2,250 to 1
3rd gear	1,440 to 1
Top gear	1,000 to 1
Reverse gear	5,590 to 1
Final drive	2,538 to 1
Drive wheels	rear

WHEELS AND TYRES:
Road wheels	alloy
Rim width	7J (front) 8J (rear)
Tyre make	Dunlop SP Sport D40
Tyre size	225 ZR 16 (front) 245/45 2R 16 (rear)
Tyre pressures (front)	250 kPa
Tyre pressures (rear)	300 kPa

BRAKES:
Front	ventilated discs
Rear	ventilated discs
Hydraulics	ABS anti-lock system
Boosting	vacuum
Handbrake position	beside driver

STEERING:
Type	rack and pinion, power assisted
Lock to lock	3 turns
Turning circle	11,5 metres

MEASUREMENTS:
Length overall	4 520 mm
Width overall	1 836 mm
Height overall	1 282 mm
Wheelbase	2 500 mm
Front track	1 551 mm
Rear track	1 546 mm
Ground clearance	120 mm
Licensing mass	1 580 kg
Mass as tested	1 660 kg

SUSPENSION:
Front	independent
Type	double cast alloy wishbones, anti-roll bar
Rear	independent
Type	lower trailing arms, upper wishbones, coils anti-roll bar

CAPACITIES:
Seating	2 + 2
Fuel tank	86 litres
Luggage trunk	154 dm³
Utility space	506 dm³

WARRANTY:
12 months unlimited km

TEST CAR FROM:
Lindsay Saker Porsche

ACCELERATION

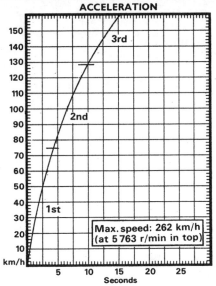

Max. speed: 262 km/h (at 5 763 r/min in top)

PERFORMANCE FACTORS:
Power/mass (W/kg) net 148,7
Frontal area (m²) 2,35
km/h per 1 000 r/min (top) 45,46
(Calculated on licensing mass, gross frontal area, gearing and I.S.O. power output.)

TEST CONDITIONS:
Altitude .... at sea level
Weather .... sunny, light wind
Fuel used .... 97 octane
Test car's odometer 7 516

GRADIENT ABILITY

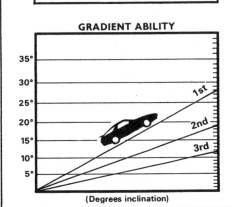

(Degrees inclination)

MAXIMUM SPEED (km/h):
True speed 262
Speedometer reading 279
(Average of runs both ways on a level road.)
Calibration:

Indicated:	60	80	100	120
True speed:	53	70	90	108

ACCELERATION (seconds):
0-60 3,30
0-80 4,76
0-100 6,61
0-120 8,73
1 km sprint 26,29
Terminal speed .... 204,3 km/h

OVERTAKING ACCELERATION:
	Drive
40-60	1,21
60-80	1,63
80-100	1,84
100-120	2,14

FUEL CONSUMPTION (litres/100 km):
(Claimed figures according to ECEA 70)
90 9,0
120 .... 10.9
Urban 17,1

BRAKING TEST:
From 100 km/h
Best stop 2,9
Worst stop 3,0
Average 2,94
(Measured in seconds with stops from true speeds at 30-second intervals on a good bitumenised surface.)

GRADIENTS IN GEARS:
Low gear .... 1 in 1,9
2nd gear .... 1 in 2,9
3rd gear .... 1 in 5,0
4th gear .... 1 in N/A
(Tabulated from Tapley (x gravity) readings, car carrying test crew of two and standard test equipment.)

GEARED SPEEDS (km/h):
Low gear	71*	75
2nd gear	212*	129
3rd gear	189*	202
Top gear	273*	291

(Calculated at engine power peak* – 6 000 r/min and at max. usable r/min – 6 400 r/min.)

INTERIOR NOISE LEVELS:
	Mech.	Wind	Road
Idling	47	–	–
60	64	–	–
80	67	73	74
100	68	75	76

(Measured in decibels, "A" weighting, averaging runs both ways on a level road: "mechanical" with car closed; "wind" with one window fully open; "road" on a coarse road surface.)

ENGINE SPEED

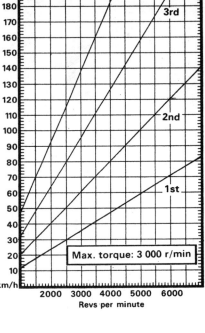

Max. torque: 3 000 r/min

BRAKING DISTANCES

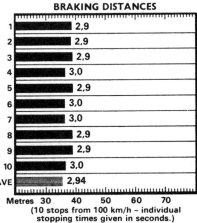

1	2,9
2	2,9
3	2,9
4	3,0
5	2,9
6	3,0
7	3,0
8	2,9
9	2,9
10	3,0
AVE	2,94

Metres 30 40 50 60 70
(10 stops from 100 km/h – individual stopping times given in seconds.)

Porsche 928GT

Speed for the serious—and the solvent.

BY ARTHUR ST. ANTOINE

• So there you are with a spare $76,500 in your pocket and an itch in your brain. Your plans to invest in flight lessons have been dashed (who'd have guessed that the FAA would object to your building a backyard dirigible hangar?). Your art collection is looking plenty comprehensive already—you've yet to figure out if you even have a wall big enough for the JFK-assassination acrylic. And only yesterday you found out that the neighborhood has zoning laws prohibiting the ranching of African gnus. Either you come up with a big-money diversion fast or the cash is going to have to go in the *bank*.

Allow us to suggest a quick remedy: the Porsche 928GT. If you have more money than encumbrances, you'll want to take a look at this brawny automotive

toy. And we do mean *toy*. So committed to speed is this latest version of the 928 that it makes casual cruising almost unpleasant. In fact, if it's high-comfort, high-exposure profiling you're after, you might as well stop reading right now.

What's that? Isn't this the famed 928 we're talking about—the Porsche of choice among the country-club set? Well, yes. And that's precisely why we thought we should have this little talk.

Introduced in 1978, the 928 has always been a serious sporting machine. Yet its luxury fittings and versatile GT profile have earned it a reputation as something of a poseur's Porsche—a car seen less often carving up mountain roads than being proudly handed over to the country-club valet. That's not Porsche's fault:

over the years the maker has steadily improved the 928 to keep it near the top of the performance class. In fact, the new manual-gearbox-only GT edition shown here is the most speed-dedicated 928 yet. But that brings us back to our warning: anyone who buys a GT looking for relaxing daily transportation is in for a shock.

The GT is a deadly serious *driver's* car. In its quest for pure performance, Porsche has chiseled off most of the 928's remaining soft edges.

There are engine refinements, of course. The GT's 5.0-liter V-8 benefits from new camshafts and a retuned intake system; the changes increase the output of the four-cam, 32-valve engine by 10 horsepower, to 326 at 6200 rpm. The automatic-equipped 928S4, on the other

PHOTOGRAPHY BY TOM DREW

114

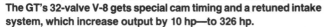

The GT's 32-valve V-8 gets special cam timing and a retuned intake system, which increase output by 10 hp—to 326 hp.

hand, produces the same 316 hp as last year's S4. The GT makes the same maximum torque as the S4—317 pound-feet—but its torque peak is 4100 rpm, 1100 rpm higher.

The extra power shows on the stopwatch. The GT rockets from 0 to 60 mph in just 5.2 seconds and through the quarter-mile in 13.7 seconds at 104 mph—improvements of 0.1 and 0.2 second, respectively, over the times generated by the five-speed 928S4 we tested in May 1987. (Not a bad showing for a 3603-pound "luxury" GT, eh?) Top speed is up a full 10 mph, to 169 mph at the engine's 6600-rpm redline.

You don't need a stopwatch to appreciate this kind of performance. Step hard into the throttle at almost any rpm and

the GT hurtles forward, the V-8 pulling with particular vigor as it ticks over the 4000-rpm mark. (The V-8's full-throttle cry, by the way, could raise the hair of a Vitalis devotee.) Wind the engine to the redline in first gear and you'll hit 45 mph. Wind it out in second and you'll muster enough speed to secure the attention of any nearby highway patrolman.

The 928GT shines when you give it the spurs. The control efforts are finely honed for speeds above 80 mph: the steering arcs with reassuring heft, the shifter chunks solidly through its racing-pattern H, and the clutch takeup is smooth and positive. Spin the speedo up to autobahn speeds and the GT really comes into its own. Suddenly, the beefy body feels not chubby but secure; racing

across the pavement at the velocities allowed in its homeland, the GT feels like a locomotive built for two.

The GT is far more agile in curvy-road dicing and slicing than you'd expect such a hefty car to be. Porsche has tamed the old 928's tail-happiness; the GT understeers resolutely through hard bends, tucking in neatly even if you suddenly snap off the throttle (it's still possible to kick the tail out with a sharp jab on the power). The four fat Bridgestone RE71s—225/50ZR-16s in front and 245/45ZR-16s in back—display commendable friction in corners: the GT circles the skidpad at 0.86 g.

To improve the relationship between tire and earth, both 1990-model 928s sport Porsche's electronically controlled

Fortified for life at 169 mph, the 928GT has sticky Bridgestones, stiff shocks, and a low-tire-pressure warning system.

limited-slip differential—a device first seen on the mighty 959. At the heart of the system is a progressively lockable multiplate clutch in-unit with the rear differential. A computer gradually engages the clutch when it detects any wheelspin at the rear; in so doing, it helps each rear tire transmit as much power as its available traction will allow. A small indicator light on the dash glows whenever the system is activated.

The GT's massive ABS-equipped disc brakes are simply superb, hauling the car down from 70 mph in just 167 feet. Fade is simply not an issue, even after repeated hard stops.

Before your performance-hungry eyes glaze over completely, however, you need to know that this stirring performance exacts a toll. There's no question that if you drive the 928GT hard—really hard—it'll reward you with some of the best moves in the auto kingdom. But if your driving is dominated by strolls over to the polo club, you're likely to think of the GT as more beast than beauty.

The GT's ride is, in a word, firm. Over the sort of fractured asphalt that blemishes most of Michigan, the car hammers and crashes so badly that you wonder if there's *any* suspension under your rear end. (Imagine riding down a log pile in an iron canoe and you'll be close.) The RE71s—not known as particularly smooth-riding tires—contribute to the harshness, as does the shock valving, which Porsche has firmed up for 1990. The unforgiving ride isn't the only strain: the shifter, the clutch, and the steering—so exemplary at high speeds—feel heavy and ponderous in city cruising. Driving the GT at six-tenths or less is *work*. Rough work.

Followers of the 928 will note that the interior is familiar (a new low-tire-pressure warning system has been added to the driver-information display). It's a fine cabin, simple and businesslike, but it's severe. You sit low, surrounded by high sills and a tall center console. All around you are stern, sensible gauges and nononsense controls. There isn't a soothing detail in sight. It's a great place from which to conduct the business of serious driving, but it's not going to do anything to brighten your mood as you thunk your way over to the club.

That's not to imply that the GT is stark. The standard-equipment list covers every imaginable power option, from heated outside mirrors and an auxiliary rear air conditioner to a ten-speaker AM/FM/cassette system—everything you'd expect in a luxury car. Then again, for $76,500, the 928GT had *better* be able to give the space shuttle a run for the "Best-Equipped Vehicle" title.

So you now realize that the 928GT is a damn serious automobile, requiring a serious investment and delivering serious performance. But the question remains: are you that serious? Since the 928's debut, a host of new and talented offerings have appeared in the luxury-GT class—

cars that offer serious speed *and* day-to-day civility. Of these, the standout is the new Nissan 300ZX Turbo—a car that delivers much of the 928GT's performance without the comfort penalty. And the Nissan costs $33,000. Do the addition and you'll realize that for the price of a 928GT you could have a 300ZX Turbo, a Lexus LS400 sedan, and enough left over for a respectable European tour. Order some of the more extravagant options—such as a custom-colored leather interior and matched-to-sample exterior paint—and you can push the price of a GT over $100,000.

Porsche plans to sell only about 100 928GTs in the U.S. this year. That should tell you plenty about this car's mass-market appeal.

The 928GT is a plaything—a leather-lined speed machine for the very well heeled. If you're looking for distinctive daily transportation and you have the GT on your short list, scratch it off—it's far too unforgiving for that. But if you've got your daily wheels and you can afford to indulge in something frivolous, well, yes, you absolutely ought to consider this potent Porsche.

Besides, it's a hell of a lot easier to park than a dirigible.

●

Vehicle type: front-engine, rear-wheel-drive, 2+2-passenger, 3-door coupe

Price as tested: $76,500

Options on test car: base Porsche 928GT, $74,545; gas-guzzler tax, $1300; freight, $655

Standard accessories: power steering, windows, seats, locks, and sunroof, A/C, cruise control, tilt steering, rear defroster and wiper

Sound system: Blaupunkt Reno 2 AM/FM-stereo radio/cassette, 10 speakers

ENGINE
Type	V-8, aluminum block and heads
Bore x stroke	3.94 x 3.11 in, 100.0 x 78.9mm
Displacement	303 cu in, 4957cc
Compression ratio	10.0:1
Engine-control system	Bosch EZK-LH-Jetronic with port fuel injection
Emissions controls	3-way catalytic converter, feedback fuel-air-ratio control, auxiliary air pump
Valve gear	belt- and chain-driven double overhead cams, 4 valves per cylinder, hydraulic lifters
Power (SAE net)	326 bhp @ 6200 rpm
Torque (SAE net)	317 lb-ft @ 4100 rpm
Redline	6600 rpm

DRIVETRAIN
Transmission 5-speed
Final-drive ratio . . . . 2.73:1, limited slip

Gear	Ratio	Mph/1000 rpm	Max. test speed
I	3.77	6.8	45 mph (6600 rpm)
II	2.51	10.2	67 mph (6600 rpm)
III	1.79	14.3	94 mph (6600 rpm)
IV	1.35	19.0	125 mph (6600 rpm)
V	1.00	25.6	169 mph (6600 rpm)

DIMENSIONS AND CAPACITIES
Wheelbase	98.4 in
Track, F/R	61.5/61.6 in
Length	178.1 in
Width	72.3 in
Height	50.5 in
Frontal area	21.3 sq ft
Ground clearance	4.7 in
Curb weight	3603 lb
Weight distribution, F/R	52.0/48.0%
Fuel capacity	22.7 gal
Oil capacity	8.0 qt
Water capacity	16.9 qt

CHASSIS/BODY
Type	unit construction
Body material	welded steel stampings and aluminum stampings

INTERIOR
SAE volume, front seat	53 cu ft
rear seat	21 cu ft
luggage space	6 cu ft
Front seats	bucket
Seat adjustments	fore and aft, seatback angle, front height, rear height
General comfort	poor fair good **excellent**
Fore-and-aft support	poor fair good **excellent**
Lateral support	poor fair **good** excellent

SUSPENSION
F: . . . . ind, unequal-length control arms, coil springs, anti-roll bar
R: . . . . ind, unequal-length control arms, coil springs, anti-roll bar

STEERING
Type	rack-and-pinion, power-assisted
Turns lock-to-lock	3.0
Turning circle curb-to-curb	38.4 ft

BRAKES
F:	12.0 x 1.3-in vented disc
R:	11.8 x 0.9-in vented disc
Power assist	vacuum with anti-lock control

WHEELS AND TIRES
Wheel size	F: 7.5 x 16 in, R: 9.0 x 16 in
Wheel type	cast aluminum
Tires	Bridgestone Potenza RE71; F: 225/50ZR-16, R: 245/45ZR-16
Test inflation pressures, F/R	36/44 psi

CAR AND DRIVER TEST RESULTS

ACCELERATION — Seconds
Zero to 30 mph	2.0
40 mph	2.9
50 mph	4.0
60 mph	5.2
70 mph	6.7
80 mph	8.3
90 mph	10.1
100 mph	12.6
110 mph	15.3
120 mph	18.5
130 mph	23.3
140 mph	30.1
150 mph	39.2
Top-gear passing time, 30–50 mph	7.1
50–70 mph	7.2
Standing ¼-mile	13.7 sec @ 104 mph
Top speed	169 mph

BRAKING
70–0 mph @ impending lockup . . . . 167 ft

Fade . . . . **none** moderate heavy

HANDLING
Roadholding, 300-ft-dia skidpad . . . . 0.86 g
Understeer . . . . minimal **moderate** excessive

COAST-DOWN MEASUREMENTS
Road horsepower @ 30 mph . . . . 6 hp
50 mph . . . . 16 hp
70 mph . . . . 32 hp

FUEL ECONOMY
EPA city driving	13 mpg
EPA highway driving	19 mpg
C/D observed fuel economy	13 mpg

INTERIOR SOUND LEVEL
Idle	55 dBA
Full-throttle acceleration	87 dBA
70-mph cruising	76 dBA
70-mph coasting	75 dBA

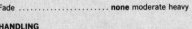

CURRENT BASE PRICE dollars x 1000
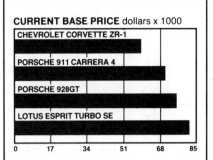
CHEVROLET CORVETTE ZR-1
PORSCHE 911 CARRERA 4
PORSCHE 928GT
LOTUS ESPRIT TURBO SE
0 17 34 51 68 85

ACCELERATION seconds
■ 0–60 mph
■ ¼-mile
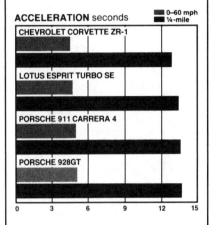
CHEVROLET CORVETTE ZR-1
LOTUS ESPRIT TURBO SE
PORSCHE 911 CARRERA 4
PORSCHE 928GT
0 3 6 9 12 15

70–0 MPH BRAKING feet
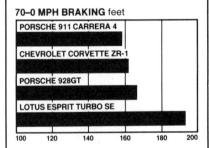
PORSCHE 911 CARRERA 4
CHEVROLET CORVETTE ZR-1
PORSCHE 928GT
LOTUS ESPRIT TURBO SE
100 120 140 160 180 200

ROADHOLDING 300-foot skidpad, g
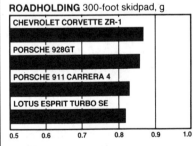
CHEVROLET CORVETTE ZR-1
PORSCHE 928GT
PORSCHE 911 CARRERA 4
LOTUS ESPRIT TURBO SE
0.5 0.6 0.7 0.8 0.9 1.0

EPA ESTIMATED FUEL ECONOMY mpg
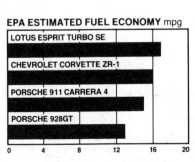
LOTUS ESPRIT TURBO SE
CHEVROLET CORVETTE ZR-1
PORSCHE 911 CARRERA 4
PORSCHE 928GT
0 4 8 12 16 20

You can drive it like a gentleman, or you can flog it like a wildman. Either way, the Porsche 928 GT cooperates. With chassis limits so high and power so linear, it's hard to imagine a situation where you'd be surprised by the road or the car.

Of course, that's precisely how a GT car is supposed to behave, and it sums up Porsche's latest, greatest 928 perfectly. The term "GT" stands for the Italian "Gran Turismo" and the Americanized "Grand Touring." In the case of the Porsche 928, the label is quite apt. Touring doesn't get much grander than this.

Porsche's 928 is one of the most familiar faces in the current sports car world, and another example of a Porsche body style that somehow transcends the fickle styling whims of popular culture. Like the 911, the 928 still looks fresh, even after years of production.

Those years have done more than just establish the 928 in the hearts and minds of sports car enthusiasts. They've

PORSCHE

THE GENTLEMAN'S EXPRESS

also presented the Porsche engineers with ample opportunity to refine the biggest, fastest car in their production inventory. The all-aluminum 5-liter V-8 that powers the manual-transmission-only GT has received four new camshafts, and the induction system has been ministered to once again. These changes push peak power up to 326

928 GT

by Jeff Karr

PHOTOGRAPHY BY SCOTT DAHLQUIST

horses at 6200 rpm. An automatic transmission is available in the 928 also, but that powertrain doesn't benefit from the GT's power-enhancing refinements, and peak power lags 10 horsepower behind.

Regardless of transmission choice, all new 928s come standard with an electronically controlled, variable-ratio limited-slip differential. An evolution of the system developed on the 959, the setup uses the ABS wheel-speed sensors to determine the amount of lockup required at any given instant, then an electronically controlled multiplate clutch adjusts in response. The result is "smarter" limited-slip operation, with just the right amount of lockup for the conditions. The other new techie tidbit is a low tire-pressure warning system.

Otherwise, the 928 GT is the same competent piece of engineering it's always been. With an as-tested price of over $77,000, you'd expect nothing less. All that money buys a car with the emphasis clearly focused on function, not on gratuitous luxury. Consider the interior, for example. Though the cockpit looks expensive and feels substantial, it has the stern, slightly impersonal appearance of a serious sports car without any overt luxo-cues. It looks more like a place of business than a throw-pillow haven for frazzled nerves. From the feel of the switches to the starkly purposeful layout, the 928 GT has a powerful am-

biance, one that speaks of attention to engineering detail and to a cost-is-no-object attitude.

The control layout is first-rate; the thick, leather-trimmed steering wheel is adjustable, and the whole instrument pod moves along with it so vital gauges are never obstructed. The wheel's center and the dashboard in front of the passenger both house airbags. The front buckets are thoughtfully shaped, so that the omission of adjustable lateral and lumbar support barely seems like an omission at all. The back seats—yes, there really are two of them back there—are tiny engineering marvels. They're deeply contoured and have flip-down backs to expand the cargo area. And each seat has its own devoted sun visor to keep the solar load through the back glass from getting too oppressive. And as if all that weren't enough, there's a center air-conditioning console between them with its own independent fan speed and temperature control. Inexplicably, those controls are mounted up front in the cabin where the back-seat riders can't possibly reach them. Apparently, you're supposed to ask the folks up front to make adjustments for you.

Such elaborate and obviously expensive measures to pamper the back-seaters seem like overkill to us, even for a car in this price range. The seats can't comfortably accommodate anyone over about 5 feet 4 inches tall, and we're doubtful that anyone who can afford such a car would subject friends or relatives to this sort of confinement for anything other than the shortest trips. We would rather have seen the money that was devoted to the rear air-conditioning instead sunk into the 928's sound system. Even with the uplevel 10-speaker CD-player option in our test car, sound quality was uninspired.

While we're complaining, we'll take a swipe at the automatic climate control system. Sometimes it overreacts to hot, direct sunlight on the top of the dash and responds by pumping copious amounts of cool air into the car when it's not really needed. To compensate, you must second-guess the system's automatic brain to keep the temperature and air flow where you want it. There's no manual control of the system. And here's an engineering curiosity: Though there's plenty of interior storage in the door armrests and glove compartment, for some reason, the Porsche people felt compelled to add a center storage console. The problem is that it's only about 1 inch deep, relegating it to the storage of pressed flowers or thinly sliced lunch meats. Yeah, sure, we're whining, but it's our job.

The important stuff is nice, real nice. The 32-valve V-8 rumbles men-

acingly under the hood. Off idle, the power is strong, but not overwhelming. Along about 3000 rpm, though, the engine gets real steamy—not in a sudden way, but in a gradual transformation. The 928 is happy to rev to redline, so steady running at high rpm is a pleasure. And in case anyone is in doubt, this engine reaffirms yet again that big, normally aspirated engines are better, more trustworthy driving companions than even the slickest turbo-motors.

Acceleration in the Porsche is, to say the least, zesty. Our car took just 5.9 seconds to accelerate 0-60 mph, and probably could have been hustled up to speed even more briskly by shifting more aggressively. The five-speed manual box does not encourage this however, since the action is stiff and the classic racing pattern slows the one-two shift down somewhat.

In keeping with the Porsche concept of mass decentralization, the 928's gearbox isn't mounted up front with the engine, but is positioned instead back by the rear axle. This design lends the car much of its legendary poise and stability at high speed. The 928 is an easy car to drive swiftly on unfamiliar roads, since it goes about its business with such regal grace and composure. The steering's solid weighting and the chassis' unerring tracking at speed make the Porsche feel like it's following a navigation wire embedded in the road surface. The smooth power delivery keeps surprises to an absolute minimum, and only a full-on effort will push the car into oversteer. You can get more aggressive, and more sideways, if you flick the car broadside at the turn entrance, but such low-percentage antics should be reserved exclusively for the racetrack. It isn't the fast way around a corner, but it sure is fun. Lifting the throttle or squeezing on the brakes won't cause problems regardless of the car's cornering attitude.

Though the 928's comforting stability by nature precludes the sort of point-and-shoot agility you'll find in the Corvette ZR-1 or 300ZX Turbo, the 928's handling balance makes a

great deal of sense for the kind of driving a grand touring car does. Point to point, the 928 is secure and swift.

The 928 GT's maximum handling numbers are respectable. On the skidpad, the car scrambles around in a mild understeer attitude to the tune of 0.85 g. The 65.6-mph slalom velocity is good, too, particularly for a car of this size and weight, without the benefit of four-wheel steering. Braking is simply amazing, with a 112-foot stopping distance from 60 mph.

All that stuff is great, but you don't have to pay the 77 grand Porsche asks for the 928 to get numbers like that, at least not these days. Cars like the Mitsubishi 3000GT VR-4 and the Dodge Stealth R/T Turbo have the same seat count, accelerate nearly as hard, and turn in even better handling numbers, plus they offer advancements like all-wheel drive and four-wheel steering and cost about 45 grand less.

This fact is of only passing interest to the couple hundred people who join the ranks of 928 GT owners each year. With the Porsche, you're not buying anything as cut and dried as simple performance numbers and breathtaking specs. There's a unique feel to the 928 that can't be found elsewhere, and a certain emotional glow you get when you strap into the car. These psychic rewards come at a high price, but if you're a sports car buyer playing in this league, you owe it to yourself to experience the Porsche 928 GT. **MT**

SECOND OPINION

I play the lottery every week for one reason. This car. The first time I saw the 928 years ago, I decided it would be the first thing I bought when my numbers came up. I already have a license plate picked out. Keep your twin turbos and techno goodies; the 928 GT, with its normally aspirated 326-horsepower V-8, excellent handling, and braking so remarkable you can start at your garage, hit mid-driveway at 60 mph, and stop the car dead before you reach the street, is in a class all by itself.

No room in the back? Tough. Hell, they can take out the passenger seat, too, as far as I'm concerned. It's the feeling you get inside, and the stares you receive outside, that make this car so special.

But alas, every year the price of my dream rises. So, I guess I'll continue to look for four-leaf clovers, rub my lucky rabbit's foot, and play my numbers, and maybe someday . . .   —*B.J. Hoffman*

Porsche 928 GT

GENERAL

Make and model	Porsche 928 GT
Importer	Porsche Cars North America, Inc., Reno, Nev.
Body style	2-door, 4-passenger
Drivetrain layout	Front engine, rear drive
Base price	$75,845
Price as tested	$77,189
Options included	CD player, $689; destination, $655
Typical market competition	Chevrolet Corvette ZR-1, Jaguar XJ-S

DIMENSIONS

Wheelbase, in./mm	98.4/2500
Track, f/r, in./mm	61.5/61.6/ 1562/1565
Length, in./mm	178.1/4525
Width, in./mm	72.3/1836
Height, in./mm	50.5/1283
Ground clearance, in./mm	4.7/119
Manufacturer's curb weight, lb	3505
Weight distribution, f/r, %	50/50
Cargo capacity, cu ft	6.30
Fuel capacity, gal	22.7
Weight/power ratio, lb/hp	10.8

ENGINE

Type	V-8, liquid cooled, cast aluminum block and heads
Bore x stroke, in./mm	3.94 x 3.11/ 100.0 x 78.9
Displacement, ci/cc	303/4957
Compression ratio	10.0:1
Valve gear	DOHC, 4 valves/cylinder
Fuel/induction system	Multipoint EFI
Horsepower, hp @ rpm, SAE net	326 @ 6200
Torque, lb-ft @ rpm, SAE net	317 @ 4100
Horsepower/liter	65.8
Redline, rpm	6600
Recommended fuel	Unleaded premium

DRIVELINE

Transmission type		5-speed man.
Gear ratios		
	(1st)	3.77:1
	(2nd)	2.51:1
	(3rd)	1.79:1
	(4th)	1.35:1
	(5th)	1.00:1
Axle ratio		2.73:1
Final drive ratio		2.73:1
Engine rpm, 60 mph in top gear		2200

CHASSIS

Suspension

Front	Upper and lower control arms, coil springs, anti-roll bar
Rear	Upper and lower control arms, coil springs, anti-roll bar

Steering

Type	Rack and pinion, power assist
Ratio	17.8:1
Turns, lock to lock	3.0
Turning circle, ft	38.4

Brakes

Front, type/dia., in.	Vented discs/12.0
Rear, type/dia., in.	Vented discs/11.8
Anti-lock	Standard

Wheels and tires

Wheel size, F/R, in.	16 x 7.5/16 x 9.0
Wheel type/material	Cast aluminum
Tire size, F/R	225/50ZR16/245/45ZR16
Tire mfr. and model	Bridgestone RE71

INSTRUMENTATION

Instruments	180-mph speedo; 7600-rpm tach; oil; fuel; temperature; battery; analog clock
Warning lamps	Oil; temperature; battery; brake; airbag; ABS; wheels; stop lamp; PSD

PERFORMANCE AND TEST DATA

Acceleration, sec

0-30 mph	2.3
0-40 mph	3.2
0-50 mph	4.7
0-60 mph	5.9
0-70 mph	7.8
0-80 mph	9.6
Standing quarter mile, sec @ mph	14.3 @ 99.7

Braking, ft

30-0 mph	33
60-0 mph	112

Handling

Lateral acceleration, g	0.85
Speed through 600-ft slalom, mph	65.6

Speedometer error, mph

Indicated	Actual
30	30
40	40
50	50
60	60

Interior noise, dBA

Idling in neutral	54
Steady 60 mph in top gear	70

FUEL ECONOMY

EPA, city/hwy., mpg	13/19
Est. range, city/hwy., miles	295/431

WHEN YOU'RE searching for the best Grand Touring car in the world, you may have to look no farther than your nearest Porsche dealer. There may be one or two exotics that can match the Porsche 928's performance and handling, another car here or there that can rival it in terms of fit and finish, but a single car isn't likely to surpass the 928 in both areas.

Though an exotic car by most standards, the 928 is hardly temperamental; reliability is one of its prime virtues. So is its surprising suitability for everyday use, which has as much to do with its myriad comfort features as with accelerative abilities.

It does accelerate, though. In 1989 the 5-speed manual model received more punch, with a different camshaft and revised intake. This has been continued for 1990. The changes raise its maximum engine speed by 200 rpm, enough to add 10 more horsepower, for a total of 326. That should shave a fraction or two from the already impressive 5.5 sec 0–60 mph sprint, and get the 928 past the 170-mph barrier.

As always, the 928 rides on double A-arms and coil springs in front, and the variable-geometry "Weissach axle" with coil springs in back. These, and the power-assisted steering rack, make the 928 almost unbeatable over enthusiast roads, yet comfortable for extended drives. ABS aids the disc brakes as well as the suspension copes with fast cornering: superbly.

Part of the 928's excellent road behavior stems from its balanced configuration. The 32-valve 5.0-liter dohc V-8 fills the engine bay right up, but the transmission—either a crisp-shifting 5-speed manual or unusually responsive 4-speed automatic lives in unit with the differential out back.

A superlative chassis wouldn't be much fun if it wasn't enveloped in style and comfort; the 928 has both in abundance. The distinctive exterior needs no comment, but the interior, with its wealth of features, is worthy of superlatives. The electrically adjustable leather seats are beyond reproach (at least the front ones are), suitable for any physique.

Want more? The steering wheel adjusts too, carrying the instrument pod—which has all the gauges you'd want—up and down with it to maintain ideal sight lines. Control groupings are optimal and the hardware, from automatic climate control to the Blaupunkt digital audio system to all the electric motors that raise and lower whatever needs to be raised and lowered, simply can't be faulted.

This is one wonderful GT car.

SPECIFICATIONS

Base price, base model **$74,545**	Fuel capacity, U.S. gal..............................**22.7**	Tires............**225/50ZR-16 f, 245/45ZR-26 r**
Country of origin ....**Germany**	Fuel economy (EPA city), mpg **13**	Steering type ....**rack & pinion (p)**
Body/seats..**3D/2+2**	Engine **326-bhp 32V V-8**	Turning circle, ft.....................................**37.7**
Layout..**F/R**	Bore x stroke, mm ....**100.0 x 78.9**	Warranty, years/miles:
Wheelbase, in.....................................**98.4**	Displacement, cc **4957**	Bumper-to-bumper **2/unlimited**
Track, f/r.................................**61.1/60.9**	Compression ratio **10.0:1**	Powertrain..............................**2/unlimited**
Length **178.1**	Bhp @ rpm, net ....**326 @ 6200**	Rust-through........................**10/unlimited**
Width..**72.3**	Torque @ rpm, lb-ft ....**317 @ 4100**	
Height...**50.5**	Transmission.................................**5M*, 4A**	
Luggage capacity, cu ft............................**6.3**	Suspension, f/r ....**ind/ind**	
Curb weight, lb **3505**	Brakes, f/r............................**disc/disc, ABS**	

*indicates model described in specifications.

PORSCHE
928

Now you see it, now you don't

PHOTOS BY RICK GRAVES

Through the years, the Porsche 928 has become something of an invisible exotic. While other cars—notably Ferrari Testarossa, Lamborghini Countach, Lotus Esprit, and even, in recent years, Corvette ZR-1—have dominated the exotic car spotlight, the 928 has soldiered on in the shadows. More recently, the introduction of its air-cooled stable mates, the 911 Carrera 2 and 4, have stolen much of the fastback's limelight. Not that it doesn't get a share of the attention; the V-8 coupe still garners a few stares. But compared to the other exotics, the big Porsche ends up like Meryl Streep at the Oscars; when Cher turns up in a see-through bodystocking, eyes turn elsewhere.

Still, that familiar face hides some fairly impressive figures. With four cams, 32 valves, and a claimed 326 horsepower (316 with the 4-speed automatic), the all-aluminum 5.0-liter V-8 has all the right numbers, and can push the coupe through the quarter-mile in 14.6 sec at 98.3 mph. From a dead stop, 60 mph comes up in 6.1 sec.

Unlike some of its more exotic brethren, however, the Porsche answers the call right now, shoving you back into the warm cozy clutches of the leather-clad buckets. All 8 cylinders snap to instantly at the behest of your right foot, more like a Detroit V-8 than anything from Hethel or Maranello. Its response, in fact, instantly brings to mind comparisons with the L98 Corvette, which might make some Por-

schephiles rend their garments, but is actually high praise indeed. Keep in mind the 928 has been around since 1978, and it's only recently that Corvettes have caught up to the 928.

Over the years, Porsche has revised the suspension tuning on the 928, giving the car stiffer springs and firmer damping for more precise wheel control and a more sporting ride. In addition, the manual wraps its Goodrich Comp T/A radials around wider pressure-cast alloy wheels; 7½ x 16 front, 9 x 16 rear, up 0.5 in. at the front and 1.0 in. at the rear over the automatic's forged-alloy rims. As a bonus, the manual gets revised cam and intake tuning, giving it an additional 10 horsepower and raises the redline 200 rpm (to 6200 rpm) over the auto.

■ **Purposeful interior is typically German with its no-nonsense decor.**

For the white-knuckle performance fan, those changes might seem like manna from heaven. The 928 corners with a pit bull's tenacity, with a grip that belies its 3505-lb heft. Last year's 928 managed 0.83g around the skidpad, and the 1990 model seems like it should easily match or exceed that figure. The company's multi-link Weissach rear axle—coupled this year with an effective, electronically controlled limited-slip differential—also effectively snubs squat during hard acceleration, something that afflicts the 944. Like its smaller sibling, however, the

928 turns in eagerly, with an exceptionally linear response. Despite its large exterior, this Porsche lives up to its reputation for quick, agile handling.

While you might expect that agility to translate to some nervousness at high speed, the 928 settles into scofflaw velocities with the comfort of an old chair. Its *Autobahn* breeding shows through particularly well once the speedo reaches triple digits, and the ride seems especially reassuring. The steering remains accurate, the car stays firmly planted, and you get the feeling that the suspension, tires and rear wing were specifically tuned for flying low.

Coming down from those speeds also lacks any drama. The big Porsche stops via a set of 12.0-in. front/11.8-in. rear discs, with ABS-controlled 4-piston calipers. A hard flog across several miles of severely twisted terrain failed to produce any fade, and the anti-lock plumbing means that duplicating our 135-ft 60–0-mph stop requires no more finesse than stepping on a cockroach. If you need to scrub off some serious speed, just lift your right foot and stomp. The harder you push, the harder you stop; the brakes convert that velocity to heat, and the suspension takes care of any nose dive.

What the suspension does to the ride, however, is not nearly so flattering—nor so pleasant. Like the early Corvettes, the 928 pounds over the pavement, jostling and thumping its passengers. Tire thump from the huge (225/50-16 front, 245/45-16 rear) T/As invades the passenger compartment with the clarity of the base line from a heavy-metal band, particularly over freeway expansion joints. While that might not seem completely out of character for a full-on performance car, it does seem a bit jarring in a $75,000 luxury coupe.

Fortunately, the interior does its best to make up for the suspension's shortcomings, providing a sumptuous, comfortable driving environment. The front buckets—leather-clad in our test car—strike a typically Teutonic compromise between comfort and support; a bit on the firm side initially, but still comfy after several hours on the road. What's more, the front seats don't require a specific body size or type, fitting drivers without regard to sex, agility or length of inseam. The back seats, as you might expect, work acceptably well for out-to-lunch short treks, but their munchkin-like dimensions rule them out for any extended tours.

The rest of the interior combines businesslike driving accommodations with the expected luxury appointments. The controls are within easy reach, and the climate control keeps close tabs on the interior atmosphere. Driver and passenger airbags allow for genuine 3-point seatbelts, just like God intended cars to have. The clutch seems a bit on the firm side, and the linkage for the rear-mounted transaxle is sometimes a bit notchy, but the driving controls are otherwise first rate.

The 928's interior does contain a few nits, of course, though the list is short for an exotic. Nevertheless, with the relatively wide B- and C-pillars, outward vision is in short supply, particularly out the rear. The hatch-mounted wing cuts directly across the driver's field of vision, which makes parking maneuvers a bit more thrilling than they might be otherwise.

Of course, the biggest thrill about the Porsche 928 is stomping on the loud pedal and feeling that 32-valve V-8 launch you toward the next corner. And if nobody else seems to notice, you can be either disappointed or relieved, depending on your purpose. If you're interested in the car for its flash appeal, there are others that will fill the bill better than the 928. If you're looking for something that will get you from here to there with a minimum of fuss and a lack of attention from the gendarmerie, the 928 has all it takes. After all, there's an advantage to invisibility, you know.—*Jim Miller*

PRICE

List price, all POE .... $74,545   Price as tested $77,189
Price as tested includes std equip. (auto. climate control, AM/FM stereo/cassette, elect. adj seats, central locking, anti-theft system, leather seats, elect. window lifts, cruise control, elect. adj mirrors, elect. sunroof, ABS, electronically controlled limited-slip differential, tire-pressure monitoring system), AM/FM stereo with CD player ($689), gas-guzzler tax ($1300)

ENGINE

Type	dohc 4-valve V-8
Displacement	4974 cc
Bore x stroke	100.1 mm x 79.0 mm
Compression ratio	10.0:1
Horsepower, (SAE)	326 bhp @ 6200 rpm
Torque	317 lb-ft @ 4100 rpm
Maximum engine speed	6200 rpm
Fuel injection	electronic port
Fuel requirement	unleaded, 91 pump oct

GENERAL

Curb weight	3505 lb
Test weight	3655 lb
Weight dist, f/r, %	52/48
Wheelbase	98.4 in.
Track, f/r	61.1 in./60.9 in.
Length	178.1 in.
Width	72.3 in.
Height	50.5 in.
Trunk space	6.3 + 7.9 cu ft

DRIVETRAIN

Transmission .... 4-sp automatic

Gear	Ratio	Overall ratio	(Rpm) Mph
1st	3.87:1	9.83:1	na
2nd	2.25:1	5.71:1	na
3rd	1.44:1	3.66:1	na
4th	1.00:1	2.54:1	na

Final drive ratio 2.54:1
Engine rpm @ 60 mph in 5th .... na

CHASSIS & BODY

Layout	front engine/rear drive
Body/frame	unit steel
Brakes, f/r	12.0-in. vented discs/
	11.8-in. vented discs, vacuum assist, ABS
Wheels	pressure cast alloy, 16 x 7½J f,
	16 x 9J r
Tires	BF Goodrich Comp T/A,
	225/50ZR-16 f, 245/45ZR-16 r
Steering	rack & pinion, power assist
Turns, lock to lock	3.0
Suspension, f/r: upper & lower A-arms, coil springs, tube shocks, anti-roll bar/upper lateral links, lower trailing arms, Weissach axle, coil springs, tube shocks, anti-roll bar	

ACCELERATION

Time to speed	Seconds
0-30 mph	2.6
0-40 mph	3.6
0-50 mph	4.8
0-60 mph	6.3
0-70 mph	7.9
0-80 mph	9.8
0-90 mph	12.3
0-100 mph	15.0
Time to distance	
0-100 ft	na
0-500 ft	na
0-1320 ft (¼ mi)	14.6 sec @ 98.3 mph

FUEL ECONOMY

Normal driving	na
EPA city/highway	15 mpg/19 mpg
Fuel capacity	22.7 gal.

BRAKING

Minimum stopping distance	
From 60 mph	135 ft
From 80 mph	247 ft
Control	excellent
Brake feel	very good
Overall brake rating	excellent

HANDLING

Lateral accel (200-ft skidpad)	0.83g[1]
Speed thru 700-ft slalom	58.3 mph[1]

[1]1990 test car.
Subjective ratings consist of excellent, very good, good, average and poor.
na means information is not available.

928GTS

Porsche brings us yet another 928 evolution, this time offering a substantial boost in performance and grip

WHEN PORSCHE LAUNCHED the 928 at the 1977 Geneva show, the V8 coupé was meant eventually to replace the 911. After it failed to reach that goal and became an independent one-car line instead, it underwent half a dozen significant changes over the succeeding years. First, Porsche added the more powerful S version, then it increased the capacity of the alloy engine from 4.5 to 5.0 litres, doubled the number of valves, introduced the facelifted 928S4 and added the emphatically sporty GT. The GTS edition, which goes on sale this spring, probably won't be the last metamorphosis of the 928 theme.

It is relatively easy to tell the GTS apart from its predecessors. Clues are flared rear wings, 17in diameter 'Turbo Cup-style' alloy wheels with integrated tyre pressure sensors, even wider tyres, more aerodynamic door mirrors, a body-colour rear wing

and a red reflective insert fixed between the tail-lights. The more muscular rear side panels and the fatter tyres give the car a more aggressive stance; beauty has finally turned into beast. The classic hatchback coupé shape has aged very well, but its space utilisation is worse than ever.

Now that the car comes with standard driver and passenger airbags, protruding knee bolsters conflict with long legs. While headroom is restricted by the tiny sunroof, the shoulder and elbow room are very generous indeed - but so they should be in a sports car that is wider than a Cadillac Fleetwood, and longer than a Renault Espace. Although this car has four seats, getting into the rear pair requires the agility of a 10 year-old. In any case, people any older than that won't be able to find room for their legs or head. The 928's hatchback versatility is a boon, but unless you fold the rear seats forward, the boot holds a cramping 5.2cu ft. Because of the strong heat intrusion from above (sun) and below (exhaust), a Porsche engineer once described the cargo deck of the 928 as the world's hottest oven on wheels.

At a glance, the 928's engine hasn't changed a bit. Don't be fooled. Capacity of the 32-valve unit has gone up from 4957cc to 5397cc, bringing a jump in maximum power from 320bhp at 6000rpm to 340bhp at 5700rpm. Even more impressive is the gain

in torque, which has soared from 311lb ft at 3000rpm to a massive 362lb ft at 4200rpm. Because of the longer stroke, the engineers had to develop a new crankshaft, which now has eight instead of four counterweights. To save weight, the cast alloy connecting rods were replaced with lighter ones made of steel. The cast aluminium low-friction pistons were modified for better efficiency and to generate a higher 10.4 to one compression ratio. The breathing apparatus is machined of ultra-lightweight magnesium, its respiratory ducts are coated to speed up the air-flow and the entire intake manifold has been fine-tuned for a more even torque supply. The

ignition boasts what Porsche calls Electronic Octane Knock Control, claimed to be the most sophisticated system of its kind. The exhaust and catalysts have been adapted to cope with the higher power output. The transmissions, though, are by and large carried over. You can choose between a five-speed manual and a four-speed auto supplied by Mercedes-Benz.

The suspension is also pretty much the way it was, although the chassis wizards reduced the tolerances and played with the ride height. They also fitted mildly recalibrated, adjustable springs and shock absorbers. There is a choice of four different tyre makes (Bridgestone, Pirelli Michelin, Yokohama); the dimensions have increased to 225/45 ZR17 in the front and to 255/40 ZR17 on the rear wheels. The power steering is a touch lighter than before, and brake performance has improved, thanks to enlarged front calipers and bigger inner-ventilated discs.

The brakes are in fact one of the strong points of the new Porsche 928GTS. They provide a maximum deceleration of 1.06*g*, which is exceptional but not best-in-class (Ferrari F40: 1.17*g*). Boasts the newly appointed board member in charge of R&D, Horst Marchart: 'The 928GTS has a maximum brake performance of 1332bhp - that's almost four times the engine's performance. The car takes a mere 8.5sec to

New 17-inch wheels, wider tyres and flared wings to house them, are the main visual changes for GTS. Performance gets another boost thanks to huge torque

accelerate from 0 to 60mph and to stop again. The stopping time from 125mph to 0 is 5.3sec.' On my drive, the four discs respond instantly no matter whether hot or cold, the brake pedal is nicely weighted, and there simply isn't any appreciable fade. The only drawback is an unrestrained urge to tramline, which turns from bad to worse on uneven surfaces.

Although the GTS's weight is a well-fed 3564lb, the car will storm from a standstill to 60mph in 5.5sec (5.6sec for the automatic version). Accelerating from 0 to 125mph is a matter of only 13.8sec, and even beyond that mark the 340bhp coupé will thunder on until it eventually runs out of steam at 172mph. On the autobahn, the big-bore 5.4-litre V8 impresses with sensational mid-range grunt which makes it so easy to pull away from the hot hatches. Our test car was equipped with the automatic transmission, which gets on very well with the torquey V8. You're always in the right gear, there is always the right amount of oomph on tap, and the shift action is quick and reasonably smooth.

The 928GTS is rather noisy for a grand tourer. The extra 20 horses gallop along loud and clear, the tyres drum like Jon Hiseman at his best, the wind always makes itself heard and the exhaust is only too willing to trumpet forth the good news. Over the first few miles, blipping the throttle thrills your ears, but after a couple of hours even the keenest will grow tired of the steamhammer symphony. Criticism goes too to the rather heavy and sticky throttle action, which makes smooth driving difficult, and to the high fuel consumption. According to the data chart, the GTS is supposed to average 20.8mpg, but when you make full use of the car's potential, you're lucky to better 14.0mpg, so despite the generous 19-gallon tank, the driving range will seldom exceed 250 miles.

Even in the softest setting, the GTS suspension is firm. Only masochists and part-time racing drivers should consider the optional sports dampers, since their effect is very close to that of no suspension at all. According to Horst Marchart, the ride quality is greatly dependent on the type of tyre fitted: our car wore Yokohama A-008 Ps, which are stiff enough to make you wonder whether they are filled with air or solid matter. On the other hand, the Yokohamas do provide terrific roadholding and grip. To keep the inherent tail happiness under control, the 928 GTS is equipped with an electronically controlled limited-slip differential (PDS). Judging by the flashing of its warning light, PDS is quite active at the limit.

The 928 GTS is very fast point-to-point, but its handling qualities are impaired by its sheer bulk, weight and size. The turning circle would be familiar to a post office van driver, and the slightly underdamped steering is not as nimble as that of more modern rivals such as the 500SL or 850i. Turn-in is a bit slow, but once you've pointed the car in the right direction it corners without much roll. Handling is generally fail-safe, but it is worth bearing in mind that the 928 doesn't like mid-corner corrections, sudden lift-off or an untimely overdose of power. The tail stays put for a long time, but when it does snap out, catching it isn't as easy as it used to be, since more oomph and stickier tyres have narrowed the warning zone.

On sale in the UK from autumn, the 928GTS replaces both the S4 and GT, and in Germany at least, the price is unchanged. It offers big performance, excellent build quality, a competent chassis, strong passive safety and lavish equipment. But despite these virtues, it's impossible to ignore the old drawbacks of harshness and overall lack of refinement. More than ever, the 928GTS is a niche vehicle for those who don't care about value for money but rate most highly the emotional values of charisma and brawny driving pleasure.

by Georg Kacher

Stretched to 5.4 litres, the 32-valve V8 now gives 340bhp and colossal 362lb ft of torque. Interior is as before, though has airbags now. UK launch this autumn

RED LEADER

PORSCHE
928 GTS

Photography Michael Bailie

The 928 has evolved again, with a bigger, more powerful engine and more grip. John Barker drives the GTS, the latest and possibly greatest 928

You could never accuse Porsche of being hasty. No car maker in the world has a model range so old and yet so competitive; the 911 is pushing 30, the 968 (nee 924) is approaching its late teens and the 928 was voted Car of the Year 1978. A Japanese company would have replaced each at least a couple of times, but that's not the Porsche way.

Porsche seems as taken with the idea of evolution as Darwin was, and has made refinement and development its speciality. Of course, it helps to have good, durable designs in the first place and that, with the exception of the 924, which after all began its life on a VW/Audi drawing board, is what Porsche has.

Since its launch in 1977, the 928's basic shape has changed little, save for a sleeker nose and tail, while on its rump the designation has changed from plain 928 to 928 S, S2, S3, S4, GT and finally GTS. The succession of badges has coincided with developments under the bonnet, the capacity of the V8 expanding gradually from 4.5 to the current 5.4 litres and gaining four valves per cylinder on the way. Its output has risen from 240 to 340bhp, and the car's top speed has climbed from 140 to over 170mph. ▶

ROAD TEST

● *928 lines are a familiar sight, having been around since 1977, but on the GTS those arches are wider than ever*

The GTS is now Germany's fastest production car and costs £64,998, around £1600 more than the out-going GT. That makes it a pricey alternative to a BMW 850CSi or Jaguar XJR-S but the 928 has always distanced itself from other big Grand Tourers by being overtly sporting in nature.

Previous models have disguised this but with its new 17-inch 'Cup Design' alloys, wider rear tyres and flared rear wheel arches, the GTS sends an unambiguous message. The latest 928 promises to be the greatest.

Performance and economy

The latest incarnation of the Porsche V8 sets out to deliver improved flexibility and more mid-range punch, the increase in capacity from 5.0 to 5.4 litres coming through a longer throw crankshaft. Thus the power of the all-alloy 32-valve V8 has increased only slightly, from 330 to 340bhp, but torque has burgeoned from 317lb ft to 369lb ft.

As with the new BMW M5, who's straight-six has been similarly upgraded, the effect of the extra torque is considerable in the mind of the driver. The V8 pulls so strongly and smoothly from low revs that it feels as if you're always in a gear lower than you actually are, and you hardly ever have to shuffle ratios to overtake, as top does for most

situations. If you wish, the engine will pull from 10mph in top without a murmur of protest.

This is not reflected convincingly by the GTS's in-gear acceleration times, however. Over the benchmarks of 30-50mph in fourth and 50-70mph in top the GTS is no quicker than the GT, recording 4.4 and 6.6 respectively. The GTS's extra muscle makes itself felt in the mid-range, which in fourth gear is between 50 and 80mph.

Interestingly, the standing start times of the GTS show a fair improvement; 60mph comes up in 5.2secs and the quarter mile in 13.7, both 0.3secs quicker than the GT. Maximum speed is unchanged at 164mph which, taking into account the Millbrook banking factor, equates to a storming170mph on the flat.

This is Ferrari 512TR performance for half the price, though there are cars like the Alpine A610 and Mazda

RX-7 which will almost keep pace where it counts for even less outlay. But then part of the satisfaction derived from driving the GTS or 512TR is knowing they're engineered to 170mph-plus standards.

If there is one flaw in the 928's case, however, it's that the V8 is not as charismatic this time around. Where on previous 928s firm acceleration illicited a smooth, creamy burble, the 5.4 of the GTS has a harsh edge which is always distant but nonetheless irksome. It doesn't deter you from taking the V8 all the way to the 6500rpm red line, but as power peaks at 5500rpm and the engine is at its glorious best between 4000 and this figure, you don't find the need to.

Although first gear is down and left on a dog leg, the gate pattern and springing of the 928's 'box are well defined so there's little chance of

wrong slotting. Besides, first gear is rarely necessary; the weighty clutch is smooth and progressive and the engine has the guts and temperament to pull away easily in second.

The fact that the 928's gearbox is in unit with the rear axle isn't usually apparent but the shift of our GTS was less than perfect, showing a tendency to baulk at rapid down-changes. Slicing through the gears on a full bore rush up the 'box was never a problem however, and if you give it a moment between shifts, the fat lever snicks home with the lightest of touches.

Economy is about as poor as you'd expect of a hard-driven, 170mph sports car. We averaged 14.5mpg, which means a useable range of around 250 miles per tankful of super unleaded, though cruising in top (good for 26mph/1000rpm) should see the range up to a more useful 300-plus miles.

Handling, ride and brakes

It's no mean feat getting a 3600lb, 74in-wide GT to handle like a much lighter and smaller car but the GTS's ride lets you know how it's done within a couple of hundred yards. Wheel control is exemplary, through a combination of firm springing and precision damping. Yet firm as it is — an XJR-S driver would feel shaken up — it never crashes or bangs, managing to round off the sharpest of ridges.

This solid composure gives the GTS's handling a responsive, predictable platform to work from which makes it terrifically exploitable, although with its wider rear tyres the tail stays more firmly glued than before. The fronts (225/45 ZR17) are the same width as on the GT but a section lower, while the rears (255/40 ZR17) are both wider and lower. Their rims are pushed out into the wider arches by spacers too, widening the

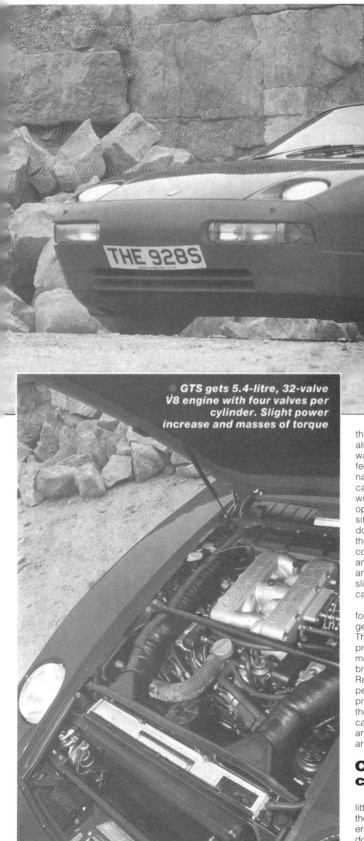

GTS gets 5.4-litre, 32-valve V8 engine with four valves per cylinder. Slight power increase and masses of torque

track, while as before Porsche's automatic locking diff is standard.

Thrown down your favourite stretch of road, the GTS feels weighty but all of a piece, not nimble but reassuringly agile. It goes just where you point it, the meaty, power assisted steering

giving plenty of feedback, the chassis' responses coming clean and swift.

Quite soon you forget about its bulk and start making the engine and tyres work for their living, and when the engine's torque wins over the grip of

the rear tyres, you've already had plenty of warning. If the front end feels anything less than nailed to the road, you can bet that full power will soon require some opposite lock. In such situations, the 928 doesn't leave you to sort things out; its composure isn't ruffled and its steering is fast and accurate, so the slide can be held or cancelled at will.

The GTS's all-disc, four-pot caliper brakes get high marks, too. There's a weighty precision about the car's major controls and the brake pedal shares it. Response is top-of-the-pedal keen, yet progressive, while under the heaviest braking you can take the system within an ace of activating the anti-lock.

Comfort and controls

Just as on the outside, little has changed inside the 928 over the years. An ergonomically sound driving position doesn't date, nor does a clear instrument panel, and fine all-round visibility is just as useful as it was 15 years ago. There's none of the offset pedal nonsense of other supercars to contend with either, and it takes only a few moments to feel settled behind the GTS's chunky, height adjustable steering wheel, electric motors taking care of the seat cushion angle. It's also worth mentioning that the 928's pop-up headlamps are — literally —

Not a luxury atmosphere inside, but a fine mixture of sport support and cruiser comforts

brilliantly effective.

The seats themselves grip in all the right places and at the right pressures, so that while you feel secure driving the GTS hard, you also emerge from a long motorway run in fine fettle. Which is more than can be said for adults lured into the rear by the perfectly formed but tiny rear buckets.

There isn't what you'd call a luxury atmosphere about the GTS's cabin. Most of the trappings are there — air conditioning, leather faced seats, trip

ROAD TEST

computer, cruise control — but its simple styling and fat, user-friendly switches give it a functional feel. It all looks and feels durable, that is apart from the fluffy, snow white carpet that our car was afflicted by.

As ever, tyre roar is the biggest source of noise, the engine giving it some competition only when extended in the lower gears. You can turn up the 10-speaker Blaupunkt stereo to drown it out of course, but

the thrum of the fat Bridgestones cancels out most of the bass, leaving it sounding a bit underpowered.

Verdict

The GTS is the best 928 ever, though that shouldn't be a surprise given Porsche's track record on developing designs. The new V8 may not make the GTS much quicker on paper but its extra torque is certainly appreciated by the driver. Response in top is so good that you rarely need to change down once you've selected it, though that would be a waste of the 928's handling.

In many ways, the chassis of the GTS is as impressive as that of the 911, as in front engine/rear drive terms it's among the very best. It possesses outstanding composure and balance, responds beautifully and dishes up a feast of feedback. Get out of it after a good hack and it's hard to believe it's such a big car.

The engine was sweeter before it was expanded to 5.4 litres and some will feel that the ride is just too firm, but in the GTS Porsche still has the best driver's car in the Grand Tourer market. The new Ferrari 465 certainly has its work cut out bettering it. ∎

Porsche 928 GTS

All tests with a crew of two and a full tank of fuel

THROUGH THE GEARS (seconds)			
0-30mph	**2.2**	0-90mph	**10.2**
0-40mph	**3.0**	0-100mph	**12.8**
0-50mph	**4.1**	0-110mph	**15.5**
0-60mph	**5.2**	0-120mph	**18.7**
0-70mph	**6.7**	0-130mph	**23.6**
0-80mph	**8.4**	0-140mph	**—**
STANDING 1/4 MILE		**13.7/104**	**(secs/mph)**
AVERAGE TOP SPEED			**164mph**

ACCELERATION in 3rd/4th/5th (seconds)			
30-50mph	3.0/4.4/6.5	80-100mph	—/4.2/6.4
40-60mph	2.9/4.2/6.5	90-110mph	—/4.8/6.6
50-70mph	2.9/3.9/6.6	100-120mph	—/5.7/7.1
60-80mph	3.1/3.9/6.3	110-130mph	—/—/8.1
70-90mph	3.5/4.1/6.2	120-140mph	—/—/—

MAX SPEEDS IN GEARS AT 6500rpm			
FIRST	46mph	FOURTH	127mph
SECOND	68mph	FIFTH	164 at 6180rpm
THIRD	96mph		
OVERALL FUEL CONS			14.5mpg
TOURING FUEL CONS*			18.5mpg

(*50% of Govn Urban cycle plus 25% of steady 56mph and 75mph)

TRACK CONDITION	Dry
TEMPERATURE	7°C
WIND SPEED	8mph
ATMOSPHERIC PRESSURE	992mb

SPECIFICATION

ENGINE TYPE			**Longitudinal V8**
DISPLACEMENT			**5397cc**
BORE	**100mm**	STROKE	**85.9mm**
COMPRESSION RATIO			**10.4:1**
FUEL AND IGNITION			**Bosch LH Motronic**
		multi-point fuel injection, electronic ignition	
MAX POWER			**340bhp@5700rpm**
MAX TORQUE			**369lb ft@4250rpm**
GEARBOX			**five-speed manual tansaxle**
RATIOS (:1)	1st **3.500**	4th	**1.034**
	2nd **1.889**	5th	**0.857**
	3rd **1.320**	Reverse	**3.455**
FINAL DRIVE RATIO			**2.727:1**
SPEED PER 1000rpm IN TOP			**26.5mph**
FRONT SUSPENSION			**Independent by double**
		wishbones, coil springs and anti-roll bar	
REAR SUSPENSION			**Independent by**
	'Weissach axle'; semi-trailing arms, upper		
	transverse link, coil springs and anti-roll bar		
STEERING			**Rack and pinion, power assisted**

BRAKES	**Ventilated discs all round. Anti-lock standard**
WHEELS	**Forged alloy, front, 7.5 x 17in, rear 9 x 17in**
TYRES	**Bridgestone, front 225/45 ZR, rear 255/40 ZR**
WHEELBASE	**98.4in**
TURNING CIRCLE	**38ft 5in**
FUEL TANK CAPACITY	**18.9gallons/86litres**
UNLADEN WEIGHT	**3616lb**
TEST WEIGHT	**3946lb**
POWER TO WEIGHT RATIO (test weight)	**193bhp/ton**
BASE PRICE	**£64,998**
PRICE AS TESTED	**£66,620**
OPTIONAL EXTRAS FITTED TO TEST CAR	
	Sunroof £1622

STAR RATINGS

ENGINE ★★★★
The new 5.4 has an excellent temperament, strong low-rev pick-up and a knockout mid-range punch. Sounds less refined than previous V8s, so only four stars.

GEARCHANGE ★★★★
Well weighted and precise lever action, shifts swiftly and positively up the gears but can baulk in rapid down-changes. Superb when not rushed.

HANDLING ★★★★
Feels like a much lighter and smaller car when hussled. Steering is superb and the chassis' composure and reactions are finely honed. Tail slides are easily caught and held. A genuine big sports car.

RIDE ★★★
Sacrificed for handling. Very firm at low speed but never harsh or uncomfortable. Improves the faster you go.

BRAKES ★★★★
More than man enough for the job. Excellent power allied to a well judged pedal that combines keenness with just the right amount of feel and progression. You don't know you've got anti-lock until you really need it.

COMFORT ★★★★
Faultless driving position makes the driver feel at ease right away. Seats are supportive in hard cornering and comfortable enough to watch countries go by from. Rear seats best used for luggage. Air conditioning standard.

INTERIOR ★★★
Functional rather than luxurious, despite having most of the trappings you'd expect of a cossetting GT. Fit and finish solid, materials ordinary.

ENJOYMENT ★★★★
Lustier, grippier and sexier looking, the GTS is the best 928 ever. Handles superbly, like a much smaller and lighter car, and has a solid composure that won't be shaken even by a tail slide. The V8 could be smoother and the ride is too firm for some, but the 928 remains the driver's choice in the Grand Tourer market.

Porsche 928 GTS
Quick! Before it melts.
BY JOE RUSZ

THIS MAY BE your last chance to own one of the world's finest *Gran Turismos*. Also, one of the most underrated. And unappreciated. It's the 928 GTS and, yes, it is a true Porsche.

That the 928 hasn't caught the public's fancy may be due to the popularity of the 911 Carrera, which continues to be Zuffenhausen's best-selling road car. Also the oldest. The 928 with its water-cooled front engine has been with us for a mere 15 years. Perhaps some designs take a bit longer to catch on. On the other hand, maybe they will never gain popular acceptance.

More's the pity because the 928 is an impressive luxury automobile whose performance level approaches that of many exotics. In fact, with a top speed of 171 mph (according to the factory, whose numbers tend to be conservative), the 928 is not only the fastest Porsche, but also one of the fastest production-built GTs in the world—behind the Lamborghini Diablo, Ferrari F40 and Testarossa and Chevrolet Corvette ZR-1.

Porsche calls this model—the fourth and final variation on the 928 theme—the GTS, which is essentially a hotted-up version of the 1991 (and early 1992) model known as the 928

GT (when equipped with 5-speed manual transmission) and 928 S4 (when fitted with 4-speed automatic). Previously, the engine of the stick shift developed 326 bhp while the automatic's powerplant was detuned to 316 bhp. Now both versions use the same engine (the manual gearbox has been fitted with an external oil pump and front-mounted oil cooler) and can take all that the new engine dishes out—namely, 345 bhp and 369 lb.-ft. of torque.

To achieve these substantial gains in horsepower and torque, the stroke of the GTS's crankshaft (now with eight, versus six, main bearings) has been lengthened by 7.0 mm, increasing displacement from 4957 to 5397 cc. Connecting rod and piston weight has been reduced (these components are now forged), and the compression ratio has been raised from 10.0 to 10.4:1. Changes in camshaft profile help reduce idle speed while increasing low-end torque in the 928's 32-valve, dohc all-aluminum V-8, which retains

the S4's dual-stage induction system (albeit with plastic-coated intake passages for reduced flow losses and Bosch LH-Jetronic electronic fuel injection).

A stronger clutch with spring-loaded pedal assist offers assurance that the engine's newfound power makes it to the 928's rear-mounted transaxle. To ensure that power is applied in proper dosage to each rear wheel, the GTS is fitted with a variable-ratio limited-slip differential, a carryover from the previous model. Unlike an ordinary limited-slip, the Porsche's is electronically controlled by a computer that takes its input from the car's ABS and provides lockup varying from 0 to 100 percent, depending on the amount of rear-wheel slippage.

The 928 GTS has a 2.7-in.-wider rear track that improves stability and necessitates flaring of the rear fenders. Distinctive Porsche Cup-style cast-alloy wheels are an inch taller, but the same width as the previous model's, and are fitted with a warning system that keeps tabs

on tire pressures. Although the springs and anti-roll bars are the same as before, the 928 GTS gets revalved shock absorbers that are a trifle softer than those of its predecessor.

Porsche brakes are among the best in the business, but just to be sure, the 928 GTS is equipped with massive 12.68-in.-diameter (versus 11.97) front discs fitted with huge Brembo 4-piston calipers.

In addition to its flared rear fenders and 17-in. wheels, the 928 GTS wears restyled taillights, which stretch across the rear of the car; a body-color rear spoiler; and reshaped side mirrors that resemble the Carrera's.

The GTS interior offers the same excellent ergonomics and high level of comfort and luxury that we've come to expect in a 928. Virtually everything is standard, including driver and passenger airbags.

Of course, along with a full complement of amenities, one can expect impressive performance, 0 to 60-mph times of 5.5 seconds (for the 5-speed) says the factory and astonishingly low passing times that are world-class. Crisp handling too, even though this is a big and heavy (3600-lb.) car. Alas, the price—$80,920—requires a heavy wallet.

Porsche 928 GTS

Plusher, plumper but quicker, the latest — perhaps last — 928 shows that extra practicality need not dilute driving appeal

Price as tested £64,998 **Top speed** 168mph
0-60mph 5.4secs **MPG** 14.8

For Tremendous performance, great handling, uncompromising character
Against Not very refined, disappointing finish in places

EXTEND THE 928 GTS on a demanding road and you understand something important about the engineers at Porsche. They drive hard. Despite the impression that Zuffenhausen's celebrated grand tourer has been polished and preened and smoothed free of all rough edges for what many believe is its final, £64,998 incarnation, it's still a big league hitter — a car for those who'd find a Mercedes 500SL altogether too polite and pampering. It may have put on a little weight (about 60kg) but its 32-valve V8 engine is stronger than ever.

The extra muscle is largely a result of a longer stroke and

PETER BURN

measure of granite stability — and virtually matches the factory's 170mph flat road claim. In our hands, only two cars have gone faster at the Bedfordshire proving ground and both were Ferrari Testarossas, the latest 512TR clocking an astonishing 175mph. That said, it does cost twice as much as the Porsche.

Maranello's fastest also eclipses the GTS in a straight sprint from rest, storming to 60 and 100mph in 5.0 and 10.7secs respectively against the 928's relatively relaxed 5.4 and 14.3secs. As you'd hope, the GTS beats its predecessor to the punch by a couple of tenths to 60mph but, disappointingly, is almost a second down at 100mph, the GT recording a storming 13.4secs. Despite holding a 1mph advantage in top speed, there's no danger of the GTS usurping the 911 Turbo (4.7/11.4secs) as Porsche's peak performer.

If you want evidence that standing start figures are a poor guide to real-world performance, though, the GTS is happy to provide it. You only have to look at the fourth-gear 50-70mph time of 3.7secs to understand the magnitude of its overtaking ability. Even the Ferrari has to drop down to third to match it (3.7secs); in fourth it's left trailing with a time of 5.5secs. This is no trick of the torque curve but it does point to the fact that the Porsche has snappier gearing than the Testarossa. Take 80-100mph in fifth — the Porsche does it in 5.9secs, the 512TR takes 7.5secs.

It's the deep-chested dig of the 32-valve V8 that makes the biggest impression on the road. With small throttle openings, the unit feels curiously torpid and apathetic but, in league with the clean response and taut driveline, this makes driving in traffic less of a bind than with some rivals. Push it towards the floor with anything approaching deliberation and its immense reserves are marshalled progressively into spine-tingling service. Far from there being any troughs in the delivery, usable power seems to be flowing over the sides. All out, there's little question that the GTS possesses Porsche's most vigorous ever V8, although it's far from the smoothest or most musical. The howling, burbling voice is there all right but is submerged beneath a hash of ancillary and transmission noise, which, while never all that loud, is more industrial than inspirational.

As already intimated, the GTS is geared for performance rather than parsimony and, given the extent of the former, few will be shocked by its 14.8mpg overall. But impressive as the Porsche's thirst is, it's no more profligate than the Ferrari's 14.7mpg or, indeed, the 928 GT's 14.2mpg. Our best return of 19.9mpg shows that there is some scope for improvement, but not much. Even with an 86-litre (18.9-gallon) tank, the practical range is about 370 miles.

The 928's five-speed gearchange isn't all that heavy but, despite Porsche's best efforts to refine it, remains clonky and prone to baulking if the driver isn't neat and positive. More taxing in its long-windedness than its weight, the clutch has a reasonably progressive, if late, take-up and plenty of bite during fast shifts.

More than with previous 928s, the GTS's chassis places far greater emphasis on grip and stability than balance and adjustability. Which isn't to say that one of the great-handling supercars has been tainted by shopping car sensibilities but, with still wider tyres and an effective electronically controlled limited slip differential (PDS), wild power slides are much harder to provoke than they once were. The system isn't so protective that it kills all the fun, though. You can zip out of junctions with little drama but if you're determined to go sideways you will; few big cars feel better on opposite lock than a 928.

As power assistance goes, the Porsche's is about as unintrusive as it comes and leaves feedback well resolved and largely unsullied. Helm responses feel precise and meaty, too. Belying its size and weight, the GTS is an easy car to place accurately in a bend and one that appears to have inexhaustible composure: it turns in with crisp fluency and has terrific body control. A mild tendency for the front wheels to run down cambers needs watching ▶

another 440cc, while still smoother running is promised by having eight crankshaft balancer weights instead of six. Further honing includes more sound deadening and a gearbox re-engineered for an easier shift.

Outputs, unsurprisingly, are at an all-time high for a 928, respectively 20bhp and 45lb ft of torque up on the GT's. The GTS's 350bhp, however, is developed 500rpm lower at 5700rpm and its 362lb ft of torque 150rpm higher at 4250rpm.

The top speed round Millbrook's speed bowl of 168mph is 4mph better than the GT posted — but achieved with a similar

The Autocar Road Test

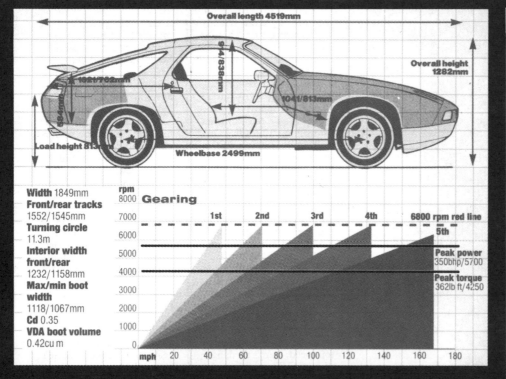

Overall length 4519mm
Overall height 1282mm
Load height 813
Wheelbase 2499mm

Width 1849mm
Front/rear tracks 1552/1545mm
Turning circle 11.3m
Interior width front/rear 1232/1158mm
Max/min boot width 1118/1067mm
Cd 0.35
VDA boot volume 0.42cu m

Gearing

rpm: 8000, 7000, 6000, 5000, 4000, 3000, 2000, 1000, 0
6800 rpm red line
1st 2nd 3rd 4th 5th
Peak power 350bhp/5700
Peak torque 362lb ft/4250
mph 20 40 60 80 100 120 140 160 180

Specification

Engine
Layout	8 cyls in vee, 5397cc
Max power	350bhp/5700rpm
Max torque	362lb ft/4250rpm
Specific output	65bhp/litre
Power to weight	216bhp/tonne
Installation	longitudinal, front, rear-wheel drive
Made of	alloy head and block
Bore/stroke	100/85.9mm
Comp ratio	10.4:1
Valves	4 per cyl, dohc
Ignition and fuel	LH-Jetronic, catalyst

Gearbox
Type 5-speed manual
Ratios/mph per 1000rpm
1st 3.77/7.0 **2nd** 2.52/10.5
3rd 1.79/14.8 **4th** 1.36/19.5
5th 1.00/26.5 **Final drive** 2.73:1

Suspension
Front double wishbones, coil springs, gas-filled dampers, anti-roll bar
Rear upper transverse links, lower semi-trailing arms, Weissach axle, gas-filled dampers, anti-roll bar

Steering
Type rack and pinion, progressive power assistance
Lock to lock 3.0 turns

Brakes
Front 322mm ventilated discs **Rear** 299mm ventilated discs **Anti-lock** std

Wheels and tyres
Size front 7.5Jx17, rear 9Jx17ins
Made of forged alloy **Tyres** front 225/45 ZR17, rear 255/40 ZR17
Spare space saver

Made and sold by
Dr Ing h.c.F. Porsche AG, Porschestrasse 42, Stuttgart-Zuffenhausen, Germany. Available in UK through Porsche Cars GB Ltd, Bath Road, Calcot, Reading, Berks RG3 7SE. Tel: 0734 303666

Performance

Maximum speeds
Top gear 168mph/6340rpm
4th 133/6800 **3rd** 100/6800
2nd 71/6800 **1st** 48/6800

Acceleration from rest
True mph	Secs	Speedo mph
30	2.2	32
40	2.9	42
50	4.1	52
60	5.4	62
70	7.1	73
80	8.9	83
90	11.2	93
100	14.3	103
110	17.5	113
120	21.5	123
130	27.7	133

Standing qtr mile 14.1secs/100mph
Standing km 25.7secs/127mph
30-70mph through gears 4.9secs

Acceleration in each gear
mph	top	4th	3rd	2nd
10-30	–	4.6	3.3	2.3
20-40	6.0	4.2	3.1	2.1
30-50	5.8	4.1	2.8	2.0
40-60	5.8	3.9	2.7	2.0
50-70	5.9	3.7	2.7	2.6
60-80	5.8	3.9	2.8	–
70-90	5.7	4.0	3.2	–
80-100	5.9	4.2	–	–
90-110	6.4	4.6	–	–
100-120	6.8	5.4	–	–
110-130	7.6	7.1	–	–
120-140	9.3	–	–	–
130-150	11.5	–	–	–

Fuel consumption
Overall mpg on test	14.8
Best/worst on test	19.9/8.2
Touring	19.9
Range	376 miles

Govt tests (mpg):
urban 13.6 **56mph** 28.7 **75mph** 23.5
Tank capacity 52 litres
(18.9 galls)

Brakes
Distance travelled under max braking (track surface: dry)
Anti-lock yes

30mph	8.8m
50mph	25.0m
70mph	48.9m
st qtr mile (98mph)	102.7m

Fade tests
Consecutive brake applications at 0.5g retardation from st qtr terminal speed
(figures on the right represent pedal pressures)
40lb 20lb 10lb 0lb

Weight
Kerb (incl half tank)	1600kg
Distribution f/r	52/48%
Max payload	n/a
Max towing weight	1600kg

1 Air vents 2 Heater controls 3 Clock 4 Headlights switch 5 Indicators/main beam stalk 6 Oil pressure gauge 7 Fuel gauge 8 Speedometer 9 Trip computer display 10 Revcounter 11 Battery condition gauge 12 Water temperature 13 Horn 14 Wipers stalk 15 Heated rear window switch

Porsche 928 GTS

down narrow, twisty lanes but grip, even in the wet, is extraordinary. As, in many respects, is the ride which, although very firm, never feels harsh or jittery.

Braking, as you might reasonably expect with massive ventilated discs all round, is vastly powerful but the spongy pedal feel saps confidence — initially at least.

Jaguar-style refinement has never been on the 928's agenda and neither is it with the GTS. Even on a light throttle the engine can be heard, but this is more a reflection of the reduction in road roar than any increase in mechanical noise.

Cosmetically plusher and better equipped for the GTS, the 928's cabin design has changed hardly at all over the years. What started out as peerless switchgear ergonomics seems a tad clumsy now, but for instrumentation presentation and clarity, driving position and seat comfort, the Porsche is the paragon it always was. Visibility is good, too, and the feeling of solidity the cabin exudes is nothing short of remarkable. The fit of the carpet on the broad sills looks like it belongs to a cheaper car, though.

Only the sadistic would call the 928 a four-seater, but the rear accommodation is fine in an emergency or for small children and, in its intended role as a mile-eating express, space for two people and their luggage is ample.

The equipment list is as thorough as a £65,000 price tag would signify and includes air conditioning, cruise control, leather upholstery, part-powered seat adjustment and an impressive-looking but ordinary-sounding 10-speaker stereo.

It would be easy to get the wrong idea about the GTS. True, it's less noisy than the GT it supplements and totes a more comfortable ride. It's a little plusher and a little plumper. But it hasn't lost sight of what the 928 is all about and that's driving. From beneath the gloss, an even clearer focus and more uncompromising nature emerges. There might be more cosseting coupes and faster supercars but none can touch the 928 for a potent combination of driver appeal and practicality. ∎

928 cabin has changed little over the years and remains very impressive. Leather sports seats have part-electric adjustment; comfort, support and driving position are superb, visibility good

Stepping into the rear is a squeeze and, once there, space is very cramped. Seats for emergencies or children but backrests fold down to increase luggage capacity. Transmission hump incorporates lockable cubby

Instruments are among the very best for presentation, clarity and readability. They're now supplemented by three digital displays for trip computer. Entire instrument pod adjusts with steering wheel

Heavy tailgate reveals shallow but reasonably long luggage bay

GTS handling combines huge grip with great stability

With 350bhp, 32-valve V8 hits new power peak. Flexibility in fourth and fifth is awesome

It's been called a German Corvette. Or the best Mercedes Porsche ever built. Because it packs a V-8 and because it's, ahem, large. Or at least larger than a Porsche is supposed to be. But does this make it any less a sports car or anything less than a Porsche? *Nein!*

In fact the 928 GTS is a no-nonsense GT that just happens to be too luxurious for its own good. And therein lies the rub: Namely, that the car is too big for those purists who demand a lean, lithe machine and too small for luxury-coupe buyers who want the extra room that, say, a Mercedes 500SL or Lexus SC 400 offers.

That's a pity, because the 928 GTS is an impressive automobile and a technical tour de force. Its all-aluminum engine (one of the first to use linerless cylinder bores with silica-crystal surfaces) is fitted with four overhead camshafts and a tuned induction system that has been re-designed over the years. Displacement increases, the introduction of 4-valve-per-cylinder heads, and electronic engine-management controls, phased-in over the cars's 16-year lifespan, have seen horsepower climb from 219 in 1977 to 345 bhp in 1993. Making the 171-mph 928 GTS one of the fastest production-built sports cars in the world.

During those 16 years the 928's suspension, with its unique Weissach rear axle, has been fine-tuned. Last year, when the 928 became the 928 GTS, rear-wheel width and tire size were increased to handle the extra power. Up front, the already powerful disc brakes received Brembo 4-piston calipers.

Exterior design changes, when executed, have been minor: a new wheel now and again; a reconfigured rear spoiler. And, in 1993, a reshaped rear end with wraparound taillights.

Nor has there been much redesign of the 928's interior. Ergonomically perfect, stylistically advanced, comfortable, it has served as a model for cars built by competitors. And while many have sought to incorporate the 928's myriad details and lavish appointments (leather, power this and adjustable that, climate control, etc) into their own designs, few manufacturers have come close to offering as complete a level of fitment. In other words, the 928 GTS is loaded, and its options list brief.

But a bit longer than the car's lifeline. Because the 928 GTS is largely unappreciated, fairly expensive and thus, not exactly a best seller, this elegant GT will be produced only as long as demand exists. A pity, because its mix of performance and luxury has not been matched by any other Porsche model. And few other GTs and sport coupes.

SPECIFICATIONS

Base price, base model	$82,260	Fuel capacity	22.7 gal.	Brakes, f/r	disc/disc, ABS
Country of origin	Germany	Fuel economy (EPA), city/highway	12/19 mpg	Tires	225/45ZR-17 f, 255/40ZR-17 r
Body/seats	3D/2+2	Base engine	345-bhp dohc 32V V-8	Steering type	rack & pinion (p)
Layout	F/R	Bore x stroke	100.1 x 85.9 mm	Turning circle	38.4 ft
Wheelbase	98.4 in.	Displacement	5395 cc	Warranty, years/miles:	
Track, f/r	61.1/63.6 in.	Compression ratio	10.4:1	Bumper-to-bumper	2/unlimited
Length	178.1 in.	Horsepower, SAE net	345 bhp @ 5700 rpm	Powertrain	2/unlimited
Width	74.4 in.	Torque	369 lb-ft @ 4250 rpm	Rust-through	10/unlimited
Height	50.5 in.	Optional engine(s)	none	Passive restraint, driver's side	airbag
Luggage capacity	6.3 cu ft	Transmission	5M, 4A	Front passenger's side	airbag
Curb weight	3590 lb	Suspension, f/r	ind/ind		